Cram101 Textbook Outlines to accompany:

Psychology and Life

Gerrig and Zimbardo, 17th Edition

An Academic Internet Publishers (AIPI) publication (c) 2007.

With Cram101.com online, you also have access to extensive reference material.

You will nail those essays and papers. Here is an example from a Cram101 Biology text:

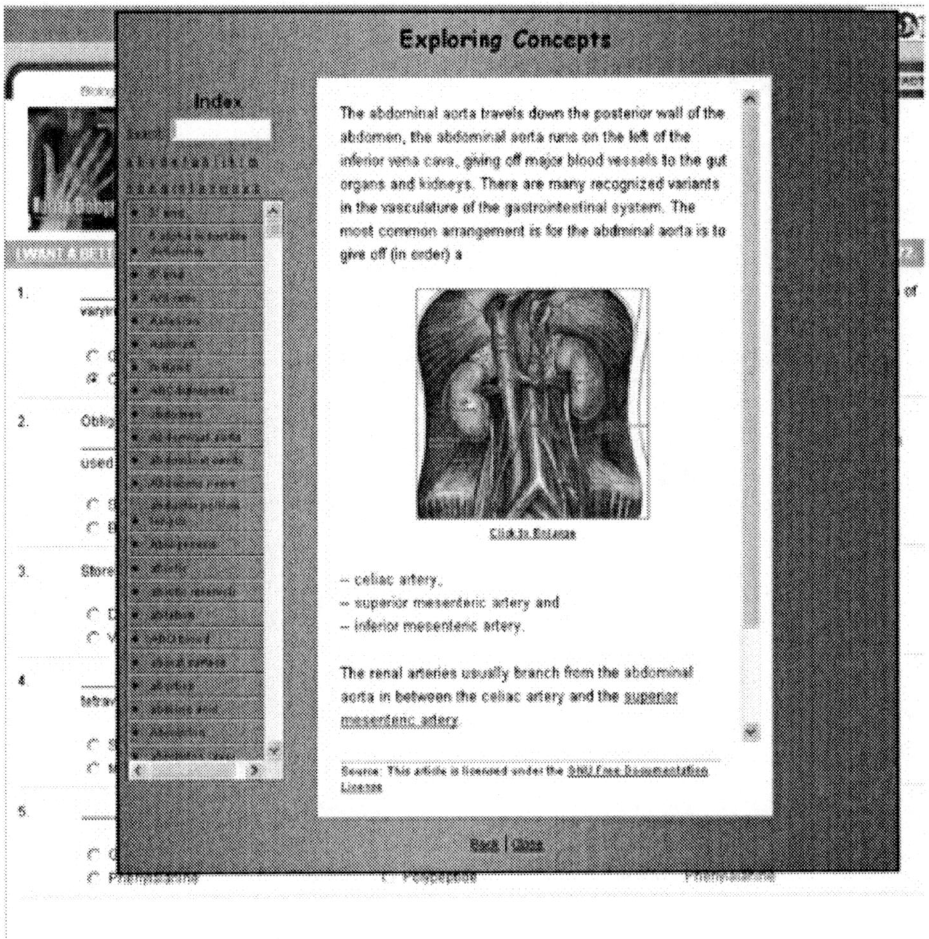

Visit **www.Cram101.com**, click Sign Up at the top of the screen, and enter DK73DW in the promo code box on the registration screen. Access to www.Cram101.com is normally $9.95, but because you have purchased this book, your access fee is only $4.95. Sign up and stop highlighting textbooks forever.

Learning System

Cram101 Textbook Outlines is a learning system. The notes in this book are the highlights of your textbook, you will never have to highlight a book again.

How to use this book. Take this book to class, it is your notebook for the lecture. The notes and highlights on the left hand side of the pages follow the outline and order of the textbook. All you have to do is follow along while your intructor presents the lecture. Circle the items emphasized in class and add other important information on the right side. With Cram101 Textbook Outlines you'll spend less time writing and more time listening. Learning becomes more efficient.

Cram101.com Online

Increase your studying efficiency by using Cram101.com's practice tests and online reference material. It is the perfect complement to Cram101 Textbook Outlines. Use self-teaching matching tests or simulate in-class testing with comprehensive multiple choice tests, or simply use Cram's true and false tests for quick review. Cram101.com even allows you to enter your in-class notes for an integrated studying format combining the textbook notes with your class notes.

Visit **www.Cram101.com**, click Sign Up at the top of the screen, and enter **DK73DW2482** in the promo code box on the registration screen. Access to www.Cram101.com is normally $9.95, but because you have purchased this book, your access fee is only $4.95. Sign up and stop highlighting textbooks forever.

 ISBN: 1-4288-0207-X

Psychology and Life
Gerrig and Zimbardo, 17th

CONTENTS

Evolution	Commonly used to refer to gradual change, evolution is the change in the frequency of alleles within a population from one generation to the next. This change may be caused by different mechanisms, including natural selection, genetic drift, or changes in population (gene flow).
Brain	The brain controls and coordinates most movement, behavior and homeostatic body functions such as heartbeat, blood pressure, fluid balance and body temperature. Functions of the brain are responsible for cognition, emotion, memory, motor learning and other sorts of learning. The brain is primarily made up of two types of cells: glia and neurons.
Human nature	Human nature is the fundamental nature and substance of humans, as well as the range of human behavior that is believed to be invariant over long periods of time and across very different cultural contexts.
Scientific method	Psychologists gather data in order to describe, understand, predict, and control behavior. Scientific method refers to an approach that can be used to discover accurate information. It includes these steps: understand the problem, collect data, draw conclusions, and revise research conclusions.
Species	Species refers to a reproductively isolated breeding population.
Mental processes	The thoughts, feelings, and motives that each of us experiences privately but that cannot be observed directly are called mental processes.
Reasoning	Reasoning is the act of using reason to derive a conclusion from certain premises. There are two main methods to reach a conclusion,deductive reasoning and inductive reasoning.
Artificial intelligence	The science of creating machines capable of performing activities that require intelligence when they are done by people is referred to as artificial intelligence.
Cognitive science	Cognitive Science is the scientific study of the mind and brain and how they give rise to behavior. The field is highly interdisciplinary and is closely related to several other areas, including psychology, artificial intelligence, linguistics and psycholinguistics, philosophy, neuroscience, logic, robotics, anthropology and biology.
Basic research	Basic research has as its primary objective the advancement of knowledge and the theoretical understanding of the relations among variables . It is exploratory and often driven by the researcher's curiosity, interest or hunch.
Mental illness	Mental illness is the term formerly used to mean psychological disorder but less preferred because it implies that the causes of the disorder can be found in a medical disease process.
Prejudice	Prejudice in general, implies coming to a judgment on the subject before learning where the preponderance of the evidence actually lies, or formation of a judgement without direct experience.
Self-esteem	Self-esteem refers to a person's subjective appraisal of himself or herself as intrinsically positive or negative to some degree.
Motivation	In psychology, motivation is the driving force (desire) behind all actions of an organism.
Peer pressure	Peer pressure comprises a set of group dynamics whereby a group of people in which one feels comfortable may override the sexual personal habits, individual moral inhibitions or idiosyncratic desires to impose a group norm of attitudes or behaviors.
Zimbardo	Zimbardo is best-known for his Stanford prison experiment. The experiment led to theories about the importance of the social situation in individual psychology that are still controversial today.
Shyness	A tendency to avoid others plus uneasiness and strain when socializing is called shyness.
Insight	Insight refers to a sudden awareness of the relationships among various elements that had previously appeared to be independent of one another.
Scientific research	Research that is objective, systematic, and testable is called scientific research.

Consciousness	The awareness of the sensations, thoughts, and feelings being experienced at a given moment is called consciousness.
Ebbinghaus	Ebbinghaus pioneered the development of experimental methods for the measurement of rote learning and memory.
Aristotle	Aristotle can be credited with the development of the first theory of learning. He concluded that ideas were generated in consciousness based on four principlesof association: contiguity, similarity, contrast, and succession. In contrast to Plato, he believed that knowledge derived from sensory experience and was not inherited.
Plato	According to Plato, people must come equipped with most of their knowledge and need only hints and contemplation to complete it. Plato suggested that the brain is the mechanism of mental processes and that one gained knowledge by reflecting on the contents of one's mind.
Free will	The idea that human beings are capable of freely making choices or decisions is free will.
Physiology	The study of the functions and activities of living cells, tissues, and organs and of the physical and chemical phenomena involved is referred to as physiology.
Experimental psychology	Experimental psychology is an approach to psychology that treats it as one of the natural sciences, and therefore assumes that it is susceptible to the experimental method.
Wundt	Wundt, considered the father of experimental psychology, created the first laboratory in psychology in 1879. His methodology was based on introspection and his body of work founded the school of thought called Voluntarism.
Perception	Perception is the process of acquiring, interpreting, selecting, and organizing sensory information.
Sensation	Sensation is the first stage in the chain of biochemical and neurologic events that begins with the impinging of a stimulus upon the receptor cells of a sensory organ, which then leads to perception, the mental state that is reflected in statements like "I see a uniformly blue wall."
Physiological psychology	Physiological psychology refers to the study of the physiological mechanisms, in the brain and elsewhere, that mediate behavior and psychological experiences.
American Psychological Association	The American Psychological Association is a professional organization representing psychology in the US. The mission statement is to "advance psychology as a science and profession and as a means of promoting health, education , and human welfare".
Stanley Hall	His laboratory at Johns Hopkins is considered to be the first American laboratory of psychology. In 1887 Stanley Hall founded the American Journal of Psychology. His interests centered around child development and evolutionary theory
Hilgard	Hilgard made headlines as a pioneer in the scientific study of hypnosis. He and his wife, Josephine, established the Laboratory of Hypnosis Research at Stanford.
Structuralism	The school of psychology that argues that the mind consists of three basic elements sensations, feelings, and images which combine to form experience is structuralism-- a term coined by Titchener. They were associationists in that they believed that complex ideas were made up of simpler ideas that were combined in accordance with the laws of association.
Titchener	Titchener attempted to classify the structures of the mind, not unlike the way a chemist breaks down chemicals into their component parts-water into hydrogen and oxygen for example. He conceived of hydrogen and oxygen as structures of a chemical compound, and sensations and thoughts as structures of the mind. This approach became known as structuralism.
Introspection	Introspection is the self report or consideration of one's own thoughts, perceptions and mental processes. Classic introspection was done through trained observers.
Wertheimer	His discovery of the phi phenomenon concerning the illusion of motion gave rise to the influential

	school of Gestalt psychology. In the latter part of his life, Wertheimer directed much of his attention to the problem of learning.
Functionalism	Functionalism was created by William James and influenced by Darwin. This school of psychology focuses on past experience and behavior. It adressed how experience permits people to function better in our environment. According to functionalism, the mental states that make up consciousness can essentially be defined as complex interactions between different functional processes.
William James	Functionalism as a psychology developed out of Pragmatism as a philosophy: To find the meaning of an idea, you have to look at its consequences. This led William James and his students towards an emphasis on cause and effect, prediction and control, and observation of environment and behavior, over the careful introspection of the Structuralists.
Habit	A habit is a response that has become completely separated from its eliciting stimulus. Early learning theorists used the term to describe S-R associations, however not all S-R associations become a habit, rather many are extinguished after reinforcement is withdrawn.
Dewey	Dewey is one of the three central figures in American pragmatism though he did not identify himself as a pragmatist per se, and instead referred to his philosophy as "instrumentalism". He established the first major educational psychology laboratory in the United States, at the University of Chicago in 1894.
Emotion	An emotion is a mental states that arise spontaneously, rather than through conscious effort. They are often accompanied by physiological changes.
Psychodynamic	Most psychodynamic approaches are centered around the idea of a maladapted function developed early in life (usually childhood) which are at least in part unconscious. This maladapted function (a.k.a. defense mechanism) does not do well in place of a normal/healthy one.
Deprivation	Deprivation, is the loss or withholding of normal stimulation, nutrition, comfort, love, and so forth; a condition of lacking. The level of stimulation is less than what is required.
Sigmund Freud	Sigmund Freud was the founder of the psychoanalytic school, based on his theory that unconscious motives control much behavior, that particular kinds of unconscious thoughts and memories are the source of neurosis, and that neurosis could be treated through bringing these unconscious thoughts and memories to consciousness in psychoanalytic treatment.
Abnormal behavior	An action, thought, or feeling that is harmful to the person or to others is called abnormal behavior.
Motives	Needs or desires that energize and direct behavior toward a goal are motives.
Early childhood	Early childhood refers to the developmental period extending from the end of infancy to about 5 or 6 years of age; sometimes called the preschool years.
Personality	Personality refers to the pattern of enduring characteristics that differentiates a person, the patterns of behaviors that make each individual unique.
Social influence	Social influence is when the actions or thoughts of individual(s) are changed by other individual(s). Peer pressure is an example of social influence.
Neo-Freudian	The Neo-Freudian psychologists were those followers of Sigmund Freud who accepted the basic tenets of his theory of psychoanalysis but altered it in some way.
Skinner	Skinner conducted research on shaping behavior through positive and negative reinforcement, and demonstrated operant conditioning, a technique which he developed in contrast with classical conditioning.
Behaviorism	The school of psychology that defines psychology as the study of observable behavior and studies relationships between stimuli and responses is called behaviorism. Behaviorism relied heavily on animal research and stated the same principles governed the behavior of both nonhumans and humans.

Variable	A variable refers to a measurable factor, characteristic, or attribute of an individual or a system.
Positive reinforcement	In positive reinforcement, a stimulus is added and the rate of responding increases.
Punishment	Punishment is the addtion of a stimulus that reduces the frequency of a response, or the removal of a stimulus that results in a reduction of the response.
Utopian	An ideal vision of society is a utopian society.
Humanistic perspective	The approach that suggests that all individuals naturally strive to grow, develop, and be in control of their lives and behavior is called the humanistic perspective.
Humanistic psychology	Humanistic psychology refers to the school of psychology that focuses on the uniqueness of human beings and their capacity for choice, growth, and psychological health.
Humanistic	Humanistic refers to any system of thought focused on subjective experience and human problems and potentials.
Self-actualization	Self-actualization (a term originated by Kurt Goldstein) is the instinctual need of a human to make the most of their unique abilities. Maslow described it as follows: Self Actualization is the intrinsic growth of what is already in the organism, or more accurately, of what the organism is.
Maslow	Maslow is mostly noted today for his proposal of a hierarchy of human needs which he often presented as a pyramid. Maslow was an instrumental player in the formation of the humanistic movement, also known as the third force in psychology.
Cognitive revolution	The cognitive revolution is a name for an intellectual movement in the 1950s that combined new thinking in psychology, anthropology and linguistics with the nascent fields of computer science and neuroscience. In psychology, the movement was a response to behaviorism.
Problem solving	An attempt to find an appropriate way of attaining a goal when the goal is not readily available is called problem solving.
Endocrine system	The endocrine system is a control system of ductless endocrine glands that secrete chemical messengers called hormones that circulate within the body via the bloodstream to affect distant organs. It does not include exocrine glands such as salivary glands, sweat glands and glands within the gastrointestinal tract.
Nervous system	The body's electrochemical communication circuitry, made up of billions of neurons is a nervous system.
Gene	A gene is an ultramicroscopic area of the chromosome. It is the smallest physical unit of the DNA molecule that carries a piece of hereditary information.
Nerve	A nerve is an enclosed, cable-like bundle of nerve fibers or axons, which includes the glia that ensheath the axons in myelin. Neurons are sometimes called nerve cells, though this term is technically imprecise since many neurons do not form nerves.
Neuroscience	A field that combines the work of psychologists, biologists, biochemists, medical researchers, and others in the study of the structure and function of the nervous system is neuroscience.
Learning	Learning is a relatively permanent change in behavior that results from experience. Thus, to attribute a behavioral change to learning, the change must be relatively permanent and must result from experience.
Brain imaging	Brain imaging is a fairly recent discipline within medicine and neuroscience. Brain imaging falls into two broad categories -- structural imaging and functional imaging.
Evolutionary perspective	A perspective that focuses on how humans have evolved and adapted behaviors required for survival against various environmental pressures over the long course is called the evolutionary perspective.
Natural	Natural selection is a process by which biological populations are altered over time, as a result of

selection	the propagation of heritable traits that affect the capacity of individual organisms to survive and reproduce.
Darwin	Darwin achieved lasting fame as originator of the theory of evolution through natural selection. His book Expression of Emotions in Man and Animals is generally considered the first text on comparative psychology.
Adaptation	Adaptation is a lowering of sensitivity to a stimulus following prolonged exposure to that stimulus. Behavioral adaptations are special ways a particular organism behaves to survive in its natural habitat.
Evolutionary psychology	Evolutionary psychology proposes that cognition and behavior can be better understood in light of evolutionary history.
Inference	Inference is the act or process of drawing a conclusion based solely on what one already knows.
Theories	Theories are logically self-consistent models or frameworks describing the behavior of a certain natural or social phenomenon. They are broad explanations and predictions concerning phenomena of interest.
Sociocultural perspective	The view that focuses on the roles of ethnicity, gender, culture, and socioeconomic status in personality formation, behavior, and mental processes is a sociocultural perspective.
Population	Population refers to all members of a well-defined group of organisms, events, or things.
Generalization	In conditioning, the tendency for a conditioned response to be evoked by stimuli that are similar to the stimulus to which the response was conditioned is a generalization. The greater the similarity among the stimuli, the greater the probability of generalization.
Displacement	An unconscious defense mechanism in which the individual directs aggressive or sexual feelings away from the primary object to someone or something safe is referred to as displacement. Displacement in linguistics is simply the ability to talk about things not present.
Attitude	An enduring mental representation of a person, place, or thing that evokes an emotional response and related behavior is called attitude.
Rape	Rape is a crime where the victim is forced into sexual activity, in particular sexual penetration, against his or her will.
Psychological disorder	Mental processes and/or behavior patterns that cause emotional distress and/or substantial impairment in functioning is a psychological disorder.
Developmental psychologist	A psychologist interested in human growth and development from conception until death is referred to as a developmental psychologist.
Acquisition	Acquisition is the process of adapting to the environment, learning or becoming conditioned. In classical conditoning terms, it is the initial learning of the stimulus response link, which involves a neutral stimulus being associated with a unconditioned stimulus and becoming a conditioned stimulus.
Survey	A method of scientific investigation in which a large sample of people answer questions about their attitudes or behavior is referred to as a survey.
Society	The social sciences use the term society to mean a group of people that form a semi-closed (or semi-open) social system, in which most interactions are with other individuals belonging to the group.
Stimulus	A change in an environmental condition that elicits a response is a stimulus.
Affect	A subjective feeling or emotional tone often accompanied by bodily expressions noticeable to others is called affect.

Operational definition	An operational definition is the definition of a concept or action in terms of the observable and repeatable process, procedures, and appartaus that illustrates the concept or action.
Observer bias	Observer bias is an error introduced into measurement when observers overemphasize behavior they expect to find and fail to notice behavior they do not expect. Observer bias can also be introduced because researchers see a behavior and interpret it according to what it means to them, whereas it may mean something else to the person showing the behavior.
Reliability	Reliability means the extent to which a test produces a consistent , reproducible score .
Scientific method	Psychologists gather data in order to describe, understand, predict, and control behavior. Scientific method refers to an approach that can be used to discover accurate information. It includes these steps: understand the problem, collect data, draw conclusions, and revise research conclusions.
Theories	Theories are logically self-consistent models or frameworks describing the behavior of a certain natural or social phenomenon. They are broad explanations and predictions concerning phenomena of interest.
Direct observation	Direct observation refers to assessing behavior through direct surveillance.
Society	The social sciences use the term society to mean a group of people that form a semi-closed (or semi-open) social system, in which most interactions are with other individuals belonging to the group.
Brain	The brain controls and coordinates most movement, behavior and homeostatic body functions such as heartbeat, blood pressure, fluid balance and body temperature. Functions of the brain are responsible for cognition, emotion, memory, motor learning and other sorts of learning. The brain is primarily made up of two types of cells: glia and neurons.
Determinism	Determinism is the philosophical proposition that every event, including human cognition and action, is causally determined by an unbroken chain of prior occurrences.
Mental processes	The thoughts, feelings, and motives that each of us experiences privately but that cannot be observed directly are called mental processes.
Hypothesis	A specific statement about behavior or mental processes that is testable through research is a hypothesis.
Scientific research	Research that is objective, systematic, and testable is called scientific research.
Motives	Needs or desires that energize and direct behavior toward a goal are motives.
Munsterberg	Munsterberg was a pioneer in industrial psychology, and held controversial views on the reliability of witness testimony.
Operationali-ation	The process of translating a hypothesis into specific, testable procedures that can be measured and observed is referred to as operationalization.
Variable	A variable refers to a measurable factor, characteristic, or attribute of an individual or a system.
Independent variable	A condition in a scientific study that is manipulated (assigned different values by a researcher) so that the effects of the manipulation may be observed is called an independent variable.
Dependent variable	A measure of an assumed effect of an independent variable is called the dependent variable.
Affect	A subjective feeling or emotional tone often accompanied by bodily expressions noticeable to

others is called affect.

Confounding variable A confounding variable is a variable which is the common cause of two things that may falsely appear to be in a causal relationship. It is the cause of a spurious relationship.

Placebo effect The placebo effect is the phenomenon that a patient's symptoms can be alleviated by an otherwise ineffective treatment, apparently because the individual expects or believes that it will work.

Insight Insight refers to a sudden awareness of the relationships among various elements that had previously appeared to be independent of one another.

Experimental manipulation The change that an experimenter deliberately produces in a situation under study is called the experimental manipulation.

Research design A research design tests a hypothesis. The basic typess are: descriptive, correlational, and experimental.

Placebo Placebo refers to a bogus treatment that has the appearance of being genuine.

Experimental effect A statistically significant difference between two groups experiencing different manipulations of the independent variable is called the experimental effect.

Baseline Measure of a particular behavior or process taken before the introduction of the independent variable or treatment is called the baseline.

Between-subjects design Between-subjects design is an experimental design in which comparisons are made between one group and another. Participants in a given group do not receive the same level of the independent variable or treatment as those in another group.

Individual differences Individual differences psychology studies the ways in which individual people differ in their behavior. This is distinguished from other aspects of psychology in that although psychology is ostensibly a study of individuals, modern psychologists invariably study groups.

Random assignment Assignment of participants to experimental and control groups by chance is called random assignment. Random assigment reduces the likelihood that the results are due to preexisiting systematic differences between the groups.

Population Population refers to all members of a well-defined group of organisms, events, or things.

Representative sample Representative sample refers to a sample of participants selected from the larger population in such a way that important subgroups within the population are included in the sample in the same proportions as they are found in the larger population.

Ethnic group An ethnic group is a culture or subculture whose members are readily distinguishable by outsiders based on traits originating from a common racial, national, linguistic, or religious source. Members of an ethnic group are often presumed to be culturally or biologically similar, although this is not in fact necessarily the case.

Within-subjects design Experimental design in which the participants receive more than one level of the independent variable is called a within-subjects design.

Emotion An emotion is a mental states that arise spontaneously, rather than through conscious effort. They are often accompanied by physiological changes.

Correlational method A research method used to establish the degree of relationship between two characteristics, events, or behaviors is called a correlational method.

Trait An enduring personality characteristic that tends to lead to certain behaviors is called a trait. The term trait also means a genetically inherited feature of an organism.

Correlation Correlation coefficient refers to a number from +1.00 to -1.00 that expresses the direction

coefficient	and extent of the relationship between two variables. The closer to 1, the stronger the relationship. The sign, + or -, indicates the direction.
Positive correlation	A relationship between two variables in which both vary in the same direction is called a positive correlation.
Negative correlation	A negative correlation refers to a relationship between two variables in which one variable increases as the other decreases.
Correlation	A statistical technique for determining the degree of association between two or more variables is referred to as correlation.
Causation	Causation concerns the time order relationship between two or more objects such that if a specific antecendent condition occurs the same consequent must always follow.
Self-esteem	Self-esteem refers to a person's subjective appraisal of himself or herself as intrinsically positive or negative to some degree.
Survey	A method of scientific investigation in which a large sample of people answer questions about their attitudes or behavior is referred to as a survey.
Psychological test	Psychological test refers to a standardized measure of a sample of a person's behavior.
Questionnaire	A self-report method of data collection or clinical assessment method in which the individual being studied checks off items on a printed list, answers multiple-choice questions, or writes out answers to essay questions aimed at producing a selfdescription is called questionnaire.
Subliminal message	A subliminal message is a signal or message designed to pass below the normal limits of perception. For example it might be inaudible to the conscious mind or might be an image transmitted briefly and unperceived consciously and yet perceived unconsciously.
Subliminal persuasion	Subliminal persuasion refers to sending persuasive messages below the recipient's level of awareness.
Anxiety	Anxiety is a complex combination of the feeling of fear, apprehension and worry often accompanied by physical sensations such as palpitations, chest pain and/or shortness of breath.
Validity	The extent to which a test measures what it is intended to measure is called validity.
Psychological testing	Psychological testing is a field characterized by the use of small samples of behavior in order to infer larger generalizations about a given individual. The technical term for psychological testing is psychometrics.
Attitude	An enduring mental representation of a person, place, or thing that evokes an emotional response and related behavior is called attitude.
Prejudice	Prejudice in general, implies coming to a judgment on the subject before learning where the preponderance of the evidence actually lies, or formation of a judgement without direct experience.
Naturalistic observation	Naturalistic observation is a method of observation that involves observing subjects in their natural habitats. Researchers take great care in avoiding making interferences with the behavior they are observing by using unobtrusive methods.
Learning	Learning is a relatively permanent change in behavior that results from experience. Thus, to attribute a behavioral change to learning, the change must be relatively permanent and must result from experience.
Laboratory	Research setting in which the behavior of interest does not naturally occur is called a

setting laboratory setting.

Shaping The concept of reinforcing successive, increasingly accurate approximations to a target behavior is called shaping. The target behavior is broken down into a hierarchy of elemental steps, each step more sophisticated then the last. By successively reinforcing each of the the elemental steps, a form of differential reinforcement, until that step is learned while extinguishing the step below, the target behavior is gradually achieved.

Stages Stages represent relatively discrete periods of time in which functioning is qualitatively different from functioning at other periods.

Behavioral observation A form of behavioral assessment that entails careful observation of a person's overt behavior in a particular situation is behavioral observation.

Case study A carefully drawn biography that may be obtained through interviews, questionnaires, and psychological tests is called a case study.

American Psychological Association The American Psychological Association is a professional organization representing psychology in the US. The mission statement is to "advance psychology as a science and profession and as a means of promoting health, education , and human welfare".

Informed consent The term used by psychologists to indicate that a person has agreed to participate in research after receiving information about the purposes of the study and the nature of the treatments is informed consent. Even with informed consent, subjects may withdraw from any experiment at any time.

Debriefing Process of informing a participant after the experiment about the nature of the experiment, clarifying any misunderstanding, and answering any questions that the participant may have concerning the experiment is called debriefing.

Mental illness Mental illness is the term formerly used to mean psychological disorder but less preferred because it implies that the causes of the disorder can be found in a medical disease process.

Drug addiction Drug addiction, or substance dependence is the compulsive use of drugs, to the point where the user has no effective choice but to continue use.

Perception Perception is the process of acquiring, interpreting, selecting, and organizing sensory information.

Research method The scope of the research method is to produce some new knowledge. This, in principle, can take three main forms: Exploratory research; Constructive research; and Empirical research.

Correlational research Research that examines the relationship between two sets of variables to determine whether they are associated is called correlational research.

Statistics Statistics is a type of data analysis which practice includes the planning, summarizing, and interpreting of observations of a system possibly followed by predicting or forecasting of future events based on a mathematical model of the system being observed.

Statistic A statistic is an observable random variable of a sample.

Cowan Cowan regards working memory not as a separate system, but as a part of long-term memory. Representations in working memory are a subset of the representations in long-term memory.

Shyness A tendency to avoid others plus uneasiness and strain when socializing is called shyness.

Reasoning Reasoning is the act of using reason to derive a conclusion from certain premises. There are two main methods to reach a conclusion,deductive reasoning and inductive reasoning.

Impulse control Deferred gratification is the ability of a person to wait for things they want. This trait is critical for life success. Those who lack this trait are said to suffer from poor impulse control, and often become criminals, as they are unwilling to work and wait for their

	paycheck.
Masculinity	Masculinity is a culturally determined value reflecting the set of characteristics of maleness.
Femininity	Femininity is the set of characteristics defined by a culture for idealized females.
Androgyny	Androgyny refers to two concepts. The first is the mixing of masculine and feminine characteristics. Secondly it describes something that is neither masculine nor feminine.
Ego	In Freud's view the Ego serves to balance our primitive needs and our moral beliefs and taboos. Relying on experience, a healthy Ego provides the ability to adapt to reality and interact with the outside world.
Descriptive statistic	A simple numerical description of observations, such as the mean of a distribution of scores, used to summarize the observations is a descriptive statistic.
Inferential statistics	Inferential statistics is the branch of statistics that is concerned with the degree of confidence that conclusions drawn about samples can be extended to the populations from which the samples were drawn .
Chance variation	Differences between events without any known influence is considered a chance variation.
Frequency distribution	In statistics, a frequency distribution is a list of the values that a variable takes in a sample. It is usually a list, ordered by quantity, showing the number of times each value appears.
Histogram	In statistics, a histogram is a graphical display of tabulated frequencies. It is the graphical version of a table which shows what proportion of cases fall into each of several or many specified categories. The categories are usually specified as nonoverlapping intervals of some variable.
Central tendency	In statistics, central tendency is an average of a set of measurements, the word average being variously construed as mean, median, or other measure of location, depending on the context. Central tendency is a descriptive statistic analogous to center of mass in physical terms.
Variability	Statistically, variability refers to how much the scores in a distribution spread out, away from the mean.
Standard deviation	In probability and statistics, the standard deviation is the most commonly used measure of statistical dispersion. Simply put, it measures how spread out the values in a data set are.
Deviation score	A test score calculated by comparing an individual's score with the scores of others is called a deviation score.
Normal curve	Normal curve refers to graphic presentation of a normal distribution, which shows a characteristic bell shape.
Statistical significance	The condition that exists when the probability that the observed findings are due to chance is very low is called statistical significance.
Normal distribution	A normal distribution is a symmetrical distribution of scores that is assumed to reflect chance fluctuations; approximately 68% of cases lie within a single standard deviation of the mean.
T-test	A t-test is any statistical hypothesis test in which the test statistic has a Student's t-distribution if the null hypothesis is true.

Anatomy
Anatomy is the branch of biology that deals with the structure and organization of living things. It can be divided into animal anatomy (zootomy) and plant anatomy (phytonomy). Major branches of anatomy include comparative anatomy, histology, and human anatomy.

Evolution
Commonly used to refer to gradual change, evolution is the change in the frequency of alleles within a population from one generation to the next. This change may be caused by different mechanisms, including natural selection, genetic drift, or changes in population (gene flow).

Heredity
Heredity is the transfer of characteristics from parent to offspring through their genes.

Nurture
Nurture refers to the environmental influences on behavior due to nutrition, culture, socioeconomic status, and learning.

Nature versus nurture
Nature versus nurture is a shorthand expression for debates about the relative importance of an individual's innate makeup versus personal experiences in determining or causing physical and behavioral traits.

Society
The social sciences use the term society to mean a group of people that form a semi-closed (or semi-open) social system, in which most interactions are with other individuals belonging to the group.

Affect
A subjective feeling or emotional tone often accompanied by bodily expressions noticeable to others is called affect.

Species
Species refers to a reproductively isolated breeding population.

Natural selection
Natural selection is a process by which biological populations are altered over time, as a result of the propagation of heritable traits that affect the capacity of individual organisms to survive and reproduce.

Survey
A method of scientific investigation in which a large sample of people answer questions about their attitudes or behavior is referred to as a survey.

Darwin
Darwin achieved lasting fame as originator of the theory of evolution through natural selection. His book Expression of Emotions in Man and Animals is generally considered the first text on comparative psychology.

Emotion
An emotion is a mental states that arise spontaneously, rather than through conscious effort. They are often accompanied by physiological changes.

Origin of Species
The Origin of Species by Charles Darwin makes the argument that groups of organisms gradually evolve through the process of natural selection. Characteristics that favor survival and reproduction are passed on to the next generation, those that do not, are gradually lost.

Population
Population refers to all members of a well-defined group of organisms, events, or things.

Trait
An enduring personality characteristic that tends to lead to certain behaviors is called a trait. The term trait also means a genetically inherited feature of an organism.

Evolutionary theory
Evolutionary theory is concerned with heritable variability rather than behavioral variations. Natural selection requirements: (1) natural variability within a species must exist, (2) only some individual differences are heritable, and (3) natural selection only takes place when there is an interaction between the inborn attributes of organisms and the environment in which they live.

Phenotype
The phenotype of an individual organism is either its total physical appearance and constitution, or a specific manifestation of a trait, such as size or eye color, that varies between individuals. Phenotype is determined to some extent by genotype, or by the identity of the alleles that an individual carries at one or more positions on the chromosomes.

Genotype
The genotype is the specific genetic makeup of an individual, usually in the form of DNA. It

codes for the phenotype of that individual. Any given gene will usually cause an observable change in an organism, known as the phenotype.

Adaptation

Adaptation is a lowering of sensitivity to a stimulus following prolonged exposure to that stimulus. Behavioral adaptations are special ways a particular organism behaves to survive in its natural habitat.

Brain

The brain controls and coordinates most movement, behavior and homeostatic body functions such as heartbeat, blood pressure, fluid balance and body temperature. Functions of the brain are responsible for cognition, emotion, memory, motor learning and other sorts of learning. The brain is primarily made up of two types of cells: glia and neurons.

Reasoning

Reasoning is the act of using reason to derive a conclusion from certain premises. There are two main methods to reach a conclusion,deductive reasoning and inductive reasoning.

Wisdom

Wisdom is the ability to make correct judgments and decisions. It is an intangible quality gained through experience. Whether or not something is wise is determined in a pragmatic sense by its popularity, how long it has been around, and its ability to predict against future events.

Learning

Learning is a relatively permanent change in behavior that results from experience. Thus, to attribute a behavioral change to learning, the change must be relatively permanent and must result from experience.

Chromosome

The DNA which carries genetic information in biological cells is normally packaged in the form of one or more large macromolecules called a chromosome. Humans normally have 46.

Genetics

Genetics is the science of genes, heredity, and the variation of organisms.

Mendel

Mendel is often called the "father of genetics" for his study of the inheritance of traits in pea plants. Mendel showed that there was particulate inheritance of traits according to his laws of inheritance.

Attention

Attention is the cognitive process of selectively concentrating on one thing while ignoring other things. Psychologists have labeled three types of attention: sustained attention, selective attention, and divided attention.

Gene

A gene is an ultramicroscopic area of the chromosome. It is the smallest physical unit of the DNA molecule that carries a piece of hereditary information.

Deoxyribonuc-eic acid

Deoxyribonucleic acid contains the genetic instructions specifying the biological development of all cellular forms of life. It is often referred to as the molecule of heredity, as it is responsible for the genetic propagation of most inherited traits.

Nucleus

In neuroanatomy, a cluster of cell bodies of neurons within the central nervous system is a nucleus.

Protein

A protein is a complex, high-molecular-weight organic compound that consists of amino acids joined by peptide bonds. It is essential to the structure and function of all living cells and viruses. Many are enzymes or subunits of enzymes.

Double helix

The double helix is the structure of DNA. Each of the two strands forms a helix, and the two helices are held together through hydrogen bonds, ionic forces, hydrophobic interactions, and van der Waals forces forming a double helix.

Human genome project

The Human Genome Project (HGP) endeavored to map the human genome down to the nucleotide (or base pair) level and to identify all the genes present in it.

Human genome

The complete sequence or mapping of genes in the human body and their locations is the human genome. It is made up of 23 chromosome pairs with a total of about 3 billion DNA base pairs.

Heritability	Heritability It is that proportion of the observed variation in a particular phenotype within a particular population, that can be attributed to the contribution of genotype. In other words: it measures the extent to which differences between individuals in a population are due their being different genetically.
Adoption studies	Research studies that assess hereditary influence by examining the resemblance between adopted children and both their biological and their adoptive parents are referred to as adoption studies. The studies have been inconclusive about the relative importance of heredity in intelligence.
Monozygotic	Identical twins occur when a single egg is fertilized to form one zygote, calld monozygotic, but the zygote then divides into two separate embryos. The two embryos develop into foetuses sharing the same womb. Monozygotic twins are genetically identical unless there has been a mutation in development, and they are almost always the same gender.
Dizygotic	Fraternal twins (commonly known as "non-identical twins") usually occur when two fertilized eggs are implanted in the uterine wall at the same time. The two eggs form two zygotes, and these twins are therefore also known as dizygotic.
Correlation	A statistical technique for determining the degree of association between two or more variables is referred to as correlation.
Perception	Perception is the process of acquiring, interpreting, selecting, and organizing sensory information.
Pitch	Pitch is the psychological interpretation of a sound or musical tone corresponding to its physical frequency
Evolutionary psychology	Evolutionary psychology proposes that cognition and behavior can be better understood in light of evolutionary history.
Evolutionary perspective	A perspective that focuses on how humans have evolved and adapted behaviors required for survival against various environmental pressures over the long course is called the evolutionary perspective.
Neuroscience	A field that combines the work of psychologists, biologists, biochemists, medical researchers, and others in the study of the structure and function of the nervous system is neuroscience.
Nerve	A nerve is an enclosed, cable-like bundle of nerve fibers or axons, which includes the glia that ensheath the axons in myelin. Neurons are sometimes called nerve cells, though this term is technically imprecise since many neurons do not form nerves.
Research method	The scope of the research method is to produce some new knowledge. This, in principle, can take three main forms: Exploratory research; Constructive research; and Empirical research.
Harlow	Harlow and his famous wire and cloth surrogate mother monkey studies demonstrated that the need for affection created a stronger bond between mother and infant than did physical needs. He also found that the more discrimination problems the monkeys solved, the better they became at solving them.
Personality	Personality refers to the pattern of enduring characteristics that differentiates a person, the patterns of behaviors that make each individual unique.
Paul Broca	Paul Broca became famous with his discovery of the speech center, the third circumvolution of the frontal lobe. He arrived at this discovery by studying the brains of aphasic patients (persons unable to talk).
Lesion	A lesion is a non-specific term referring to abnormal tissue in the body. It can be caused by any disease process including trauma (physical, chemical, electrical), infection, neoplasm,

metabolic and autoimmune.

Electrode — Any device used to electrically stimulate nerve tissue or to record its activity is an electrode.

Anxiety — Anxiety is a complex combination of the feeling of fear, apprehension and worry often accompanied by physical sensations such as palpitations, chest pain and/or shortness of breath.

Phineas Gage — As a result of an injury to his brain, Phineas Gage reportedly had significant changes in personality and temperament, which provided some of the first evidence that specific parts of the brain, particularly the frontal lobes, might be involved in specific psychological processes dealing with emotion, personality and problem solving.

Microelectrode — An electrical wire so small that it can be used either to monitor the electrical activity of a single neuron or to stimulate activity within it is a microelectrode.

Electroencep-alogram — Electroencephalography is the neurophysiologic measurement of the electrical activity of the brain by recording from electrodes placed on the scalp, or in the special cases on the cortex. The resulting traces are known as an electroencephalogram and represent so-called brainwaves.

Stroke — A stroke occurs when the blood supply to a part of the brain is suddenly interrupted by occlusion, by hemorrhage, or other causes

Descartes — Descartes was concerned with the sharp contrast between the certainty of mathematics and the controversial nature of philosophy, and came to believe that the sciences could be made to yield results as certain as those of mathematics. He introduced the method of rationalism for arriving at knowledge. He also saw the human condition as a competition between the body and soul, introducing the concept of dualism.

Magnetic resonance imaging — Magnetic resonance imaging is a method of creating images of the inside of opaque organs in living organisms as well as detecting the amount of bound water in geological structures. It is primarily used to demonstrate pathological or other physiological alterations of living tissues and is a commonly used form of medical imaging.

Nervous system — The body's electrochemical communication circuitry, made up of billions of neurons is a nervous system.

Neuron — The neuron is the primary cell of the nervous system. They are found in the brain, the spinal cord, in the nerves and ganglia of the peripheral nervous system. It is a specialized cell that conducts impulses through the nervous system and contains three major parts: cell body, dendrites, and an axon. It can have many dendrites but only one axon.

Peripheral nervous system — The peripheral nervous system consists of the nerves and neurons that serve the limbs and organs. It is not protected by bone or the blood-brain barrier, leaving it exposed to toxins and mechanical injuries. The peripheral nervous system is divided into the somatic nervous system and the autonomic nervous system.

Central nervous system — The vertebrate central nervous system consists of the brain and spinal cord.

Spinal cord — The spinal cord is a part of the vertebrate nervous system that is enclosed in and protected by the vertebral column (it passes through the spinal canal). It consists of nerve cells. The spinal cord carries sensory signals and motor innervation to most of the skeletal muscles in the body.

Sensory receptor — A sensory receptor is a structure that recognizes a stimulus in the environment of an organism. In response to stimuli the sensory receptor initiates sensory transduction by creating graded potentials or action potentials in the same cell or in an adjacent one.

Spinal nerve	The term spinal nerve generally refers to the mixed spinal nerve, which is formed from the dorsal and ventral roots that come out of the spinal cord. The spinal nerve passes out of the vertebrae through the intervertebral foramen.
Gland	A gland is an organ in an animal's body that synthesizes a substance for release such as hormones, often into the bloodstream or into cavities inside the body or its outer surface.
Somatic nervous system	The somatic nervous system is the part of the peripheral nervous system associated with the voluntary control of body movements through the action of skeletal muscles. The somatic nervous system consists of afferent fibers which receive information from external sources, and efferent fibers which are responsible for muscle contraction.
Skeletal muscle	Skeletal muscle is a type of striated muscle, attached to the skeleton. They are used to facilitate movement, by applying force to bones and joints; via contraction. They generally contract voluntarily (via nerve stimulation), although they can contract involuntarily.
Feedback	Feedback refers to information returned to a person about the effects a response has had.
Autonomic nervous system	A division of the peripheral nervous system, the autonomic nervous system, regulates glands and activities such as heartbeat, respiration, digestion, and dilation of the pupils. It is responsible for homeostasis, maintaining a relatively constant internal environment .
Anesthesia	Anesthesia is the process of blocking the perception of pain and other sensations. This allows patients to undergo surgery and other procedures without the distress and pain they would otherwise experience.
Parasympathetic	The parasympathetic nervous system is one of two divisions of the autonomic nervous system. It conserves energy as it slows the heart rate, increases intestinal and gland activity, and relaxes sphincter muscles. In another words, it acts to reverse the effects of the Sympathetic nervous system.
Sympathetic	The sympathetic nervous system activates what is often termed the "fight or flight response". It is an automatic regulation system, that is, one that operates without the intervention of conscious thought.
Conservation	Conservation refers to the recognition that basic properties of substances such as weight and mass remain the same even when transformations merely alter their appearance.
Pupil	In the eye, the pupil is the opening in the middle of the iris. It appears black because most of the light entering it is absorbed by the tissues inside the eye. The size of the pupil is controlled by involuntary contraction and dilation of the iris, in order to regulate the intensity of light entering the eye. This is known as the pupillary reflex.
Brain stem	The brain stem is the stalk of the brain below the cerebral hemispheres. It is the major route for communication between the forebrain and the spinal cord and peripheral nerves. It also controls various functions including respiration, regulation of heart rhythms, and primary aspects of sound localization.
Limbic system	The limbic system is a group of brain structures that are involved in various emotions such as aggression, fear, pleasure and also in the formation of memory. The limbic system affects the endocrine system and the autonomic nervous system. It consists of several subcortical structures located around the thalamus.
Motivation	In psychology, motivation is the driving force (desire) behind all actions of an organism.
Cerebrum	The cerebrum (the portion of the brain that performs motor and sensory functions and a variety of mental activities) is divided into four lobes - the frontal, temporal, parietal and occipital lobes.
Cerebral cortex	The cerebral cortex is the outermost layer of the cerebrum and has a grey color. It is made

up of four lobes and it is involved in many complex brain functions including memory, perceptual awareness, "thinking", language and consciousness. The cerebral cortex receives sensory information from many different sensory organs eg: eyes, ears, etc. and processes the information.

Cerebellum

The cerebellum is located in the inferior posterior portion of the head (the hindbrain), directly dorsal to the brainstem and pons, inferior to the occipital lobe. The cerebellum is a region of the brain that plays an important role in the integration of sensory perception and fine motor output.

Thalamus

An area near the center of the brain involved in the relay of sensory information to the cortex and in the functions of sleep and attention is the thalamus.

Reticular formation

Reticular formation is a part of the brain which is involved in stereotypical actions, such as walking, sleeping, and lying down. The reticular formation, phylogenetically one of the oldest portions of the brain, is a poorly-differentiated area of the brain stem.

Hypothalamus

The hypothalamus is a region of the brain located below the thalamus, forming the major portion of the ventral region of the diencephalon and functioning to regulate certain metabolic processes and other autonomic activities.

Acquisition

Acquisition is the process of adapting to the environment, learning or becoming conditioned. In classical conditoning terms, it is the initial learning of the stimulus response link, which involves a neutral stimulus being associated with a unconditioned stimulus and becoming a conditioned stimulus.

Hippocampus

The hippocampus is a part of the brain located inside the temporal lobe. It forms a part of the limbic system and plays a part in memory and navigation.

Amygdala

Located in the brain's medial temporal lobe, the almond-shaped amygdala is believed to play a key role in the emotions. It forms part of the limbic system and is linked to both fear responses and pleasure. Its size is positively correlated with aggressive behavior across species.

Seizure

A seizure is a temporary alteration in brain function expressed as a changed mental state, tonic or clonic movements and various other symptoms. They are due to temporary abnormal electrical activity of a group of brain cells.

Homeostasis

Homeostasis is the property of an open system, especially living organisms, to regulate its internal environment so as to maintain a stable condition, by means of multiple dynamic equilibrium adjustments controlled by interrelated regulation mechanisms.

Endocrine system

The endocrine system is a control system of ductless endocrine glands that secrete chemical messengers called hormones that circulate within the body via the bloodstream to affect distant organs. It does not include exocrine glands such as salivary glands, sweat glands and glands within the gastrointestinal tract.

Lateral fissure

The lateral fissure is one of the most prominent structures of the human brain. It divides the frontal lobe and parietal lobe above from the temporal lobe below.

Central sulcus

The central sulcus is a prominent landmark of the brain, separating the parietal lobe from the frontal lobe. The central sulcus is the site of the primary motor cortex in mammals, a group of cells that controls voluntary movements of the body.

Lobes

The four major sections of the cerebral cortex: frontal, parietal, temporal, and occipital are called lobes.

Frontal lobe

The frontal lobe comprises four major folds of cortical tissue: the precentral gyrus, superior gyrus and the middle gyrus of the frontal gyri, the inferior frontal gyrus. It has been found to play a part in impulse control, judgement, language, memory, motor function,

problem solving, sexual behavior, socialization and spontaneity.

Occipital lobe	The occipital lobe is the smallest of four true lobes in the human brain. Located in the rearmost portion of the skull, the occipital lobe is part of the forebrain structure. It is the visual processing center.
Cerebral hemisphere	Either of the two halves that make up the cerebrum is referred to as a cerebral hemisphere. The hemispheres operate together, linked by the corpus callosum, a very large bundle of nerve fibers, and also by other smaller commissures.
Temporal lobe	The temporal lobe is part of the cerebrum. It lies at the side of the brain, beneath the lateral or Sylvian fissure. Adjacent areas in the superior, posterior and lateral parts of the temporal lobe are involved in high-level auditory processing.
Motor cortex	Motor cortex refers to the section of cortex that lies in the frontal lobe, just across the central fissure from the sensory cortex. Neural impulses in the motor cortex are linked to muscular responses throughout the body.
Somatosensory cortex	The primary somatosensory cortex is across the central sulcus and behind the primary motor cortex configured to generally correspond with the arrangement of nearby motor cells related to specific body parts. It is the main sensory receptive area for the sense of touch.
Parietal lobe	The parietal lobe is positioned above (superior to) the occipital lobe and behind (posterior to) the frontal lobe. It plays important roles in integrating sensory information from various senses, and in the manipulation of objects.
Visual cortex	The visual cortex is the general term applied to both the primary visual cortex and the visual association area. Anatomically, the visual cortex occupies the entire occipital lobe, the inferior temporal lobe (IT), posterior parts of the parietal lobe, and a few small regions in the frontal lobe.
Retina	The retina is a thin layer of cells at the back of the eyeball. It is the part of the eye which converts light into nervous signals. The retina contains photoreceptor cells which receive the light; the resulting neural signals then undergo complex processing by other neurons of the retina, and are transformed into action potentials in retinal ganglion cells whose axons form the optic nerve.
Association cortex	Region of the cerebral cortex in which the highest intellectual functions, including thinking and problem solving, occur is the association cortex.
Association areas	Association areas refer to the site of the higher mental processes such as thought, language, memory, and speech.
Verbal Behavior	Verbal Behavior is a book written by B.F. Skinner in which the author presents his ideas on language. For Skinner, speech, along with other forms of communication, was simply a behavior. Skinner argued that each act of speech is an inevitable consequence of the speaker's current environment and his behavioral and sensory history.
Nerve impulse	A nerve impulse is a change in the electric potential of a neuron; a wave of depolarization spreads along the neuron and causes the release of a neurotransmitter.
Somatosensory	Somatosensory system consists of the various sensory receptors that trigger the experiences labelled as touch or pressure, temperature, pain, and the sensations of muscle movement and joint position including posture, movement, and facial expression.
Coding	In senation, coding is the process by which information about the quality and quantity of a stimulus is preserved in the pattern of action potentials sent through sensory neurons to the central nervous system.
Gyrus	A gyrus is a ridge on the cerebral cortex. It is generally surrounded by one or more sulci.

Synchrony | In child development, synchrony is the carefully coordinated interaction between the parent and the child or adolescent in which, often unknowingly, they are attuned to each other's behavior.

Larynx | The larynx, or voicebox, is an organ in the neck of mammals involved in protection of the trachea and sound production. The larynx houses the vocal cords, and is situated at the point where the upper tract splits into the trachea and the esophagus.

Left hemisphere | The left hemisphere of the cortex controls the right side of the body, coordinates complex movements, and, in 95% of people, controls the production of speech and written language.

Aphasia | Aphasia is a loss or impairment of the ability to produce or comprehend language, due to brain damage. It is usually a result of damage to the language centers of the brain.

Epilepsy | Epilepsy is a chronic neurological condition characterized by recurrent unprovoked neural discharges. It is commonly controlled with medication, although surgical methods are used as well.

Split-brain | Split-brain is a lay term to describe the result when the corpus callosum connecting the two halves of the brain is severed to some degree. The surgical operation to produce this condition is called corpus callosotomy. It is rarely performed, usually to treat epilepsy; people with generalized seizures who injure themselves during falls may have less violent seizures, and hence less injury during those seizures, after the procedure.

Corpus callosum | The corpus callosum is the largest white matter structure in the brain. It consists of mostly of contralateral axon projections. The corpus callosum connects the left and right cerebral hemispheres. Most communication between regions in different halves of the brain are carried over the corpus callosum.

Gazzaniga | Gazzaniga worked under the guidance of Roger Sperry, with primary responsibility for initiating human split-brain research. In his subsequent work he has made important advances in our understanding of functional lateralization in the brain and how the cerebral hemispheres communicate with one another.

Sperry | Sperry separated the corpus callosum, the area of the brain used to transfer signals between the right and left hemispheres, to treat epileptics. He then tested these patients with tasks that were known to be dependant on specific hemispheres of the brain and demonstrated that the two halves of the brain now had independent functions.

Right hemisphere | The brain is divided into left and right cerebral hemispheres. The right hemisphere of the cortex controls the left side of the body.

Optic nerve | The optic nerve is the nerve that transmits visual information from the retina to the brain. The optic nerve is composed of retinal ganglion cell axons and support cells.

American Sign Language | The American Sign Language is a language of hand gestures used by deaf and hearing impaired persons.

Lateralization | Lateralization refers to the dominance of one hemisphere of the brain for specific functions.

Brain imaging | Brain imaging is a fairly recent discipline within medicine and neuroscience. Brain imaging falls into two broad categories -- structural imaging and functional imaging.

Endocrine gland | An endocrine gland is one of a set of internal organs involved in the secretion of hormones into the blood. The other major type of gland is the exocrine glands, which secrete substances—usually digestive juices—into the digestive tract or onto the skin.

Pituitary gland | The pituitary gland is an endocrine gland about the size of a pea that sits in the small, bony cavity at the base of the brain. The pituitary gland secretes hormones regulating a wide variety of bodily activities, including trophic hormones that stimulate other endocrine

glands.

Pancreas The pancreas is a retroperitoneal organ that serves two functions: it produces juice containing digestive enzymes; and it produces several important hormones including insulin, glucagon, and several other hormones.

Thyroid In anatomy, the thyroid is the largest endocrine gland in the body. The primary function of the thyroid is production of hormones.

Hormone A hormone is a chemical messenger from one cell (or group of cells) to another. The best known are those produced by endocrine glands, but they are produced by nearly every organ system. The function of hormones is to serve as a signal to the target cells; the action of the hormone is determined by the pattern of secretion and the signal transduction of the receiving tissue.

Stages Stages represent relatively discrete periods of time in which functioning is qualitatively different from functioning at other periods.

Receptor A sensory receptor is a structure that recognizes a stimulus in the internal or external environment of an organism. In response to stimuli the sensory receptor initiates sensory transduction by creating graded potentials or action potentials in the same cell or in an adjacent one.

Adrenaline Adrenaline refers to a hormone produced by the adrenal medulla that stimulates sympathetic ANS activity and generally arouses people and heightens their emotional responsiveness.

Growth hormone Growth hormone is a polypeptide hormone synthesised and secreted by the anterior pituitary gland which stimulates growth and cell reproduction in humans and other vertebrate animals.

Testosterone Testosterone is a steroid hormone from the androgen group. It is the principal male sex hormone and the "original" anabolic steroid.

Testes Testes are the male reproductive glands or gonads; this is where sperm develop and are stored.

Maturation The orderly unfolding of traits, as regulated by the genetic code is called maturation.

Blocking If the one of the two members of a compound stimulus fails to produce the CR due to an earlier conditioning of the other member of the compound stimulus, blocking has occurred.

Dendrite A dendrite is a slender, typically branched projection of a nerve cell, or "neuron," which conducts the electrical stimulation received from other cells to the body or soma of the cell from which it projects. This stimulation arrives through synapses, which typically are located near the tips of the dendrites and away from the soma.

Cytoplasm Cytoplasm is the colloidal, semi-fluid matter contained within the cell's plasma membrane, in which organelles are suspended. In contrast to the protoplasm, the cytoplasm does not include the cell nucleus, the interior of which is made up of nucleoplasm.

Soma The soma, or cell body, is the bulbous end of a neuron, containing the nucleus. The cell nucleus is a key feature of the soma. The nucleus is the source of most of the RNA that is produced in neurons and most proteins are produced from mRNAs that do not travel far from the nucleus.

Axon An axon, or "nerve fiber," is a long slender projection of a nerve cell, or "neuron," which conducts electrical impulses away from the neuron's cell body or soma.

Terminal buttons Terminal buttons are small bulges at the end of axons that send messages to other neurons.

Sensory neuron A sensory neuron is an afferent nerve cell within the nervous system responsible for converting external stimuli from the organism's environment into internal electrical

impulses. It carries messages from a sensory organ, through a nerve, into the brain or spinal cord.

Motor neuron A motor neuron is an efferent neuron that originates in the spinal cord and synapses with muscle fibers to facilitate muscle contraction and with muscle spindles to modify proprioceptive sensitivity.

Interneuron An interneuron (also called relay neuron or association neuron) is a neuron that communicates only to other neurons.

Neurotransmitter A neurotransmitter is a chemical that is used to relay, amplify and modulate electrical signals between a neurons and another cell.

Glial Glial cells are non-neuronal cells that provide support and nutrition, maintain homeostasis, form myelin, and participate in signal transmission in the nervous system.

Myelin Myelin is an electrically insulating fatty layer that surrounds the axons of many neurons, especially those in the peripheral nervous system. The main consequence of a myelin sheath is an increase in the speed at which impulses propagate along the myelinated fiber. The sheath continues to develop throughout childhood.

Astrocyte An astrocyte, also known as astroglia, is a characteristic star-shaped cell in the brain. They are the biggest cells found in brain tissue and outnumber the neurons ten to one. A commonly accepted function is to structure physically the brain. A second function is to provide neurons with nutrients such as glucose. They regulate the flow of nutrients provided by capillaries by forming the blood-brain barrier.

Action potential The electrical impulse that provides the basis for the conduction of a neural impulse along an axon of a neuron is the action potential. When a biological cell or patch of membrane undergoes an action potential, or electrical excitation, the polarity of the transmembrane voltage swings rapidly from negative to positive and back.

Ion An ion is an atom or group of atoms with a net electric charge. The energy required to detach an electron in its lowest energy state from an atom or molecule of a gas with less net electric charge is called the ionization potential, or ionization energy.

Resting state Resting state is a negative electrical charge of about 270 millivolts within a neuron.

Resting potential The resting potential of a cell is the membrane potential that would be maintained if there were no action potentials, synaptic potentials, or other active changes in the membrane potential. In most cells the resting potential has a negative value, which by convention means that there is excess negative charge inside compared to outside.

Ion channel An Ion channel is a pore-forming protein that help establish the small voltage gradient that exists across the membrane of all living cells, by controlling the flow of ions. They are present in the membranes that surround all biological cells.

Cell membrane A component of every biological cell, the selectively permeable cell membrane is a thin and structured bilayer of phospholipid and protein molecules that envelopes the cell. It separates a cell's interior from its surroundings and controls what moves in and out.

All-or-none All-or-none indicates a situation in which there are two possibilities (a binary choice set), one of which is 100% and one of which is 0%. It is a phrase commonly used to describe action potentials of neurons, which, if they fire at all, propagate from the beginning to the end of the axonal process.

Threshold In general, a threshold is a fixed location or value where an abrupt change is observed. In the sensory modalities, it is the minimum amount of stimulus energy necessary to elicit a sensory response.

Nodes of Ranvier	Nodes of Ranvier are regularly spaced gaps in the myelin sheath around an axon or nerve fiber. About one micrometer in length, these gaps expose the membrane of the axon to the surrounding liquid. Ion flow occurs only at the nodes of Ranvier.
Multiple sclerosis	Multiple sclerosis affects neurons, the cells of the brain and spinal cord that carry information, create thought and perception, and allow the brain to control the body. Surrounding and protecting these neurons is a layer of fat, called myelin, which helps neurons carry electrical signals. MS causes gradual destruction of myelin (demyelination) in patches throughout the brain and/or spinal cord, causing various symptoms depending upon which signals are interrupted.
Tremor	Tremor is the rhythmic, oscillating shaking movement of the whole body or just a certain part of it, caused by problems of the neurons responsible from muscle action.
Absolute refractory period	The refractory period in a neuron occurs after an action potential. The action potential ends when voltage-gated ion channels allow positively charged potassium ions to leave the cell, between the 2nd and 3rd millisecond after the action potential. During this repolarization period when the potassium ion-channels are open, it is impossible to have another action potential. As a result, this is known as the absolute refractory period.
Refractory period	Refractory period refers to a phase following firing during which a neuron is less sensitive to messages from other neurons and will not fire. In the sexual response cycle, it is a period of time following orgasm during which an individual is not responsive to sexual stimulation.
Immune system	The most important function of the human immune system occurs at the cellular level of the blood and tissues. The lymphatic and blood circulation systems are highways for specialized white blood cells. These cells include B cells, T cells, natural killer cells, and macrophages. All function with the primary objective of recognizing, attacking and destroying bacteria, viruses, cancer cells, and all substances seen as foreign.
Stimulus	A change in an environmental condition that elicits a response is a stimulus.
Depolarization	Depolarization is any change that decreases the absolute value of a cell's membrane potential. Thus, changes in membrane voltage in which the membrane potential becomes less positive or less negative are both depolarizations.
Synaptic cleft	Synaptic cleft refers to a microscopic gap between the terminal button of a neuron and the cell membrane of another neuron.
Enzyme	An enzyme is a protein that catalyzes, or speeds up, a chemical reaction. Enzymes are essential to sustain life because most chemical reactions in biological cells would occur too slowly, or would lead to different products, without enzymes.
Synapse	A synapse is specialized junction through which cells of the nervous system signal to one another and to non-neuronal cells such as muscles or glands.
Psychological disorder	Mental processes and/or behavior patterns that cause emotional distress and/or substantial impairment in functioning is a psychological disorder.
Drug addiction	Drug addiction, or substance dependence is the compulsive use of drugs, to the point where the user has no effective choice but to continue use.
Acetylcholine	The chemical compound acetylcholine was the first neurotransmitter to be identified. It plays a role in learning, memory, and rapid eye movement sleep and causes the skeletal muscle fibers to contract.
Curare	Curare is a drug that once entered into the bloodstream and reaches the muscles it blocks the receptors on the muscles, paralyzing the muscles.

Gamma-aminobutyric acid	Gamma-aminobutyric acid is a neurotransmitter that reduces activity across the synapse and thus inhibits a range of behaviors and emotions, especially generalized anxiety.
Psychopathology	Psychopathology refers to the field concerned with the nature and development of mental disorders.
Anxiety disorder	Anxiety disorder is a blanket term covering several different forms of abnormal anxiety, fear, phobia and nervous condition, that come on suddenly and prevent pursuing normal daily routines.
Norepinephrine	Norepinephrine is released from the adrenal glands as a hormone into the blood, but it is also a neurotransmitter in the nervous system. As a stress hormone, it affects parts of the human brain where attention and impulsivity are controlled. Along with epinephrine, this compound effects the fight-or-flight response, activating the sympathetic nervous system to directly increase heart rate, release energy from fat, and increase muscle readiness.
Serotonin	Serotonin, a neurotransmitter, is believed to play an important part of the biochemistry of depression, bipolar disorder and anxiety. It is also believed to be influential on sexuality and appetite.
Dopamine	Dopamine is critical to the way the brain controls our movements and is a crucial part of the basal ganglia motor loop. It is commonly associated with the 'pleasure system' of the brain, providing feelings of enjoyment and reinforcement to motivate us to do, or continue doing, certain activities.
Schizophrenia	Schizophrenia is characterized by persistent defects in the perception or expression of reality. A person suffering from untreated schizophrenia typically demonstrates grossly disorganized thinking, and may also experience delusions or auditory hallucinations
Depression	In everyday language depression refers to any downturn in mood, which may be relatively transitory and perhaps due to something trivial. This is differentiated from Clinical depression which is marked by symptoms that last two weeks or more and are so severe that they interfere with daily living.
Hallucinogenic	Certain drugs can affect the subjective qualities of perception, thought or emotion, resulting in altered interpretations of sensory input, alternate states of consciousness, or hallucinations. The term hallucinogenic is often broadly applied, especially in current scientific literature, to some or all of these substances.
Lysergic acid	Lysergic acid is a precursor for a wide range of ergoline alkaloids that are produced by the ergot fungus and some plants. Amides of lysergic acid, commonly called lysergamides, are widely used as pharmaceuticals and as hallucinogenic drugs (LSD).
Neuromodulator	A neuromodulator is a substance other than a neurotransmitter, released by a neuron at a synapse and conveying information to adjacent or distant neurons, either enhancing or damping their activities.
Antidepressant	An antidepressant is a medication used primarily in the treatment of clinical depression. They are not thought to produce tolerance, although sudden withdrawal may produce adverse effects. They create little if any immediate change in mood and require between several days and several weeks to take effect.
Endorphin	An endorphin is an endogenous opioid biochemical compound. They are peptides produced by the pituitary gland and the hypothalamus, and they resemble the opiates in their abilities to produce analgesia and a sense of well-being. In other words, they work as "natural pain killers."
Receptor site	A location on the dendrite of a receiving neuron that is tailored to receive a specific

neurotransmitter is a receptor site.

Morphine — Morphine, the principal active agent in opium, is a powerful opioid analgesic drug. According to recent research, it may also be produced naturally by the human brain. Morphine is usually highly addictive, and tolerance and physical and psychological dependence develop quickly.

Opium — Opium is a narcotic analgesic drug which is obtained from the unripe seed pods of the opium poppy. Regular use, even for a few days, invariably leads to physical tolerance and dependence. Various degrees of psychological addiction can occur, though this is relatively rare when opioids are properly used..

Placebo — Placebo refers to a bogus treatment that has the appearance of being genuine.

Neurogenesis — Neurogenesis literally means "birth of neurons". Neurogenesis is most prevalent during pre-natal development and is the process by which neurons are created to populate the growing brain.

Plasticity — The capacity for modification and change is referred to as plasticity.

Stem cells — Stem cells are primal undifferentiated cells which retain the ability to differentiate into other cell types. This ability allows them to act as a repair system for the body, replenishing other cells as long as the organism is alive.

Embryo — A developed zygote that has a rudimentary heart, brain, and other organs is referred to as an embryo.

Fetus — A fetus develops from the end of the 8th week of pregnancy (when the major structures have formed), until birth.

Mental processes — The thoughts, feelings, and motives that each of us experiences privately but that cannot be observed directly are called mental processes.

Long-term memory — Long-term memory is memory that lasts from over 30 seconds to years.

Metabolism — Metabolism is the biochemical modification of chemical compounds in living organisms and cells.

Bottom-up	In Bottom-up design individual parts of the system are specified in detail. The parts are then linked together to form larger components, which are in turn linked until a complete system is formed. Strategies based on the bottom-up information flow seem potentially necessary and sufficient because they are based on the knowledge of all variables that may affect the elements of the system.
Priming	A phenomenon in which exposure to a word or concept later makes it easier to recall related information, even when one has no conscious memory of the word or concept is called priming.
Senses	The senses are systems that consist of a sensory cell type that respond to a specific kind of physical energy, and that correspond to a defined region within the brain where the signals are received and interpreted.
Perception	Perception is the process of acquiring, interpreting, selecting, and organizing sensory information.
Sensation	Sensation is the first stage in the chain of biochemical and neurologic events that begins with the impinging of a stimulus upon the receptor cells of a sensory organ, which then leads to perception, the mental state that is reflected in statements like "I see a uniformly blue wall."
Stages	Stages represent relatively discrete periods of time in which functioning is qualitatively different from functioning at other periods.
Sensory receptor	A sensory receptor is a structure that recognizes a stimulus in the environment of an organism. In response to stimuli the sensory receptor initiates sensory transduction by creating graded potentials or action potentials in the same cell or in an adjacent one.
Neural impulse	Neural impulse refers to the electrochemical discharge of a nerve cell, or neuron.
Brain	The brain controls and coordinates most movement, behavior and homeostatic body functions such as heartbeat, blood pressure, fluid balance and body temperature. Functions of the brain are responsible for cognition, emotion, memory, motor learning and other sorts of learning. The brain is primarily made up of two types of cells: glia and neurons.
Nerve	A nerve is an enclosed, cable-like bundle of nerve fibers or axons, which includes the glia that ensheath the axons in myelin. Neurons are sometimes called nerve cells, though this term is technically imprecise since many neurons do not form nerves.
Stimulus	A change in an environmental condition that elicits a response is a stimulus.
Attitude	An enduring mental representation of a person, place, or thing that evokes an emotional response and related behavior is called attitude.
Theories	Theories are logically self-consistent models or frameworks describing the behavior of a certain natural or social phenomenon. They are broad explanations and predictions concerning phenomena of interest.
Proximal	Students can set both long-term (distal) and short-term (proximal) goals .
Retina	The retina is a thin layer of cells at the back of the eyeball. It is the part of the eye which converts light into nervous signals. The retina contains photoreceptor cells which receive the light; the resulting neural signals then undergo complex processing by other neurons of the retina, and are transformed into action potentials in retinal ganglion cells whose axons form the optic nerve.
Visual perception	Visual perception is one of the senses, consisting of the ability to detect light and interpret it. Vision has a specific sensory system.
Proximal stimulus	A proximal stimulus refers to the energies that impinge directly on sensory receptors.

Illusion	An illusion is a distortion of a sensory perception.
Ambiguous stimuli	Patterns that allow more than one perceptual organization are called ambiguous stimuli.
Bottom-up processing	Using the parts of a pattern to recognize, or form an image of, the originating pattern is called bottom-up processing.
Motivation	In psychology, motivation is the driving force (desire) behind all actions of an organism.
Top-down	In the Top-down model an overview of the system is formulated, without going into detail for any part of it. Each part of the system is then refined by designing it in more detail. Each new part may then be refined again, defining it in yet more detail until the entire specification is detailed enough to validate the Model.
Variability	Statistically, variability refers to how much the scores in a distribution spread out, away from the mean.
Invariance	Invariance is the property of perception whereby simple geometrical objects are recognized independent of rotation, translation, and scale, as well as several other variations such as elastic deformations, different lighting, and different component features.
Physiology	The study of the functions and activities of living cells, tissues, and organs and of the physical and chemical phenomena involved is referred to as physiology.
Hallucination	A hallucination is a sensory perception experienced in the absence of an external stimulus, as distinct from an illusion, which is a misperception of an external stimulus. They may occur in any sensory modality - visual, auditory, olfactory, gustatory, tactile, or mixed.
Visual illusion	Visual illusion refers to a discrepancy or incongruency between reality and the perceptual representation of it.
Psychophysics	Psychophysics refers to the study of the mathematical relationship between the physical aspects of stimuli and our psychological experience of them.
Threshold	In general, a threshold is a fixed location or value where an abrupt change is observed. In the sensory modalities, it is the minimum amount of stimulus energy necessary to elicit a sensory response.
Construct	A generalized concept, such as anxiety or gravity, is a construct.
Fechner	Fechner founded psychophysics or the scientific investigation of the functional relations of dependency between body and mind.
Absolute threshold	An absolute threshold is the minimum amount of stimulation required for a person to detect a stimulus fifty percent of the time.
Psychometric	Psychometric study is concerned with the theory and technique of psychological measurement, which includes the measurement of knowledge, abilities, attitudes, and personality traits. The field is primarily concerned with the study of differences between individuals
Operational definition	An operational definition is the definition of a concept or action in terms of the observable and repeatable process, procedures, and appartaus that illustrates the concept or action.
Adaptation	Adaptation is a lowering of sensitivity to a stimulus following prolonged exposure to that stimulus. Behavioral adaptations are special ways a particular organism behaves to survive in its natural habitat.
Sensory adaptation	Sensory adaptation is a change over time in the responsiveness of the sensory system to a constant stimulus. It is usually experienced as a change in the stimulus.
Signal	Signal detection theory is a means to quantify the ability to discern between signal and

detection theory	noise. According to the theory, there are a number of psychological determiners of how we will detect a signal, and where our threshold levels will be. Experience, expectations, physiological state (e.g, fatigue) and other factors affect thresholds.
Difference threshold	Difference threshold refers to the minimal difference in intensity required between two sources of energy so that they will be perceived as being different 50 percent of the time.
Ernst Weber	Ernst Weber discovered that the just-noticeable differences in the intensity of various stimuli are proportional to the intensity of the original stimulus. His work latter became known as Weber's Law.
Just noticeable difference	The minimal amount by which a source of energy must be increased or decreased so that a difference in intensity will be perceived is called just noticeable difference.
Transduction	Transduction in the nervous system typically refers to synaptic events wherein an electrical signal, known as an action potential, is converted into a chemical one via the release of neurotransmitters. Conversely, in sensory transduction a chemical or physical stimulus is transduced by sensory receptors into an electrical signal.
Nervous system	The body's electrochemical communication circuitry, made up of billions of neurons is a nervous system.
Neuron	The neuron is the primary cell of the nervous system. They are found in the brain, the spinal cord, in the nerves and ganglia of the peripheral nervous system. It is a specialized cell that conducts impulses through the nervous system and contains three major parts: cell body, dendrites, and an axon. It can have many dendrites but only one axon.
Association cortex	Region of the cerebral cortex in which the highest intellectual functions, including thinking and problem solving, occur is the association cortex.
Cornea	The cornea is the transparent front part of the eye that covers the iris, pupil, and anterior chamber and provides most of an eye's optical power. Together with the lens, the cornea refracts light and consequently helps the eye to focus.
Optic nerve	The optic nerve is the nerve that transmits visual information from the retina to the brain. The optic nerve is composed of retinal ganglion cell axons and support cells.
Aqueous humor	The aqueous humor is the clear, watery fluid that fills the complex space in the front of the eye which is bounded at the front by the cornea and at the rear by the front surface or face of the vitreous humor.
Pupil	In the eye, the pupil is the opening in the middle of the iris. It appears black because most of the light entering it is absorbed by the tissues inside the eye. The size of the pupil is controlled by involuntary contraction and dilation of the iris, in order to regulate the intensity of light entering the eye. This is known as the pupillary reflex.
Iris	The iris is the most visible part of the eye. The iris is an annulus (or flattened ring) consisting of pigmented fibrovascular tissue known as a stroma. The stroma connects a sphincter muscle, which contracts the pupil, and a set of dialator muscles which open it.
Crystalline lens	The crystalline lens is a transparent, biconvex structure in the eye that, along with the cornea, helps to refract light to focus on the retina. The lens is flexible and its curvature is controlled by ciliary muscles. By changing the curvature of the lens, one can focus the eye on objects at different distances from it. This process is called accommodation.
Variable	A variable refers to a measurable factor, characteristic, or attribute of an individual or a system.
Ciliary muscle	The ciliary muscle is a smooth muscle that affects zonules in the eye (fibers that suspend the lens in position during accommodation), enabling changes in lens shape for light

focusing.

Accommodation Piaget's developmental process of accommodation is the modification of currently held schemes or new schemes so that new information inconsistent with the existing schemes can be integrated and understood.

Receptor A sensory receptor is a structure that recognizes a stimulus in the internal or external environment of an organism. In response to stimuli the sensory receptor initiates sensory transduction by creating graded potentials or action potentials in the same cell or in an adjacent one.

Cones Cones are photoreceptors that transmit sensations of color, function in bright light, and used in visual acuity. Infants prior to months of age can only distinguish green and red indicating the cones are not fully developed; they can see all of the colors by 2 months of

Rods Rods are cylindrical shaped photoreceptors that are sensitive to the intensity of light. Rods require less light to function than cone cells, and therefore are the primary source of visual information at night.

Dark adaptation Dark adaptation is the tendency for the peak sensitivity of the human eye to shift toward the blue end of the color spectrum at low illumination levels.

Fovea The fovea, a part of the eye, is a spot located in the center of the macula. The fovea is responsible for sharp central vision, which is necessary in humans for reading, watching television or movies, driving, and any activity where visual detail is of primary importance.

Ganglion cell A ganglion cell is a type of neuron located in the retina of the eye that receives visual information from photoreceptors via various intermediate cells such as bipolar cells, amacrine cells, and horizontal cells. Retinal ganglion cells' axons are myelinated.

Bipolar cell As a part of the retina, the bipolar cell exists between photoreceptors and ganglion cells. Bipolar cells are so-named as they have a central body from which two sets of processes arise. At one end, they form synapses with either a single cone cell, or a number of rod cells. At the other end, they form synapses with ganglion cells, which fire action potentials along the optic nerve (cranial nerve II). They effectively transfer information from rods and cones to ganglion cells.

Axon An axon, or "nerve fiber," is a long slender projection of a nerve cell, or "neuron," which conducts electrical impulses away from the neuron's cell body or soma.

Nerve impulse A nerve impulse is a change in the electric potential of a neuron; a wave of depolarization spreads along the neuron and causes the release of a neurotransmitter.

Blind spot In anatomy, the blind spot is the region of the retina where the optic nerve and blood vessels pass through to connect to the back of the eye. Since there are no light receptors there, a part of the field of vision is not perceived.

Primary visual cortex Primary visual cortex refers to the area at the rear of the occipital lobes where vision registers in the cerebral cortex.

Occipital lobe The occipital lobe is the smallest of four true lobes in the human brain. Located in the rearmost portion of the skull, the occipital lobe is part of the forebrain structure. It is the visual processing center.

Optic tract The optic tract is a part of the visual system in the brain. It is a continuation of the optic nerve and runs from the optic chiasm (where half of the information from each eye crosses sides, and half stays on the same side) to the lateral geniculate nucleus.

Receptive field The receptive field of a sensory neuron is a region of sensitivity in which the presence of a stimulus will alter the firing of that neuron.

Visual cortex	The visual cortex is the general term applied to both the primary visual cortex and the visual association area. Anatomically, the visual cortex occupies the entire occipital lobe, the inferior temporal lobe (IT), posterior parts of the parietal lobe, and a few small regions in the frontal lobe.
Temporal lobe	The temporal lobe is part of the cerebrum. It lies at the side of the brain, beneath the lateral or Sylvian fissure. Adjacent areas in the superior, posterior and lateral parts of the temporal lobe are involved in high-level auditory processing.
Hypothesis	A specific statement about behavior or mental processes that is testable through research is a hypothesis.
Ganglion	A ganglion is a tissue mass that contains the dendrites and cell bodies (or "somas") of nerve cells, in most case ones belonging to the peripheral nervous system. Within the central nervous system such a mass is often called a nucleus.
Photoreceptor	Photoreceptor cells are contained in the retina and are responsible for transducing, or converting, light into signals that can be ultimately transmitted to the brain via the optic nerve. A photoreceptor cell contains a membranous protein called an opsin which contains a pigment molecule called retinal.
Hue	A hue refers to the gradation of color within the optical spectrum, or visible spectrum, of light. Hue may also refer to a particular color within this spectrum, as defined by its dominant wavelength, or the central tendency of its combined wavelengths.
Visible light	The part of the electromagnetic spectrum that stimulates the eye and produces visual sensations is called visible light.
Saturation	Saturation refers to the degree to which the light waves producing a color are of the same wavelength. It is the purity of a color.
Brightness	The dimension of visual sensation that is dependent on the intensity of light reflected from a surface and that corresponds to the amplitude of the light wave is called brightness.
Complementary colors	Pairs of colors that produce gray tones when added together are referred to as complementary colors. Due to the cytology of the human eye, all perceived colors are based on combinations of red, green, and blue.
Color blindness	Color blindness in humans is the inability to perceive differences between some or all colors that other people can distinguish. It is most often of genetic nature, but may also occur because of eye, nerve, or brain damage, or due to exposure to certain chemicals.
Afterimage	An afterimage is an optical illusion that occurs after looking away from a direct gaze at an image. This is closely related to the phenomenon called the persistence of vision, which is used in animation and cinema.
X chromosome	The sex chromosomes are one of the 23 pairs of human chromosomes. Each person normally has one pair of sex chromosomes in each cell. Females have two X chromosomes, while males have one X and one Y chromosome. The X chromosome carries hundreds of genes but few, if any, of these have anything to do directly with sex determination.
Gene	A gene is an ultramicroscopic area of the chromosome. It is the smallest physical unit of the DNA molecule that carries a piece of hereditary information.
Trait	An enduring personality characteristic that tends to lead to certain behaviors is called a trait. The term trait also means a genetically inherited feature of an organism.
Thomas Young	Thomas Young discovered that light was composed of waves through his famous double-slit experiment and described the process of accomodation of vision as a result of the change of the curvature of the lens. He also argued that color perception depends on the presence in

the retina of three kinds of nerve fibres which respond respectively to red, green and violet light.

Trichromatic theory The trichromatic theory was postulated by Young and later by Helmholtz. They demonstrated that most colors can be matched by superimposing three separate light sources known as primaries; a process known as additive mixing. The Young-Helmholtz theory of color vision was built around the assumption of there being three classes of receptors.

Helmholtz Helmholtz a pioneer of the new science of psychology, was a rigorous experimental physiologist and philospher. He gave us the distinction betwen sensation and peception and is well known for his theories of color perception and hearing.

Hering Hering disagreed with the trichromatic theory of color perception which held that the human eye perceived all colors in terms of three primary colors. (Red, Green, Blue). He believed that the visual system worked based on a system of color opponency, a system of six primary colors.

Opponent-process theory The opponent-process theory is a color theory that states that the human visual system interprets information about color by processing signals from cones in an antagonistic manner.

Primary color A primary color cannot be created by mixing other colors in the gamut of a given color space.

Amplitude Amplitude is a nonnegative scalar measure of a wave's magnitude of oscillation.

Loudness Loudness is the quality of a sound that is the primary psychological correlate of physical intensity. Loudness is often approximated by a power function with an exponent of 0.6 when plotted vs. sound pressure or 0.3 when plotted vs. sound intensity.

Timbre The distinctive quality of a sound that distinguishes it from other sounds of the same pitch and loudness is called timbre.

Pitch Pitch is the psychological interpretation of a sound or musical tone corresponding to its physical frequency

Auditory system The auditory system is the sensory system for the sense of hearing. On its path from the outside world to the forebrain, sound information is preserved and modified in many ways. It changes media twice, first from air to fluid, then from fluid to action potentials.

Pinna The pinna is the visible part of the ear that resides outside of the head. It acts as a funnel, amplifying the sound and directing it to the ear canal. While reflecting from the pinna, sound also goes through a filtering process which adds directional information to the sound.

Outer ear Outer ear consists of the pinna and the external auditory canal.

Tympanic membrane The tympanic membrane, colloquially known as eardrum, is a thin membrane that separates the outer ear from the middle ear. Its function is to transmit sound from the air to the ossicles inside the middle ear.

Eardrum The tympanum or tympanic membrane, colloquially known as the eardrum, is a thin membrane that separates the outer ear from the middle ear. Its function is to transmit sound from the air to the ossicles inside the middle ear. The malleus bone connects the eardrum to the other ossicles.

Middle ear The middle ear consists of the eardrum, hammer, anvil, and stirrup.

Cochlea The Cochlea is the bony tube that contains the basilar membrane and the organ of Corti. The cochlea consists of three fluid-filled chambers - scala tympani and scala vestibuli and scala media.

Basilar membrane | The basilar membrane within the cochlea of the inner ear is the part of the auditory system that decomposes incoming auditory signals into their frequency components. This allows higher neural processing of sound information to focus on the frequency spectrum of input, rather than just the time domain waveform.

Semicircular canals | The semicircular canals are three half-circular, interconnected tubes located inside each ear that are the equivalent of three gyroscopes located in three planes perpendicular (at right angles) to each other.

Auditory nerve | The vestibulocochlear nerve is the eighth of twelve cranial nerves, and also known as the auditory nerve. It is the nerve along which the sensory cells (the hair cells) of the inner ear transmit information to the brain. It consists of the cochlear nerve, carrying information about hearing, and the vestibular nerve, carrying information about balance.

Facial nerve | The facial nerve is seventh of twelve paired cranial nerves. Its main function is motor control of most of the facial muscles and muscles of the inner ear.

Oval window | The oval window is a membrane-covered opening which leads from the middle ear to the vestibule of the inner ear.

Hair cells | Hair cells are the sensory cells of both the auditory system and the vestibular system. The auditory hair cells are located within the organ of Corti on a thin basilar membrane in the cochlea of the inner ear.

Cerebral hemisphere | Either of the two halves that make up the cerebrum is referred to as a cerebral hemisphere. The hemispheres operate together, linked by the corpus callosum, a very large bundle of nerve fibers, and also by other smaller commissures.

Conduction deafness | Deafness that occurs when the ossicles of the middle ear become rigid and cannot carry sounds inward from the tympanic membrane to the cochlea is called conduction deafness.

Place theory | Place theory is a theory of hearing which states that our perception of sound depends on where each component frequency produces vibrations along the basilar membrane. It was first discovered by Helmholtz.

Inner ear | The inner ear consists of the oval window, cochlea, and basilar membrane.

Frequency theory | Békésy's theory that the pitch of a sound is reflected in the frequency of the neural impulses that are generated in response to the sound is called frequency theory. However, frequences above 1000 Hz nerve impulses cannot follow the wave form.

Volley principle | The volley principle describes a cluster of nerve cells that can fire neural impulses in rapid succession, producing a volley of impulses.

Coding | In senation, coding is the process by which information about the quality and quantity of a stimulus is preserved in the pattern of action potentials sent through sensory neurons to the central nervous system.

Sound localization | Sound localization is a listener's ability to identify the location of origin of a detected sound. There are two general methods for sound localization, binaural cues and monaural cues.

Attention | Attention is the cognitive process of selectively concentrating on one thing while ignoring other things. Psychologists have labeled three types of attention: sustained attention, selective attention, and divided attention.

Protein | A protein is a complex, high-molecular-weight organic compound that consists of amino acids joined by peptide bonds. It is essential to the structure and function of all living cells and viruses. Many are enzymes or subunits of enzymes.

Olfactory bulb | The olfactory bulb is a part of the brain that is a distinct outgrowth from the forebrain. It plays a major role in olfaction, which is the perception of smells. The olfactory bulb

	receives direct input from olfactory nerve, made up of the axons from approximately 10 million olfactory receptor neurons in the olfactory mucosa, a region of the nasal cavity.
Frontal lobe	The frontal lobe comprises four major folds of cortical tissue: the precentral gyrus, superior gyrus and the middle gyrus of the frontal gyri, the inferior frontal gyrus. It has been found to play a part in impulse control, judgement, language, memory, motor function, problem solving, sexual behavior, socialization and spontaneity.
Cerebrum	The cerebrum (the portion of the brain that performs motor and sensory functions and a variety of mental activities) is divided into four lobes - the frontal, temporal, parietal and occipital lobes.
Action potential	The electrical impulse that provides the basis for the conduction of a neural impulse along an axon of a neuron is the action potential. When a biological cell or patch of membrane undergoes an action potential, or electrical excitation, the polarity of the transmembrane voltage swings rapidly from negative to positive and back.
Ion channel	An Ion channel is a pore-forming protein that help establish the small voltage gradient that exists across the membrane of all living cells, by controlling the flow of ions. They are present in the membranes that surround all biological cells.
Species	Species refers to a reproductively isolated breeding population.
Pheromone	A pheromone is any chemical produced by a living organism that transmits a message to other members of the same species. There are alarm pheromones, food trail pheromones, sex pheromones, and many others. Their use among insects has been particularly well documented, although many vertebrates also communicate using pheromones. Their use by humans is controversial.
Olfactory nerve	The olfactory nerve is the first of twelve cranial nerves. It consists of a collection of sensory nerve fibers that extend down from the olfactory bulb and pass through the many openings of the cribriform plate, a sieve-like structure. The specialized olfactory receptor neurons of the olfactory nerve are located in the olfactory mucosa of the upper parts of the nasal cavity.
Dendrite	A dendrite is a slender, typically branched projection of a nerve cell, or "neuron," which conducts the electrical stimulation received from other cells to the body or soma of the cell from which it projects. This stimulation arrives through synapses, which typically are located near the tips of the dendrites and away from the soma.
Papillae	The bumps on the tongue that contain taste buds, the receptors for taste, are papillae.
Feedback	Feedback refers to information returned to a person about the effects a response has had.
Taste bud	The taste bud (or lingual papillae) is a small structure on the upper surface of the tongue that provides information about the taste of food being eaten. It is known that there are five taste sensations: Sweet, Bitter, Umami, Salty and Sour.
Vestibular sense	Vestibular sense is the sensory system that provides the dominant input about our movement and orientation in space. Together with the cochlea, the auditory organ, it is situated in the vestibulum in the inner ear.
Vestibular system	The vestibular system, or balance system, is the sensory system that provides the dominant input about our movement and orientation in space. Together with the cochlea, the auditory organ, it is situated in the vestibulum in the inner ear.
Kinesthetic sense	The sense providing information about relative position and movement of body parts is the kinesthetic sense.
Congenital	A condition existing at birth is referred to as congenital.

Chronic	Chronic refers to a relatively long duration, usually more than a few months.
Cerebral cortex	The cerebral cortex is the outermost layer of the cerebrum and has a grey color. It is made up of four lobes and it is involved in many complex brain functions including memory, perceptual awareness, "thinking", language and consciousness. The cerebral cortex receives sensory information from many different sensory organs eg: eyes, ears, etc. and processes the information.
Spinal cord	The spinal cord is a part of the vertebrate nervous system that is enclosed in and protected by the vertebral column (it passes through the spinal canal). It consists of nerve cells. The spinal cord carries sensory signals and motor innervation to most of the skeletal muscles in the body.
Thalamus	An area near the center of the brain involved in the relay of sensory information to the cortex and in the functions of sleep and attention is the thalamus.
Endorphin	An endorphin is an endogenous opioid biochemical compound. They are peptides produced by the pituitary gland and the hypothalamus, and they resemble the opiates in their abilities to produce analgesia and a sense of well-being. In other words, they work as "natural pain killers."
Receptor site	A location on the dendrite of a receiving neuron that is tailored to receive a specific neurotransmitter is a receptor site.
Morphine	Morphine, the principal active agent in opium, is a powerful opioid analgesic drug. According to recent research, it may also be produced naturally by the human brain. Morphine is usually highly addictive, and tolerance and physical and psychological dependence develop quickly.
Blocking	If the one of the two members of a compound stimulus fails to produce the CR due to an earlier conditioning of the other member of the compound stimulus, blocking has occurred.
Inhibitory message	A chemical message that prevents a receiving neuron from firing is called an inhibitory message.
Attentional processes	In Bandura's theory of vicarious learning, any activity by an observer that aids in the observation of relevant aspects of a model's behavior and its consequences is referred to as attentional processes.
Dichotic listening	Dichotic Listening is a procedure used for investigating selective attention in the auditory domain. Two messages are presented to both the left and right ears, normally using a set of headphones. Normally, participants are asked to pay attention to either one, or both of the messages and may later be asked about the content of both.
Cowan	Cowan regards working memory not as a separate system, but as a part of long-term memory. Representations in working memory are a subset of the representations in long-term memory.
Consciousness	The awareness of the sensations, thoughts, and feelings being experienced at a given moment is called consciousness.
Gestalt psychology	According to Gestalt psychology, people naturally organize their perceptions according to certain patterns. The tendency is to organize perceptions into wholes and to integrate separate stimuli into meaningful patterns.
Wertheimer	His discovery of the phi phenomenon concerning the illusion of motion gave rise to the influential school of Gestalt psychology. In the latter part of his life, Wertheimer directed much of his attention to the problem of learning.
Koffka	Koffka was cofounder of the Gestalt school of psychology. They stressed the approach that psychological phenomena cannot be interpreted as combinations of elements: parts derive their meaning from the whole, and people perceive complex entities rather than their elements.

Kohler	Kohler applied Gestalt principles to study chimpanzees and recorded their ability to devise and use tools and solve problems. In 1917, he published and gained fame with The Mentality of Apes, in which he argued that his subjects, like humans, were capable of insight learning. His work led to a radical revision of learning theory.
Fixation	Fixation in abnormal psychology is the state where an individual becomes obsessed with an attachment to another human, animal or inanimate object. Fixation in vision refers to maintaining the gaze in a constant direction. .
Motion perception	Motion perception is the process of inferring the "true" velocity and direction of motion in a visual scene given some visual input.
Retinal disparity	A binocular cue for depth based on the difference in the image cast by an object on the retinas of the eyes as the object moves closer or farther away, is called retinal disparity.
Displacement	An unconscious defense mechanism in which the individual directs aggressive or sexual feelings away from the primary object to someone or something safe is referred to as displacement. Displacement in linguistics is simply the ability to talk about things not present.
Motion parallax	A monocular cue for depth, motion parallax is the apparent relative motion of several stationary objects against a background when the observer moves gives hints about their relative distance. This effect can be seen clearly when driving in a car, nearby things pass quickly, while far off objects appear stationary.
Occlusion	The monocular depth cue occlusion is the blocking of sight of objects by other objects. It creates a "ranking" of nearness, and does not give any insight as to actual distances. In the absence of color or binocular vision, it often serves as the method of last resort for rudimentary depth perception.
Linear perspective	A monocular depth cue, linear perspective is the property of parallel lines converging at infinity allowing us to reconstruct the relative distance of two parts of an object, or of landscape features.
Texture gradient	Texture gradient is a monocular cue for depth based on the perception that closer objects appear to have rougher surfaces. Objects appear denser as they go further away.
Relative size	Relative size is a monocular cue where an an automobile that is close to us seems larger than one that is far away. The visual system exploits the relative size of similar (or familiar) objects to judge distance.
Projection	Attributing one's own undesirable thoughts, impulses, traits, or behaviors to others is referred to as projection.
Ponzo	The Ponzo Illusion illustrates that the human mind judges an objects size based on its background. Two identical lines are drawn across a pair of converging lines, similar to railway tracks. The upper bar looked wider because it spans a greater apparent distance between the rails.
Depth cues	Perceptual features that impart information about distance and three-dimensional space are called depth cues.
Perceptual constancy	Perceptual constancy is the recognition that objects are constant and unchanging even though sensory input about them is changing.
Size constancy	The tendency to perceive an object as being the same size even as the size of its retinal image changes according to the object's distance is referred to as size constancy.
Ames room	An Ames room is a distorted room that is used to create an optical illusion. As a result of the optical illusion, a person standing in one corner appears to the observer to be a giant

	while a person standing in the other corner appears to be a midget.
Shape constancy	The tendency to perceive an object as being the same shape although the retinal image varies in shape as it rotates, is shape constancy.
Lightness constancy	Lightness constancy refers to the perceptual tendency to perceive a surface as having the same degree of lightness or darkness regardless of the amount of light that illuminates it.
Empirical	Empirical means the use of working hypotheses which are capable of being disproved using observation or experiment.
Affect	A subjective feeling or emotional tone often accompanied by bodily expressions noticeable to others is called affect.
Mental set	The tendency to respond to a new problem with an approach that was used successfully with similar problems, is called mental set.
Problem solving	An attempt to find an appropriate way of attaining a goal when the goal is not readily available is called problem solving.
Perceptual set	A predisposition or readiness to perceive something in a particular way is called a perceptual set.
Olfaction	Olfaction, the sense of odor (smell), is the detection of chemicals dissolved in air. Smells are sensed by the olfactory epithelium located in the nose and processed by the olfactory system.
Pictorial cues	Pictorial cues for depth perception operate on real scenes and when viewing pictures. They include occlusion, relative image size for familiar objects, linear perspective, texture gradient, differential lighting of surfaces, and position relative location.

Brain — The brain controls and coordinates most movement, behavior and homeostatic body functions such as heartbeat, blood pressure, fluid balance and body temperature. Functions of the brain are responsible for cognition, emotion, memory, motor learning and other sorts of learning. The brain is primarily made up of two types of cells: glia and neurons.

Consciousness — The awareness of the sensations, thoughts, and feelings being experienced at a given moment is called consciousness.

Stream of consciousness — James' concept that the mind is a continuous flow of sensations, images, thoughts, and feelings is stream of consciousness. Accordingly, consiousness cannot be reduced into elements.

William James — Functionalism as a psychology developed out of Pragmatism as a philosophy: To find the meaning of an idea, you have to look at its consequences. This led William James and his students towards an emphasis on cause and effect, prediction and control, and observation of environment and behavior, over the careful introspection of the Structuralists.

Introspection — Introspection is the self report or consideration of one's own thoughts, perceptions and mental processes. Classic introspection was done through trained observers.

Titchener — Titchener attempted to classify the structures of the mind, not unlike the way a chemist breaks down chemicals into their component parts-water into hydrogen and oxygen for example. He conceived of hydrogen and oxygen as structures of a chemical compound, and sensations and thoughts as structures of the mind. This approach became known as structuralism.

Wundt — Wundt, considered the father of experimental psychology, created the first laboratory in psychology in 1879. His methodology was based on introspection and his body of work founded the school of thought called Voluntarism.

Preconscious — In psychodynamic theory, material that is not in awareness but that can be brought into awareness by focusing one's attention is referred to as preconscious.

Attention — Attention is the cognitive process of selectively concentrating on one thing while ignoring other things. Psychologists have labeled three types of attention: sustained attention, selective attention, and divided attention.

Cowan — Cowan regards working memory not as a separate system, but as a part of long-term memory. Representations in working memory are a subset of the representations in long-term memory.

Motives — Needs or desires that energize and direct behavior toward a goal are motives.

Locke — In 1690, Locke wrote his Essay Concerning Human Understanding. The essay arugued for empiricism, that ideas come only from experience. In other words, there are no innate ideas. The tabula rasa or blank slate was his metaphor.

Mental processes — The thoughts, feelings, and motives that each of us experiences privately but that cannot be observed directly are called mental processes.

Personality — Personality refers to the pattern of enduring characteristics that differentiates a person, the patterns of behaviors that make each individual unique.

Hypothesis — A specific statement about behavior or mental processes that is testable through research is a hypothesis.

Dennett — Dennett is a leading proponent of the theory known by some as Neural Darwinism. He is also well known for his argument against qualia, which claims that the concept is so confused that it cannot be put to any use or understood in any non-contradictory way, and therefore does not constitute a valid refutation of physicalism.

Survey — A method of scientific investigation in which a large sample of people answer questions about their attitudes or behavior is referred to as a survey.

Natural selection	Natural selection is a process by which biological populations are altered over time, as a result of the propagation of heritable traits that affect the capacity of individual organisms to survive and reproduce.
Species	Species refers to a reproductively isolated breeding population.
Sensory receptor	A sensory receptor is a structure that recognizes a stimulus in the environment of an organism. In response to stimuli the sensory receptor initiates sensory transduction by creating graded potentials or action potentials in the same cell or in an adjacent one.
Stimulus	A change in an environmental condition that elicits a response is a stimulus.
Individual differences	Individual differences psychology studies the ways in which individual people differ in their behavior. This is distinguished from other aspects of psychology in that although psychology is ostensibly a study of individuals, modern psychologists invariably study groups.
Society	The social sciences use the term society to mean a group of people that form a semi-closed (or semi-open) social system, in which most interactions are with other individuals belonging to the group.
Predisposition	Predisposition refers to an inclination or diathesis to respond in a certain way, either inborn or acquired. In abnormal psychology, it is a factor that lowers the ability to withstand stress and inclines the individual toward pathology.
Affect	A subjective feeling or emotional tone often accompanied by bodily expressions noticeable to others is called affect.
Subjective self-awareness	The ability of an organism to differentiate itself, however crudely, from its physical and social environment is called subjective self-awareness.
Objective self-awareness	Objective self-awareness refers to an organism's capacity to be the object of its own attention, to be aware of its own state of mind, and to know that it knows and remember that it remembers.
Acquisition	Acquisition is the process of adapting to the environment, learning or becoming conditioned. In classical conditoning terms, it is the initial learning of the stimulus response link, which involves a neutral stimulus being associated with a unconditioned stimulus and becoming a conditioned stimulus.
Adaptation	Adaptation is a lowering of sensitivity to a stimulus following prolonged exposure to that stimulus. Behavioral adaptations are special ways a particular organism behaves to survive in its natural habitat.
Circadian rhythm	The circadian rhythm is a name given to the "internal body clock" that regulates the (roughly) 24 hour cycle of biological processes in animals and plants.
Synchrony	In child development, synchrony is the carefully coordinated interaction between the parent and the child or adolescent in which, often unknowingly, they are attuned to each other's behavior.
Receptor	A sensory receptor is a structure that recognizes a stimulus in the internal or external environment of an organism. In response to stimuli the sensory receptor initiates sensory transduction by creating graded potentials or action potentials in the same cell or in an adjacent one.
Cones	Cones are photoreceptors that transmit sensations of color, function in bright light, and used in visual acuity. Infants prior to months of age can only distinguish green and red indicating the cones are not fully developed; they can see all of the colors by 2 months of
Rods	Rods are cylindrical shaped photoreceptors that are sensitive to the intensity of light. Rods require less light to function than cone cells, and therefore are the primary source of

visual information at night.

Variable — A variable refers to a measurable factor, characteristic, or attribute of an individual or a system.

Sleep cycle — Sleep cycle refers to a cycle of sleep lasting about 90 minutes and including one or more stages of NREM sleep followed by a period of REM sleep.

Electroencep-alogram — Electroencephalography is the neurophysiologic measurement of the electrical activity of the brain by recording from electrodes placed on the scalp, or in the special cases on the cortex. The resulting traces are known as an electroencephalogram and represent so-called brainwaves.

Rapid Eye Movement — Rapid eye movement is the stage of sleep during which the most vivid (though not all) dreams occur. During this stage, the eyes move rapidly, and the activity of the brain's neurons is quite similar to that during waking hours. It is the lightest form of sleep in that people awakened during REM usually feel alert and refreshed.

Stages — Stages represent relatively discrete periods of time in which functioning is qualitatively different from functioning at other periods.

Stage 1 sleep — The state of transition between wakefulness and sleep, characterized by relatively rapid, low-voltage brain waves is called stage 1 sleep.

Sleep spindles — Sleep spindles refer to distinctive bursts of brain-wave activity that indicate a person is asleep.

Deep sleep — Deep sleep refers to stage 4 sleep; the deepest form of normal sleep.

Rem sleep — Sleep characterized by rapid eye movements, paralysis of large muscles, fast and irregular heart rate and respiration rate, increased brain-wave activity, and vivid dreams is referred to as REM sleep. An infant spends about half the time in REM sleep when sleeping.

Delta wave — A delta wave is a large, slow brain wave associated with deep sleep. They are present only in stage-three sleep, stage -four sleep, and coma.

Alpha wave — The brain wave associated with deep relaxation is referred to as the alpha wave. Recorded by electroencephalography (EEG) , they are synchronous and coherent (regular like sawtooth) and in the frequency range of 8 - 12 Hz. It is also called Berger's wave in memory of the founder of EEG.

Theta wave — A theta wave is an electroencephalogram pattern normally produced while awake but relaxed or drowsy. The pattern has a frequency of 3.5 to 7.5 Hz. They are strong during internal focus, meditation, prayer, and spiritual awareness.

Sleep patterns — The order and timing of daily sleep and waking periods are called sleep patterns.

Conservation — Conservation refers to the recognition that basic properties of substances such as weight and mass remain the same even when transformations merely alter their appearance.

Neurotransmitter — A neurotransmitter is a chemical that is used to relay, amplify and modulate electrical signals between a neurons and another cell.

Neuromodulator — A neuromodulator is a substance other than a neurotransmitter, released by a neuron at a synapse and conveying information to adjacent or distant neurons, either enhancing or damping their activities.

Infancy — The developmental period that extends from birth to 18 or 24 months is called infancy.

Nerve — A nerve is an enclosed, cable-like bundle of nerve fibers or axons, which includes the glia that ensheath the axons in myelin. Neurons are sometimes called nerve cells, though this term is technically imprecise since many neurons do not form nerves.

Learning	Learning is a relatively permanent change in behavior that results from experience. Thus, to attribute a behavioral change to learning, the change must be relatively permanent and must result from experience.
Emotion	An emotion is a mental states that arise spontaneously, rather than through conscious effort. They are often accompanied by physiological changes.
Insomnia	Insomnia is a sleep disorder characterized by an inability to sleep and/or to remain asleep for a reasonable period during the night.
Cognition	The intellectual processes through which information is obtained, transformed, stored, retrieved, and otherwise used is cognition.
Narcolepsy	A serious sleep disorder characterized by excessive daytime sleepiness and sudden, uncontrollable attacks of REM sleep is called narcolepsy.
Cataplexy	Sudden loss of muscle tone that accompanies narcolepsy is called cataplexy.
Sleep apnea	Sleep apnea refers to a sleep disorder involving periods during sleep when breathing stops and the person must awaken briefly in order to breathe; major symptoms are excessive daytime sleepiness and loud snoring.
Apnea	Apnea is the absence of external breathing. During apnea there is no movement of the muscles of respiration and the volume of the lungs initially remains unchanged. .
Hormone	A hormone is a chemical messenger from one cell (or group of cells) to another. The best known are those produced by endocrine glands, but they are produced by nearly every organ system. The function of hormones is to serve as a signal to the target cells; the action of the hormone is determined by the pattern of secretion and the signal transduction of the receiving tissue.
Somnambulism	Sleepwalking that occurs during a partial arousal from Stage 4 sleep is referred to as somnambulism.
Stage 4 sleep	The deepest stage of sleep, during which we are least responsive to outside stimulation is referred to as stage 4 sleep.
Reaction time	The amount of time required to respond to a stimulus is referred to as reaction time.
Deprivation	Deprivation, is the loss or withholding of normal stimulation, nutrition, comfort, love, and so forth; a condition of lacking. The level of stimulation is less than what is required.
Nocturnal	A person who exhibits nocturnal habits is referred to as a night owl.
Psychoanalyst	A psychoanalyst is a specially trained therapist who attempts to treat the individual by uncovering and revealing to the individual otherwise subconscious factors that are contributing to some undesirable behavor.
Dream analysis	Dream analysis is a part of psychoanalysis that intends to look beneath the manifest content of a dream, i.e., what we perceive in the dream, to the latent content of a dream, i.e., the meaning of the dream and the reason we dreamt it.
Sigmund Freud	Sigmund Freud was the founder of the psychoanalytic school, based on his theory that unconscious motives control much behavior, that particular kinds of unconscious thoughts and memories are the source of neurosis, and that neurosis could be treated through bringing these unconscious thoughts and memories to consciousness in psychoanalytic treatment.
Manifest content	In psychodynamic theory, the reported content of dreams is referred to as manifest content.
Latent content	In psychodynamic theory, the symbolized or underlying content of dreams is called latent content.

The Interpretation of Dreams	The Interpretation of Dreams is a book by Sigmund Freud. The book introduces the Id, the Ego, and the Superego, and describes Freud's theory of the unconscious with respect to Dream interpretation. Widely considered to be his most important contribution to Psychology.
Metaphor	A metaphor is a rhetorical trope where a comparison is made between two seemingly unrelated subjects
Uterus	The uterus or womb is the major female reproductive organ. The main function of the uterus is to accept a fertilized ovum which becomes implanted into the endometrium, and derives nourishment from blood vessels which develop exclusively for this purpose.
Genitals	Genitals refers to the internal and external reproductive organs.
Dream symbols	Images in dreams whose personal or emotional meanings differ from their literal meanings are called dream symbols.
Fisher	Fisher was a eugenicist, evolutionary biologist, geneticist and statistician. He has been described as "The greatest of Darwin's successors", and a genius who almost single-handedly created the foundations for modern statistical science inventing the techniques of maximum likelihood and analysis of variance.
Theories	Theories are logically self-consistent models or frameworks describing the behavior of a certain natural or social phenomenon. They are broad explanations and predictions concerning phenomena of interest.
Brain stem	The brain stem is the stalk of the brain below the cerebral hemispheres. It is the major route for communication between the forebrain and the spinal cord and peripheral nerves. It also controls various functions including respiration, regulation of heart rhythms, and primary aspects of sound localization.
Nightmare	Nightmare was the original term for the state later known as waking dream, and more currently as sleep paralysis, associated with rapid eye movement (REM) periods of sleep.
Trauma	Trauma refers to a severe physical injury or wound to the body caused by an external force, or a psychological shock having a lasting effect on mental life.
Rape	Rape is a crime where the victim is forced into sexual activity, in particular sexual penetration, against his or her will.
Polygraph	A polygraph is a device which measures and records several physiological variables such as blood pressure, heart rate, respiration and skin conductivity while a series of questions is being asked, in an attempt to detect lies.
Lucid dream	A dream during which the dreamer is aware of dreaming and is often able to influence the content of the dream while it is in progress is a lucid dream.
Hypnosis	Hypnosis is a psychological state whose existence and effects are strongly debated. Some believe that it is a state under which the subject's mind becomes so suggestible that the hypnotist, the one who induces the state, can establish communication with the subconscious mind of the subject and command behavior that the subject would not choose to perform in a conscious state.
Motivation	In psychology, motivation is the driving force (desire) behind all actions of an organism.
Perception	Perception is the process of acquiring, interpreting, selecting, and organizing sensory information.
Hilgard	Hilgard made headlines as a pioneer in the scientific study of hypnosis. He and his wife, Josephine, established the Laboratory of Hypnosis Research at Stanford.
Correlation	Correlation coefficient refers to a number from +1.00 to -1.00 that expresses the direction

coefficient and extent of the relationship between two variables. The closer to 1, the stronger the relationship. The sign, + or -, indicates the direction.

Adolescence The period of life bounded by puberty and the assumption of adult responsibilities is adolescence.

Personality trait According to the Diagnostic and Statistical Manual of the American Psychiatric Association, a personality trait is a "prominent aspect of personality that is exhibited in a wide range of important social and personal contexts. ...".

Fraternal twins Fraternal twins usually occur when two fertilized eggs are implanted in the uterine wall at the same time. The two eggs form two zygotes, and these twins are therefore also known as dizygotic. Dizygotic twins are no more similar genetically than any siblings.

Identical twins Identical twins occur when a single egg is fertilized to form one zygote (monozygotic) but the zygote then divides into two separate embryos. The two embryos develop into foetuses sharing the same womb. Monozygotic twins are genetically identical unless there has been a mutation in development, and they are almost always the same gender.

Conformity Conformity is the degree to which members of a group will change their behavior, views and attitudes to fit the views of the group. The group can influence members via unconscious processes or via overt social pressure on individuals.

Simulation A simulation is an imitation of some real device or state of affairs. Simulation attempts to represent certain features of the behavior of a physical or abstract system by the behavior of another system.

Loudness Loudness is the quality of a sound that is the primary psychological correlate of physical intensity. Loudness is often approximated by a power function with an exponent of 0.6 when plotted vs. sound pressure or 0.3 when plotted vs. sound intensity.

Hypnotic susceptibility One's capacity for becoming hypnotized is referred to as hypnotic susceptibility. People who are more easily put into a state of hypnosis are also more suggestible.

Analgesia Analgesia refers to insensitivity to pain without loss of consciousness.

Natural childbirth The natural childbirth technique attempts to minimize medical intervention, particularly anaesthetics, during childbirth.

Anesthesia Anesthesia is the process of blocking the perception of pain and other sensations. This allows patients to undergo surgery and other procedures without the distress and pain they would otherwise experience.

Self-hypnosis Self-hypnosis is a process by which an individual trains the subconscious mind to believe something, or systematically schematizes the person's own mental associations, usually for a given purpose. This is accomplished through repetitive, constant self-affirmations, and may be seen as a form of self-induced brainwashing.

Meditation Meditation usually refers to a state in which the body is consciously relaxed and the mind is allowed to become calm and focused.

Concentrative meditation Mental exercise based on attending to a single object or thought is a concentrative meditation.

Anxiety Anxiety is a complex combination of the feeling of fear, apprehension and worry often accompanied by physical sensations such as palpitations, chest pain and/or shortness of breath.

Health psychology The field of psychology that studies the relationships between psychological factors and the prevention and treatment of physical illness is called health psychology.

Hallucination	A hallucination is a sensory perception experienced in the absence of an external stimulus, as distinct from an illusion, which is a misperception of an external stimulus. They may occur in any sensory modality - visual, auditory, olfactory, gustatory, tactile, or mixed.
Psychoactive drug	A psychoactive drug or psychotropic substance is a chemical that alters brain function, resulting in temporary changes in perception, mood, consciousness, or behavior. Such drugs are often used for recreational and spiritual purposes, as well as in medicine, especially for treating neurological and psychological illnesses.
Delirium tremens	Delirium tremens refers to a condition characterized by sweating, restlessness, disorientation, and hallucinations. It occurs in some chronic alcohol users when there is a sudden decrease in usage.
Alcoholism	A disorder that involves long-term, repeated, uncontrolled, compulsive, and excessive use of alcoholic beverages and that impairs the drinker's health and work and social relationships is called alcoholism.
Peyote	Peyote is a hallucinogen obtained from the root of the peyote cactus. The active ingredient is mescaline, an alkaloid.
Insight	Insight refers to a sudden awareness of the relationships among various elements that had previously appeared to be independent of one another.
Ecstasy	Ecstasy as an emotion is to be outside oneself, in a trancelike state in which an individual transcends ordinary consciousness and as a result has a heightened capacity for exceptional thought or experience. Ecstasy also refers to a relatively new hallucinogen that is chemically similar to mescaline and the amphetamines.
Strychnine	Strychnine is a very toxic, colorless crystalline alkaloid used as a pesticide, particularly for killing small vertebrates such as rodents. Strychnine causes muscular convulsions and eventually asphyxia or sheer exhaustion.
Amnesia	Amnesia is a condition in which memory is disturbed. The causes of amnesia are organic or functional. Organic causes include damage to the brain, through trauma or disease, or use of certain (generally sedative) drugs.
Nitrous oxide	Nitrous oxide is a chemical compound with chemical formula N_2O. Under room conditions it is a colorless non-flammable gas, with a pleasant, slightly sweet odor. It is commonly known as laughing gas due to the exhilarating effects of inhaling it, and because it can cause spontaneous laughter in some users.
Substance abuse	Substance abuse refers to the overindulgence in and dependence on a stimulant, depressant, or other chemical substance, leading to effects that are detrimental to the individual's physical or mental health, or the welfare of others.
Blocking	If the one of the two members of a compound stimulus fails to produce the CR due to an earlier conditioning of the other member of the compound stimulus, blocking has occurred.
Addiction	Addiction is an uncontrollable compulsion to repeat a behavior regardless of its consequences. Many drugs or behaviors can precipitate a pattern of conditions recognized as addiction, which include a craving for more of the drug or behavior, increased physiological tolerance to exposure, and withdrawal symptoms in the absence of the stimulus.
Withdrawal symptoms	Withdrawal symptoms are physiological changes that occur when the use of a drug is stopped or dosage decreased.
Psychological dependence	Psychological dependence may lead to psychological withdrawal symptoms. Addictions can theoretically form for any rewarding behavior, or as a habitual means to avoid undesired activity, but typically they only do so to a clinical level in individuals who have emotional, social, or psychological dysfunctions, taking the place of normal positive stimuli

	not otherwise attained
Drug dependence	Drug dependence refers to the condition, which may or may not stem from physiological withdrawal symptoms, in which a person feels compelled to take a particular drug on a regular basis.
Habit	A habit is a response that has become completely separated from its eliciting stimulus. Early learning theorists used the term to describe S-R associations, however not all S-R associations become a habit, rather many are extinguished after reinforcement is withdrawn.
Hallucinogen	Certain drugs can affect the subjective qualities of perception, thought or emotion, resulting in altered interpretations of sensory input, alternate states of consciousness, or hallucinations. The term hallucinogen is often broadly applied, especially in current scientific literature, to some or all of these substances.
MDMA	MDMA, most commonly known today by the street name ecstasy, is a synthetic entactogen of the phenethylamine family whose primary effect is to stimulate the secretion of large amounts of serotonin as well as dopamine and noradrenaline in the brain, causing a general sense of openness, empathy, energy, euphoria, and well-being.
Hallucinogenic	Certain drugs can affect the subjective qualities of perception, thought or emotion, resulting in altered interpretations of sensory input, alternate states of consciousness, or hallucinations. The term hallucinogenic is often broadly applied, especially in current scientific literature, to some or all of these substances.
Serotonin	Serotonin, a neurotransmitter, is believed to play an important part of the biochemistry of depression, bipolar disorder and anxiety. It is also believed to be influential on sexuality and appetite.
Neuron	The neuron is the primary cell of the nervous system. They are found in the brain, the spinal cord, in the nerves and ganglia of the peripheral nervous system. It is a specialized cell that conducts impulses through the nervous system and contains three major parts: cell body, dendrites, and an axon. It can have many dendrites but only one axon.
Cannabinoids	Family of chemicals in marijuana believed to be responsible for its mood- and behavior-altering ability are called cannabinoids.
Hippocampus	The hippocampus is a part of the brain located inside the temporal lobe. It forms a part of the limbic system and plays a part in memory and navigation.
Marijuana	Marijuana is the dried vegetable matter of the Cannabis sativa plant. It contains large concentrations of compounds that have medicinal and psychoactive effects when consumed, usually by smoking or eating.
Anandamide	Anandamide is a naturally occurring neurotransmitter found in the brain of animals, as well as other organs. Anandamide receptors were originally discovered as being sensitive to tetrahydrocannabinol, which is among the psychoactive cannabinoids found in marijuana.
Heroin	Heroin is widely and illegally used as a powerful and addictive drug producing intense euphoria, which often disappears with increasing tolerance. Heroin is a semi-synthetic opioid. It is the 3,6-diacetyl derivative of morphine and is synthesised from it by acetylation.
Endorphin	An endorphin is an endogenous opioid biochemical compound. They are peptides produced by the pituitary gland and the hypothalamus, and they resemble the opiates in their abilities to produce analgesia and a sense of well-being. In other words, they work as "natural pain killers."
Barbiturate	A barbiturate is a drug that acts as a central nervous system (CNS) depressant, and by virtue of this produces a wide spectrum of effects, from mild sedation to anesthesia.

Depressant	A depressant is a chemical agent that diminishes a body function or activity. The term is used in particular with regard to the central nervous system where these chemicals are known as neurotransmitters. They tend to act on the CNS by increasing the activity of a particular neurotransmitter known as gamma-aminobutyric acid (GABA).
Synapse	A synapse is specialized junction through which cells of the nervous system signal to one another and to non-neuronal cells such as muscles or glands.
Date rape	Date rape refers to non-consensual sexual activity between people who are already acquainted, or who know each other socially where it is alleged that consent for sexual activity was not given, or was given under duress.
Psychoactive substance	A psychoactive substance is a chemical that alters brain function, resulting in temporary changes in perception, mood, consciousness, or behavior. Such drugs are often used for recreational and spiritual purposes, as well as in medicine, especially for treating neurological and psychological illnesses.
Dopamine	Dopamine is critical to the way the brain controls our movements and is a crucial part of the basal ganglia motor loop. It is commonly associated with the 'pleasure system' of the brain, providing feelings of enjoyment and reinforcement to motivate us to do, or continue doing, certain activities.
Pupil	In the eye, the pupil is the opening in the middle of the iris. It appears black because most of the light entering it is absorbed by the tissues inside the eye. The size of the pupil is controlled by involuntary contraction and dilation of the iris, in order to regulate the intensity of light entering the eye. This is known as the pupillary reflex.
Physical dependence	Physical dependence describes increased tolerance of a drug combined with a physical need of the drug to function. Abrupt cessation of the drug is typically associated with negative physical withdrawal symptoms. Physical dependence is distinguished from addiction. While addiction tends to describe psychological and behavioral attributes, physical dependence is defined primarily using physical and biological concepts.
Amphetamine	Amphetamine is a synthetic stimulant used to suppress the appetite, control weight, and treat disorders including narcolepsy and ADHD. It is also used recreationally and for performance enhancement.
Stimulant	A stimulant is a drug which increases the activity of the sympathetic nervous system and produces a sense of euphoria or awakeness.
Cocaine	Cocaine is a crystalline tropane alkaloid that is obtained from the leaves of the coca plant. It is a stimulant of the central nervous system and an appetite suppressant, creating what has been described as a euphoric sense of happiness and increased energy.
Norepinephrine	Norepinephrine is released from the adrenal glands as a hormone into the blood, but it is also a neurotransmitter in the nervous system. As a stress hormone, it affects parts of the human brain where attention and impulsivity are controlled. Along with epinephrine, this compound effects the fight-or-flight response, activating the sympathetic nervous system to directly increase heart rate, release energy from fat, and increase muscle readiness.
Nicotine	Nicotine is an organic compound, an alkaloid found naturally throughout the tobacco plant, with a high concentration in the leaves. It is a potent nerve poison and is included in many insecticides. In lower concentrations, the substance is a stimulant and is one of the main factors leading to the pleasure and habit-forming qualities of tobacco smoking.
Addictive drugs	Addictive drugs produce a biological or psychological dependence in the user; withdrawal from them leads to a craving for the drug that in some cases can be nearly irresistible.
Construct	A generalized concept, such as anxiety or gravity, is a construct.

Nervous system	The body's electrochemical communication circuitry, made up of billions of neurons is a nervous system.
Opiates	A group of narcotics derived from the opium poppy that provide a euphoric rush and depress the nervous system are referred to as opiates.

Behaviorism	The school of psychology that defines psychology as the study of observable behavior and studies relationships between stimuli and responses is called behaviorism. Behaviorism relied heavily on animal research and stated the same principles governed the behavior of both nonhumans and humans.
Conditioning	Conditioning describes the process by which behaviors can be learned or modified through interaction with the environment.
Learning	Learning is a relatively permanent change in behavior that results from experience. Thus, to attribute a behavioral change to learning, the change must be relatively permanent and must result from experience.
Observational learning	The acquisition of knowledge and skills through the observation of others rather than by means of direct experience is observational learning. Four major processes are thought to influence the observational learning: attentional, retentional, behavioral production, and motivational.
Cognition	The intellectual processes through which information is obtained, transformed, stored, retrieved, and otherwise used is cognition.
Species	Species refers to a reproductively isolated breeding population.
Attitude	An enduring mental representation of a person, place, or thing that evokes an emotional response and related behavior is called attitude.
Affect	A subjective feeling or emotional tone often accompanied by bodily expressions noticeable to others is called affect.
Maturation	The orderly unfolding of traits, as regulated by the genetic code is called maturation.
Brain	The brain controls and coordinates most movement, behavior and homeostatic body functions such as heartbeat, blood pressure, fluid balance and body temperature. Functions of the brain are responsible for cognition, emotion, memory, motor learning and other sorts of learning. The brain is primarily made up of two types of cells: glia and neurons.
John Watson	John Watson, the father of behaviorism, developed the term "Behaviorism" as a name for his proposal to revolutionize the study of human psychology in order to put it on a firm experimental footing.
Introspection	Introspection is the self report or consideration of one's own thoughts, perceptions and mental processes. Classic introspection was done through trained observers.
Sensation	Sensation is the first stage in the chain of biochemical and neurologic events that begins with the impinging of a stimulus upon the receptor cells of a sensory organ, which then leads to perception, the mental state that is reflected in statements like "I see a uniformly blue wall."
Consciousness	The awareness of the sensations, thoughts, and feelings being experienced at a given moment is called consciousness.
Skinner	Skinner conducted research on shaping behavior through positive and negative reinforcement, and demonstrated operant conditioning, a technique which he developed in contrast with classical conditioning.
Radical behaviorism	Skinner defined behavior to include everything that an organism does, including thinking, feeling and speaking and argued that these phenomena were valid subject matters of psychology. The term Radical Behaviorism refers to "everything an organism does is a behavior."
Evolution	Commonly used to refer to gradual change, evolution is the change in the frequency of alleles within a population from one generation to the next. This change may be caused by different

mechanisms, including natural selection, genetic drift, or changes in population (gene flow).

Reinforcement In operant conditioning, reinforcement is any change in an environment that (a) occurs after the behavior, (b) seems to make that behavior re-occur more often in the future and (c) that reoccurence of behavior must be the result of the change.

Deprivation Deprivation, is the loss or withholding of normal stimulation, nutrition, comfort, love, and so forth; a condition of lacking. The level of stimulation is less than what is required.

Elaboration The extensiveness of processing at any given level of memory is called elaboration. The use of elaboration changes developmentally. Adolescents are more likely to use elaboration spontaneously than children.

Classical conditioning Classical conditioning is a simple form of learning in which an organism comes to associate or anticipate events. A neutral stimulus comes to evoke the response usually evoked by a natural or unconditioned stimulus by being paired repeatedly with the unconditioned stimulus.

Operant Conditioning A simple form of learning in which an organism learns to engage in behavior because it is reinforced is referred to as operant conditioning. The consequences of a behavior produce changes in the probability of the behavior's occurence.

Stimulus A change in an environmental condition that elicits a response is a stimulus.

Innate Innate behavior is not learned or influenced by the environment, rather, it is present or predisposed at birth.

Pavlov Pavlov first described the phenomenon now known as classical conditioning in experiments with dogs.

Pavlovian conditioning Pavlovian conditioning, synonymous with classical conditioning is a type of learning found in animals, caused by the association (or pairing) of two stimuli or what Ivan Pavlov described as the learning of conditional behavior, therefore called conditioning.

Variable A variable refers to a measurable factor, characteristic, or attribute of an individual or a system.

Reflex A simple, involuntary response to a stimulus is referred to as reflex. Reflex actions originate at the spinal cord rather than the brain.

Pupil In the eye, the pupil is the opening in the middle of the iris. It appears black because most of the light entering it is absorbed by the tissues inside the eye. The size of the pupil is controlled by involuntary contraction and dilation of the iris, in order to regulate the intensity of light entering the eye. This is known as the pupillary reflex.

Unconditioned stimulus In classical conditioning, an unconditioned stimulus elicits a response from an organism prior to conditioning. It is a naturally occurring stimulus and a naturally occurring response..

Necessary condition A circumstance required for a particular phenomenon to occur is a necessary condition if and only if the condition does not occur in the absense of the circumstance.

Unconditioned response An Unconditioned Response is the response elicited to an unconditioned stimulus. It is a natural, automatic response.

Neutral stimulus A stimulus prior to conditioning that does not naturally result in the response of interest is called a neutral stimulus.

Conditioned response A conditioned response is the response to a stimulus that occurs when an animal has learned to associate the stimulus with a certain positive or negative effect.

Conditioned stimulus A previously neutral stimulus that elicits the conditioned response because of being repeatedly paired with a stimulus that naturally elicited that response, is called a

conditioned stimulus.

Acquisition

Acquisition is the process of adapting to the environment, learning or becoming conditioned. In classical conditoning terms, it is the initial learning of the stimulus response link, which involves a neutral stimulus being associated with a unconditioned stimulus and becoming a conditioned stimulus.

Extinction

In operant extinction, if no reinforcement is delivered after the response, gradually the behavior will no longer occur in the presence of the stimulus. The process is more rapid following continuous reinforcement rather than after partial reinforcement. In Classical Conditioning, repeated presentations of the CS without being followed by the US results in the extinction of the CS.

Trace conditioning

A classical conditioning procedure in which the CS is presented and then removed before the US is presented is called trace conditioning.

Simultaneous conditioning

A classical conditioning procedure in which the CS and US are presented at the same time is referred to as simultaneous conditioning.

Spontaneous recovery

The recurrence of an extinguished response as a function of the passage of time is referred to as spontaneous recovery.

Paradigm

Paradigm refers to the set of practices that defines a scientific discipline during a particular period of time. It provides a framework from which to conduct research, it ensures that a certain range of phenomena, those on which the paradigm focuses, are explored thoroughly. Itmay also blind scientists to other, perhaps more fruitful, ways of dealing with their subject matter.

Generalization

In conditioning, the tendency for a conditioned response to be evoked by stimuli that are similar to the stimulus to which the response was conditioned is a generalization. The greater the similarity among the stimuli, the greater the probability of generalization.

Stimulus generalization

When animals are trained to respond to a single stimulus and test stimuli are introduced that differ from the training stimulus, generally along a single dimension, the systematic decrement in responding typically found has been called the gradient of stimulus generalization.

Stimulus discrimination

The tendency to make a response when stimuli previously associated with reinforcement are present and to withhold the response when not present, is stimulus discrimination.

Discrimination training

Teaching an organism to show a response in the presence of only one of a series of similar stimuli is discrimination training. It is accomplished by alternating the stimuli and reinforcing only the target stimulus.

Discrimination

In Learning theory, discrimination refers the ability to distinguish between a conditioned stimulus and other stimuli. It can be brought about by extensive training or differential reinforcement. In social terms, it is the denial of privileges to a person or a group on the basis of prejudice.

Pitch

Pitch is the psychological interpretation of a sound or musical tone corresponding to its physical frequency

Hue

A hue refers to the gradation of color within the optical spectrum, or visible spectrum, of light. Hue may also refer to a particular color within this spectrum, as defined by its dominant wavelength, or the central tendency of its combined wavelengths.

Rescorla

Rescorla agreed with Pavlov that for learning to take place, the CS had to be a useful predictor of the US. But he disagreed on what made the CS a useful predictor. It was more complicated than the number of CS-US pairings. He maintained that it was the contingency between the CS and US.

Emotion	An emotion is a mental states that arise spontaneously, rather than through conscious effort. They are often accompanied by physiological changes.
Attention	Attention is the cognitive process of selectively concentrating on one thing while ignoring other things. Psychologists have labeled three types of attention: sustained attention, selective attention, and divided attention.
Fear response	In the Mowrer-Miller theory, a response to a threatening or noxious situation that is covert but that is assumed to function as a stimulus to produce measurable physiological changes in the body and observable overt behavior is referred to as the fear response.
Little Albert	The Little Albert experiment was an experiment showing empirical evidence of classical conditioning in children. The actual experiment with Little Albert on conditioned fear involved exposing the child to a loud sound while being presented with a white rat.
Opiates	A group of narcotics derived from the opium poppy that provide a euphoric rush and depress the nervous system are referred to as opiates.
Homeostasis	Homeostasis is the property of an open system, especially living organisms, to regulate its internal environment so as to maintain a stable condition, by means of multiple dynamic equilibrium adjustments controlled by interrelated regulation mechanisms.
Conditioned compensatory response	A homeostatic response that counteracts a drug's effect after repeated exposures is a conditioned compensatory response.
Heroin	Heroin is widely and illegally used as a powerful and addictive drug producing intense euphoria, which often disappears with increasing tolerance. Heroin is a semi-synthetic opioid. It is the 3,6-diacetyl derivative of morphine and is synthesised from it by acetylation.
Drug tolerance	Drug tolerance occurs when a subject's reaction to a drug (such as a painkiller or intoxicant) decreases so that larger doses are required to achieve the same effect. In addicted patients, the resulting pattern of uncontrolled escalating doses may lead to drug overdose.
Drug addiction	Drug addiction, or substance dependence is the compulsive use of drugs, to the point where the user has no effective choice but to continue use.
Law of Effect	The law of effect is a principle of psychology described by Edward Thorndike in 1898. It holds that responses to stimuli that produce a satisfying or pleasant effect in a particular situation are more likely to occur again in the situation. Conversely, responses that produce a discomforting or unpleasant effect are less likely to occur again in the situation
Thorndike	Thorndike worked in animal behavior and the learning process leading to the theory of connectionism. Among his most famous contributions were his research on cats escaping from puzzle boxes, and his formulation of the Law of Effect.
Inference	Inference is the act or process of drawing a conclusion based solely on what one already knows.
Bottom-up	In Bottom-up design individual parts of the system are specified in detail. The parts are then linked together to form larger components, which are in turn linked until a complete system is formed. Strategies based on the bottom-up information flow seem potentially necessary and sufficient because they are based on the knowledge of all variables that may affect the elements of the system.
Theories	Theories are logically self-consistent models or frameworks describing the behavior of a certain natural or social phenomenon. They are broad explanations and predictions concerning phenomena of interest.

Trial and error	Trial and error is an approach to problem solving in which one solution after another is tried in no particular order until an answer is found.
Puzzle Box	The puzzle box experiments were motivated in part by Thorndike's dislike for statements that animals made use of extraordinary factulties such as insight in their problem solving. He reasoned that if the animals were showing insight, then their time to escape would suddenly drop to a negligible period, which would also be shown in the learning curve as an abrupt drop; while animals using a more ordinary method of trial and error would show gradual curves. His finding was that cats consistently showed gradual learning. He asserted that the connection between the box and the motions the cat used to escape was strengthened by each escape.
Operant chamber	An operant chamber (usually Skinner box) is a laboratory apparatus used in experimental psychology to study animal behavior. It is used to study both classical conditioning (especially autoshaping) and operant conditioning.
Reinforcement contingencies	The circumstances or rules that determine whether responses lead to the presentation of reinforcers are referred to as reinforcement contingencies. Skinner defined culture as a set of reinforcement contingencies.
Reinforcer	In operant conditioning, a reinforcer is any stimulus that increases the probability that a preceding behavior will occur again. In Classical Conditioning, the unconditioned stimulus (US) is the reinforcer.
Aversive stimulus	A stimulus that elicits pain, fear, or avoidance is an aversive stimulus.
Negative Reinforcement	During negative reinforcement, a stimulus is removed and the frequency of the behavior or response increases.
Escape conditioning	In escape conditioning, the response results in getting away from a present undesired stimulus.
Avoidance conditioning	The operant conditioning scenario in which the behavior reinforced prevents something from happening is called avoidance conditioning. It involves both S-S and R-S expectancies.
Positive reinforcement	In positive reinforcement, a stimulus is added and the rate of responding increases.
Negative punishment	Negative punishment occurs when a response decreases as a positive stimulus is removed from the situation.
Punishment	Punishment is the addtion of a stimulus that reduces the frequency of a response, or the removal of a stimulus that results in a reduction of the response.
Punisher	Punisher refers to any event that decreases the probability or frequency of the response it follows.
Positive punishment	In operant conditioning, when the presentation of a stimulus after a response occurs decreases the likelihood that the response will be repeated, you have positive punishment.
Discriminative stimulus	In operant conditioning, a stimulus that indicates that reinforcement is available upon the apporpriate response, is called the discriminative stimulus.
Three-Term Contingency	Skinner believed that, in order to experimentally analyze human and animal behavior, each behavioral act can be broken down into three key parts. These three parts constitute his three-term contingency: discriminative stimulus, operant response, and reinforcer/punisher. The three-term contingency is fundamental to the study of operant conditioning.
Conditioned reinforcer	A conditioned reinforcer is a stimulus or situation that has acquired reinforcing power after being paired in the environment with an unconditioned reinforcer or an earlier conditioned

	reinforcer.
Primary Reinforcer	Any stimulus whose reinforcing effect is immediate and not a function of previous experience is a primary reinforcer (eg, food, water, warmth).
Operant Response	An operant response refers to any behavioral response that produces some reliable effect on the environment that influences the likelihood that the individual will produce that response again.
Corporal punishment	Corporal punishment is the use of physical force with the intention of causing pain, but not injury.
Wisdom	Wisdom is the ability to make correct judgments and decisions. It is an intangible quality gained through experience. Whether or not something is wise is determined in a pragmatic sense by its popularity, how long it has been around, and its ability to predict against future events.
Depression	In everyday language depression refers to any downturn in mood, which may be relatively transitory and perhaps due to something trivial. This is differentiated from Clinical depression which is marked by symptoms that last two weeks or more and are so severe that they interfere with daily living.
Suicide	Suicide behavior is rare in childhood but escalates in adolescence. The suicide rate increases in a linear fashion from adolescence through late adulthood.
Premack principle	That any high-frequency response can be used to reinforce a low-frequency response is called the Premack Principle.
Perception	Perception is the process of acquiring, interpreting, selecting, and organizing sensory information.
Schedules of Reinforcement	Different combinations of frequency and timing of reinforcement following a behavior are referred to as schedules of reinforcement. They are either continuous (the behavior is reinforced each time it occurs) or intermittent (the behavior is reinforced only on certain occasions).
Fixed-ratio	In a fixed-ratio schedule, reinforcement is provided after a fixed number of correct responses.
Continuous reinforcement	In continuous reinforcement, every response results in reinforcement.
Correlation	A statistical technique for determining the degree of association between two or more variables is referred to as correlation.
Stretching the ratio	The procedure of gradually increasing the number of responses required for reinforcement is called stretching the ratio.
Variable-ratio	In a variable-ratio schedule of reinforcement reinforcement is provided after a variable number of correct responses.
Resistance to extinction	Resistance to extinction is the phenomenon that occurs when an organism continues to make a response even after the delivery of the reinforcer for the response has been all or partially eliminated.
Fixed-interval	A reinforcement schedule in which a fixed amount of time must elapse between the previous and subsequent times that reinforcement is available is the fixed-interval schedule.
Response rate	The response rate is usually calculated by dividing the total number of responses by the time available for the response.
Variable-	A reinforcement schedule in which a variable amount of time must elapse between the previous

interval	and subsequent times that reinforcement is available is a variable-interval schedule.
Shaping	The concept of reinforcing successive, increasingly accurate approximations to a target behavior is called shaping. The target behavior is broken down into a hierarchy of elemental steps, each step more sophisticated then the last. By successively reinforcing each of the the elemental steps, a form of differential reinforcement, until that step is learned while extinguishing the step below, the target behavior is gradually achieved.
Successive approximations	In operant conditioning, a series of behaviors that gradually become more similar to a target behavior are called successive approximations.
Positive reinforcer	In operant conditioning, a stimulus that is presented after a response that increases the likelihood that the response will be repeated is a positive reinforcer.
Adaptation	Adaptation is a lowering of sensitivity to a stimulus following prolonged exposure to that stimulus. Behavioral adaptations are special ways a particular organism behaves to survive in its natural habitat.
Hume	Hume was the ultimate skeptic, reducing matter, mind, religion, and science to a matter of sense impressions and memories. He was a strong empiricist.
Preparedness	The species-specific biological predisposition to learn in certain ways is called preparedness.
Chemotherapy	Chemotherapy is the use of chemical substances to treat disease. In its modern-day use, it refers almost exclusively to cytostatic drugs used to treat cancer.In its non-oncological use, the term may also refer to antibiotics.
Conditioned aversion	A learned dislike or conditioned negative emotional response to a particular stimulus is a conditioned aversion.
Cognitive map	A mental representation of spatial locations and directions is a cognitive map. The concept was introduced by Tolman to explain latent learning. Controversy developed from Tolman's theory of latent learning, but several investigators demonstrated that rats do learn in the absence of rewards.
Tolman	Tolman coined the term "cognitive map", which was an internal perceptual representation of external environmental features and landmarks. He is virtually the only behaviorist who found the Stimulus-Response theory unacceptable, because reinforcement was not necessary for learning to occur. He felt behavior was holistic, purposive, and cognitive.
Conceptual Behavior	Conceptual behavior is seen when an organism makes the same response to a group of discriminably different objects. An organism is said to respond conceptually when it responds similarly to stimuli within the same class and when it responds differently to stimuli in different classes.
Bandura	Bandura is best known for his work on social learning theory or Social Cognitivism. His famous Bobo doll experiment illustrated that people learn from observing others.
Bobo doll	The Bobo doll experiment was conducted by Bandura to study aggressive patterns of behavior. One of the experiment's conclusions was that people can learn through vicarious reinforcement.
Rape	Rape is a crime where the victim is forced into sexual activity, in particular sexual penetration, against his or her will.
Desensitization	Desensitization refers to the type of sensory or behavioral adaptation in which we become less sensitive to constant stimuli.
Maladaptive	In psychology, a behavior or trait is adaptive when it helps an individual adjust and function well within their social environment. A maladaptive behavior or trait is

counterproductive to the individual.

Vicarious reinforcement | A behavior response that increases as a result of observing other people's behaviors being reinforced is referred to as vicarious reinforcement.

Amnesia	Amnesia is a condition in which memory is disturbed. The causes of amnesia are organic or functional. Organic causes include damage to the brain, through trauma or disease, or use of certain (generally sedative) drugs.
Brain	The brain controls and coordinates most movement, behavior and homeostatic body functions such as heartbeat, blood pressure, fluid balance and body temperature. Functions of the brain are responsible for cognition, emotion, memory, motor learning and other sorts of learning. The brain is primarily made up of two types of cells: glia and neurons.
Attention	Attention is the cognitive process of selectively concentrating on one thing while ignoring other things. Psychologists have labeled three types of attention: sustained attention, selective attention, and divided attention.
Ebbinghaus	Ebbinghaus pioneered the development of experimental methods for the measurement of rote learning and memory.
Empirical	Empirical means the use of working hypotheses which are capable of being disproved using observation or experiment.
Nonsense syllable	A nonsense syllable is a consonant-vowel-consonant combination that does not spell a word. It is an expermental methodology invented by Ebbinghaus to control for the meaningfulness of the material in studies of memory.
Learning	Learning is a relatively permanent change in behavior that results from experience. Thus, to attribute a behavioral change to learning, the change must be relatively permanent and must result from experience.
Rote	Rote learning, is a learning technique which avoids grasping the inner complexities and inferences of the subject that is being learned and instead focuses on memorizing the material so that it can be recalled by the learner exactly the way it was read or heard.
Forgetting curve	Ebbinghaus' forgetting curve illustrates the decline of memory retention in time. A typical graph of the forgetting curve shows that humans tend to halve their memory of newly learned knowledge in a matter of days or weeks unless they consciously review the learned material.
Savings score	The percentage of time saved in relearning material over the amount of time or number of learning trials required for the original learning, is called the savings score.
Explicit memory	Intentional or conscious recollection of information is referred to as explicit memory. Children under age three are usually poorest at explicit memory which may be due to the immaturity of the prefrontal lobes of the brain, which are believed to play an important role in memory for events.
Consciousness	The awareness of the sensations, thoughts, and feelings being experienced at a given moment is called consciousness.
Acquisition	Acquisition is the process of adapting to the environment, learning or becoming conditioned. In classical conditoning terms, it is the initial learning of the stimulus response link, which involves a neutral stimulus being associated with a unconditioned stimulus and becoming a conditioned stimulus.
Theories	Theories are logically self-consistent models or frameworks describing the behavior of a certain natural or social phenomenon. They are broad explanations and predictions concerning phenomena of interest.
Procedural memory	Procedural memory is the long-term memory of skills and procedures, or "how to" knowledge.
Mental processes	The thoughts, feelings, and motives that each of us experiences privately but that cannot be observed directly are called mental processes.

Retrieval	Retrieval is the location of stored information and its subsequent return to consciousness. It is the third stage of information processing.
Encoding	Encoding refers to interpreting; transforming; modifying information so that it can be placed in memory. It is the first stage of information processing.
Mental Representation	Stage six of the sensorimotor substages, Mental representation, 18 months to 2 years, marks the beginnings of insight, or true creativity. This marks the passage into unique thought in Piaget's later three areas of development.
Sensory memory	Sensory memory is our ability to retain impressions of sensory information after the original stimulus has ceased.
Iconic memory	The sensory register that briefly holds mental representations of visual stimuli is called iconic memory.
Icon	A mental representation of a visual stimulus that is held briefly in sensory memory is called icon.
Long-term memory	Long-term memory is memory that lasts from over 30 seconds to years.
Working Memory	Working memory is the collection of structures and processes in the brain used for temporarily storing and manipulating information. Working memory consists of both memory for items that are currently being processed, and components governing attention and directing the processing itself.
Sperling	Sperling has studied cognitive psychology and was a prominent researcher in memory. He is responsible for the concept of iconic memory.
Eidetic imagery	The maintenance of detailed visual memories over several minutes is called eidetic imagery.
Echoic memory	Sensory memory is our ability to retain impressions of sensory information after the original stimulus has ceased. The sensory register that briefly holds mental representations of auditory stimuli is called echoic memory.
Echoic	In order to learn any skill, a child must have an imitation repertoire. The echoic is the verbal operant that relates to vocal imitation. An echoic is verbal behavior whose form is controlled by someone else's verbal behavior with point-to-point (1:1) correspondence.
Darwin	Darwin achieved lasting fame as originator of the theory of evolution through natural selection. His book Expression of Emotions in Man and Animals is generally considered the first text on comparative psychology.
Stimulus	A change in an environmental condition that elicits a response is a stimulus.
Limited capacity	Limited capacity refers to the concept that one's information processing ability is restricted. Metaphors for capacity include mental space, mental energy or effort, and time.
Memory span	The second key concept associated with a short-term memory is that it has a finite capacity. Prior to the creation of current memory models, George Miller argued that human short-term memory has a forward memory span of approximately seven items plus or minus two.
George Miller	George Miller provided two theoretical ideas that are fundamental to the information processing framework and cognitive psychology: chunking and the capacity of short term memory.
Variable interval	In a variable interval schedule of reinforcement, reinforcement occurs after the passage of a varying length of time around an average, provided that at least one response occurred in that period.
Short-term memory	Short-term memory is that part of memory which stores a limited amount of information for a limited amount of time (roughly 30-45 seconds). The second key concept associated with a

	short-term memory is that it has a finite capacity.
Chunking	In cognitive psychology and mnemonics, chunking refers to a strategy for making more efficient use of short-term memory by recoding information.
Baddeley	Baddeley introduced a multicomponent model of working memory for the temporary maintenance and manipulation of information. It emphasizes the functional importance of such a system rather than its use as the unitary short-term store proposed by Atkinson and Shiffrin.
Sternberg	Sternberg proposed the triarchic theory of intelligence: componential, experiential, and practical. His notion of general intelligence or the g-factor, is a composite of intelligence scores across multiple modalities.
Dependent variable	A measure of an assumed effect of an independent variable is called the dependent variable.
Analogy	An analogy is a comparison between two different things, in order to highlight some form of similarity. Analogy is the cognitive process of transferring information from a particular subject to another particular subject.
Phonological loop	The phonological loop in Baddeley's theory is a component of working memory responsible for holding verbal information.
Problem solving	An attempt to find an appropriate way of attaining a goal when the goal is not readily available is called problem solving.
Cognition	The intellectual processes through which information is obtained, transformed, stored, retrieved, and otherwise used is cognition.
Affect	A subjective feeling or emotional tone often accompanied by bodily expressions noticeable to others is called affect.
Emotion	An emotion is a mental states that arise spontaneously, rather than through conscious effort. They are often accompanied by physiological changes.
Context-dependent memory	Information that is better retrieved in the context in which it was encoded and stored, or learned is called context-dependent memory.
Hypothesis	A specific statement about behavior or mental processes that is testable through research is a hypothesis.
Serial position effect	In what is known as the serial position effect, items at the beginning of a list are the easiest to recall, followed by the items near the end of a list. Items in the middle are the least likely to be remembered.
Primacy effect	The primacy effect is a cognitive bias that results from disproportionate salience of initial stimuli or observations. If, for example, a subject reads a sufficiently-long list of words, he or she is more likely to remember words read toward the beginning than words read in the middle.
Recency effect	Recency effect refers to the tendency to recall the last items in a series of items. The tendency to evaluate others in terms of the most recent impression.
Free recall	In memory research, a task in which a subject recalls information without specific cues or prompts is referred to as free recall.
Retrieval cue	Any stimulus or bit of information that aids in the retrieval of particular information from long-term memory is a retrieval cue.
Episodic memory	Episodic memory is the explicit memory of events. It includes time, place, and associated emotions (which affect the quality of the memorization).

Semantic memory | Semantic memory refers to the memory of meanings, understandings, and other knowledge.

Paired associate | Paired associate is a method where subjects learn pairs of items so that when they are shown one member of the pair, they can respond with the other.

Retroactive interference | Retroactive interference occurs when the material learned later disrupts retrieval of information learned earlier, so old information overlaps with new information.

Proactive interference | Proactive interference occurs when information learned earlier disrupts the recall of material learned later. This can become a problem when new information cannot be used correctly as it is interfered with by the older information.

Elaboration | The extensiveness of processing at any given level of memory is called elaboration. The use of elaboration changes developmentally. Adolescents are more likely to use elaboration spontaneously than children.

Implicit memory | Implicit memory is the long-term memory of skills and procedures, or "how to" knowledge. It is often not easily verbalized, but can be used without consciously thinking about it.

Priming | A phenomenon in which exposure to a word or concept later makes it easier to recall related information, even when one has no conscious memory of the word or concept is called priming.

Elaborative rehearsal | A method for increasing retention of new information by relating it to information that is well known is an elaborative rehearsal.

Mnemonic | A mnemonic is a memory aid. They are often verbal, are sometimes in verse form, and are often used to remember lists.

Method of loci | Method of loci is a mnemonic device that involves taking an imaginary walk along a familiar path where images of items to be remembered are associated with certain locations.

Metamemory | Metamemory refers to self-awareness of the ways in which memory functions, allowing the person to encode, store, and retrieve information effectively.

Sensation | Sensation is the first stage in the chain of biochemical and neurologic events that begins with the impinging of a stimulus upon the receptor cells of a sensory organ, which then leads to perception, the mental state that is reflected in statements like "I see a uniformly blue wall."

Intuition | Quick, impulsive thought that does not make use of formal logic or clear reasoning is referred to as intuition.

Instinct | Instinct is the word used to describe inherent dispositions towards particular actions. They are generally an inherited pattern of responses or reactions to certain kinds of situations.

Memory structure | Patterns of associations among bits of information stored in memory is a memory structure.

Prototype | A concept of a category of objects or events that serves as a good example of the category is called a prototype.

Construct | A generalized concept, such as anxiety or gravity, is a construct.

Exemplars | Exemplars refer to the individual instances of a concept that are stored in memory from personal experience.

Schema | Schema refers to a way of mentally representing the world, such as a belief or an expectation, that can influence perception of persons, objects, and situations.

Generalization | In conditioning, the tendency for a conditioned response to be evoked by stimuli that are similar to the stimulus to which the response was conditioned is a generalization. The greater the similarity among the stimuli, the greater the probability of generalization.

Personality | Personality refers to the pattern of enduring characteristics that differentiates a person,

	the patterns of behaviors that make each individual unique.
Stereotype	A stereotype is considered to be a group concept, held by one social group about another.They are often used in a negative or prejudicial sense and are frequently used to justify certain discriminatory behaviors. This allows powerful social groups to legitimize and protect their dominant position
Social psychologists	Social psychologists study the nature and causes of human social behavior, emphasizing on how people think and relate towards each other.
Trait	An enduring personality characteristic that tends to lead to certain behaviors is called a trait. The term trait also means a genetically inherited feature of an organism.
Reasoning	Reasoning is the act of using reason to derive a conclusion from certain premises. There are two main methods to reach a conclusion,deductive reasoning and inductive reasoning.
Frederic Bartlett	Frederic Bartlett demonstrated that learning processes are reliant on our past experiences and memories. He was one of the forerunners of cognitive psychology.
Social psychology	Social psychology is the study of the nature and causes of human social behavior, with an emphasis on how people think towards each other and how they relate to each other.
Constructive processes	Constructive processes are processes in which memories are influenced by the meaning we give to events.
Illusion	An illusion is a distortion of a sensory perception.
Loftus	Loftus works on human memory and how it can be changed by facts, ideas, suggestions and other forms of post-event information. One of her famous studies include the "car accident" study, which was an example of the misinformation effect.
Stages	Stages represent relatively discrete periods of time in which functioning is qualitatively different from functioning at other periods.
Plaques	Plaques refer to small, round areas composed of remnants of lost neurons and beta-amyloid, a waxy protein deposit; present in the brains of patients with Alzheimer's disease.
Tangles	Tangles are twisted fibers that build up inside nerve cells.
Neuron	The neuron is the primary cell of the nervous system. They are found in the brain, the spinal cord, in the nerves and ganglia of the peripheral nervous system. It is a specialized cell that conducts impulses through the nervous system and contains three major parts: cell body, dendrites, and an axon. It can have many dendrites but only one axon.
Anatomy	Anatomy is the branch of biology that deals with the structure and organization of living things. It can be divided into animal anatomy (zootomy) and plant anatomy (phytonomy). Major branches of anatomy include comparative anatomy, histology, and human anatomy.
Lashley	Lashley failed to find a single biological locus of memory suggesting to him that memories were not localized to one part of the brain, but were widely distributed throughout the cortex.
Engram	An engram is said to be a memory trace, one possible explanation for the persistence of memory. Fundamentally, an engram is posited to be a physical, biochemical change in the brain (and other neural tissue) in response to external stimuli, thus forming a memory.
Conditioned response	A conditioned response is the response to a stimulus that occurs when an animal has learned to associate the stimulus with a certain positive or negative effect.
Cerebellum	The cerebellum is located in the inferior posterior portion of the head (the hindbrain), directly dorsal to the brainstem and pons, inferior to the occipital lobe. The cerebellum is a region of the brain that plays an important role in the integration of sensory perception

	and fine motor output.
Forebrain	The forebrain is the highest level of the brain. Key structures in the forebrain are the limbic system, thalamus, basal ganglia, hypothalamus, and cerebral cortex.
Habit	A habit is a response that has become completely separated from its eliciting stimulus. Early learning theorists used the term to describe S-R associations, however not all S-R associations become a habit, rather many are extinguished after reinforcement is withdrawn.
Cerebral cortex	The cerebral cortex is the outermost layer of the cerebrum and has a grey color. It is made up of four lobes and it is involved in many complex brain functions including memory, perceptual awareness, "thinking", language and consciousness. The cerebral cortex receives sensory information from many different sensory organs eg: eyes, ears, etc. and processes the information.
Declarative memory	Declarative memory is the aspect of memory that stores facts and events. It applies to standard textbook learning and knowledge. It is based on pairing the stimulus and the correct response.
Amygdala	Located in the brain's medial temporal lobe, the almond-shaped amygdala is believed to play a key role in the emotions. It forms part of the limbic system and is linked to both fear responses and pleasure. Its size is positively correlated with aggressive behavior across species.
Anterograde amnesia	Anterograde amnesia is a form of amnesia where new events are not transferred to long-term memory, so the sufferer will not be able to remember anything that occurs after the onset of this type of amnesia for more than a few moments.
Retrograde amnesia	Retrograde amnesia is a form of amnesia where someone will be unable to recall events that occurred before the onset of amnesia.
Dissociation	Dissociation is a psychological state or condition in which certain thoughts, emotions, sensations, or memories are separated from the rest.
Brain imaging	Brain imaging is a fairly recent discipline within medicine and neuroscience. Brain imaging falls into two broad categories -- structural imaging and functional imaging.
Prefrontal cortex	The prefrontal cortex is the anterior part of the frontal lobes of the brain, lying in front of the motor and associative areas. It has been implicated in planning complex cognitive behaviors, personality expression and moderating correct social behavior. The prefrontal cortex continues to develop until around age 6.
Hippocampus	The hippocampus is a part of the brain located inside the temporal lobe. It forms a part of the limbic system and plays a part in memory and navigation.
Neuroscience	A field that combines the work of psychologists, biologists, biochemists, medical researchers, and others in the study of the structure and function of the nervous system is neuroscience.
Insight	Insight refers to a sudden awareness of the relationships among various elements that had previously appeared to be independent of one another.
Gyrus	A gyrus is a ridge on the cerebral cortex. It is generally surrounded by one or more sulci.
Information processing	Information processing is an approach to the goal of understanding human thinking. The essence of the approach is to see cognition as being essentially computational in nature, with mind being the software and the brain being the hardware.
Maintenance rehearsal	The repetition of information in order to keep it in memory is called maintenance rehearsal.

Deductive reasoning	Deductive reasoning refers to a form of reasoning about arguments in which conclusions are determined from the premises. The conclusions are true if the premises are true.
Inductive reasoning	A form of reasoning in which we reason from individual cases or particular facts to a general conclusion is referred to as inductive reasoning. The conclusion can be said to follow with a probability rather than certainty.
Problem solving	An attempt to find an appropriate way of attaining a goal when the goal is not readily available is called problem solving.
Expert system	An expert system is a class of computer programs developed by researchers in artificial intelligence. In essence, they are programs made up of a set of rules that analyze information about a specific class of problems, as well as provide analysis of the problem(s), and, depending upon their design, recommend a course of user action in order to implement corrections.
Cognition	The intellectual processes through which information is obtained, transformed, stored, retrieved, and otherwise used is cognition.
Heuristic	A heuristic is a simple, efficient rule of thumb proposed to explain how people make decisions, come to judgments and solve problems, typically when facing complex problems or incomplete information. These rules work well under most circumstances, but in certain cases lead to systematic cognitive biases.
Reasoning	Reasoning is the act of using reason to derive a conclusion from certain premises. There are two main methods to reach a conclusion,deductive reasoning and inductive reasoning.
Cognitive psychology	Cognitive psychology is the psychological science which studies the mental processes that are hypothesised to underlie behavior. This covers a broad range of research domains, examining questions about the workings of memory, attention, perception, knowledge representation, reasoning, creativity and problem solving.
Cognitive science	Cognitive Science is the scientific study of the mind and brain and how they give rise to behavior. The field is highly interdisciplinary and is closely related to several other areas, including psychology, artificial intelligence, linguistics and psycholinguistics, philosophy, neuroscience, logic, robotics, anthropology and biology.
Mental processes	The thoughts, feelings, and motives that each of us experiences privately but that cannot be observed directly are called mental processes.
Donders	Donders discovered that farsightedness was caused by too shallow an eyeball and that astigmatism was caused by uneven curvature of the cornea or lens.
Stimulus	A change in an environmental condition that elicits a response is a stimulus.
Insight	Insight refers to a sudden awareness of the relationships among various elements that had previously appeared to be independent of one another.
Premise	A premise is a statement presumed true within the context of a discourse, especially of a logical argument.
Metaphor	A metaphor is a rhetorical trope where a comparison is made between two seemingly unrelated subjects
Reaction time	The amount of time required to respond to a stimulus is referred to as reaction time.
Attention	Attention is the cognitive process of selectively concentrating on one thing while ignoring other things. Psychologists have labeled three types of attention: sustained attention, selective attention, and divided attention.
Brain	The brain controls and coordinates most movement, behavior and homeostatic body functions

	such as heartbeat, blood pressure, fluid balance and body temperature. Functions of the brain are responsible for cognition, emotion, memory, motor learning and other sorts of learning. The brain is primarily made up of two types of cells: glia and neurons.
Neuroscience	A field that combines the work of psychologists, biologists, biochemists, medical researchers, and others in the study of the structure and function of the nervous system is neuroscience.
Theories	Theories are logically self-consistent models or frameworks describing the behavior of a certain natural or social phenomenon. They are broad explanations and predictions concerning phenomena of interest.
Controlled processes	Controlled processes refer to the most alert states of consciousness.
Cingulate cortex	The part of the limbic system that is believed to process cognitive information in emotion is the cingulate cortex. The cingulate cortex is part of the brain and situated roughly in the middle of the cortex.
Affect	A subjective feeling or emotional tone often accompanied by bodily expressions noticeable to others is called affect.
Left hemisphere	The left hemisphere of the cortex controls the right side of the body, coordinates complex movements, and, in 95% of people, controls the production of speech and written language.
Inference	Inference is the act or process of drawing a conclusion based solely on what one already knows.
Species	Species refers to a reproductively isolated breeding population.
Habit	A habit is a response that has become completely separated from its eliciting stimulus. Early learning theorists used the term to describe S-R associations, however not all S-R associations become a habit, rather many are extinguished after reinforcement is withdrawn.
Sapir	Sapir proposed an alternative view of language in 1921, asserting that language influences the ways in which people think. Sapir's idea was adopted and developed during the 1940s by Whorf and eventually became the Sapir-Whorf Hypothesis.
Linguistic relativity	Linguistic relativity is the idea that one's language determines the nature of one's thought.
Hypothesis	A specific statement about behavior or mental processes that is testable through research is a hypothesis.
Hue	A hue refers to the gradation of color within the optical spectrum, or visible spectrum, of light. Hue may also refer to a particular color within this spectrum, as defined by its dominant wavelength, or the central tendency of its combined wavelengths.
Mental rotation	The ability to change the position of an image in mental space is called mental rotation.
Anchor	An anchor is a sample of work or performance used to set the specific performance standard for a rubric level .
Problem space	The problem space is the set of possible pathways to a solution considered by the problem solver.
Newell	Newell contributed to the Information Processing Language (1956) and two of the earliest AI programs, the Logic Theory Machine (1956) and the General Problem Solver (1957) (with Herbert Simon).
Algorithm	A systematic procedure for solving a problem that works invariably when it is correctly applied is called an algorithm.

Meditation	Meditation usually refers to a state in which the body is consciously relaxed and the mind is allowed to become calm and focused.
Variable	A variable refers to a measurable factor, characteristic, or attribute of an individual or a system.
Functional fixedness	Functional fixedness is a cognitive bias that limits a person to using an object only in the way it is traditionally used.
Perception	Perception is the process of acquiring, interpreting, selecting, and organizing sensory information.
Aristotle	Aristotle can be credited with the development of the first theory of learning. He concluded that ideas were generated in consciousness based on four principlesof association: contiguity, similarity, contrast, and succession. In contrast to Plato, he believed that knowledge derived from sensory experience and was not inherited.
Syllogism	In traditional logic, a syllogism is an inference in which one proposition (the conclusion) follows of necessity from two others (known as premises).
Mental Representation	Stage six of the sensorimotor substages, Mental representation, 18 months to 2 years, marks the beginnings of insight, or true creativity. This marks the passage into unique thought in Piaget's later three areas of development.
Construct	A generalized concept, such as anxiety or gravity, is a construct.
Janis	Janis is famous for his theory of "groupthink" which described the systematic errors made by groups when taking collective decisions. He also collaborated with Carl Hovland on his studies of attitude change, including the sleeper effect.
Alcoholic	An alcoholic is dependent on alcohol as characterized by craving, loss of control, physical dependence and withdrawal symptoms, and tolerance.
Schema	Schema refers to a way of mentally representing the world, such as a belief or an expectation, that can influence perception of persons, objects, and situations.
Deduction	Deduction refers to reasoning from the general to the particular, as in the case of creating an expected hypothesis for a particular experiment from a general theoretical statement.
Mental set	The tendency to respond to a new problem with an approach that was used successfully with similar problems, is called mental set.
Attitude	An enduring mental representation of a person, place, or thing that evokes an emotional response and related behavior is called attitude.
Right hemisphere	The brain is divided into left and right cerebral hemispheres. The right hemisphere of the cortex controls the left side of the body.
Herbert Simon	Herbert Simon was a pioneer in the field of artificial intelligence, creating with Allen Newell the Logic Theory Machine (1956) and the General Problem Solver (GPS) (1957) programs. GPS was possibly the first method of separating problem solving strategy from information about particular problems.
Kahneman	Kahneman is famous for collaboration with Amos Tversky and others in establishing a cognitive basis for common human errors using heuristics and in developing prospect theory.
Tversky	Tversky was a pioneer of cognitive science. With Kahneman, he originated prospect theory to explain irrational human economic choices.
Illusion	An illusion is a distortion of a sensory perception.
Analogy	An analogy is a comparison between two different things, in order to highlight some form of

	similarity. Analogy is the cognitive process of transferring information from a particular subject to another particular subject.
Learning	Learning is a relatively permanent change in behavior that results from experience. Thus, to attribute a behavioral change to learning, the change must be relatively permanent and must result from experience.
Anchoring	Anchoring or focalism is a term used in psychology to describe the common human tendency to rely too heavily, or "anchor," on one trait or piece of information when making decisions.
Availability heuristic	The availability heuristic is a rule of thumb, or heuristic, which occurs when people estimate the probability of an outcome based on how easy that outcome is to imagine.
Biased sample	A biased sample is one that is falsely taken to be typical of a population from which it is drawn.
Mood-congruent	Symptoms are said to be mood-congruent if they are consistent with a patient's mood or mental disorder.
Correlation	A statistical technique for determining the degree of association between two or more variables is referred to as correlation.
Population	Population refers to all members of a well-defined group of organisms, events, or things.
Representati-eness heuristic	Under the representativeness heuristic, we judge things as being similar based on how closely they resemble each other using prima facie, often superficial qualities, rather than essential characteristics.
Framing	Framing refers to the way information is presented so as to emphasize either a potential gain or a potential loss as the outcome.
Individual differences	Individual differences psychology studies the ways in which individual people differ in their behavior. This is distinguished from other aspects of psychology in that although psychology is ostensibly a study of individuals, modern psychologists invariably study groups.

Psychometric	Psychometric study is concerned with the theory and technique of psychological measurement, which includes the measurement of knowledge, abilities, attitudes, and personality traits. The field is primarily concerned with the study of differences between individuals
Sternberg	Sternberg proposed the triarchic theory of intelligence: componential, experiential, and practical. His notion of general intelligence or the g-factor, is a composite of intelligence scores across multiple modalities.
Theories	Theories are logically self-consistent models or frameworks describing the behavior of a certain natural or social phenomenon. They are broad explanations and predictions concerning phenomena of interest.
Triarchic Theory of Intelligence	The Triarchic Theory of Intelligence was formulated by Robert J. Sternberg. It proposes that intelligence consists of componential intelligence, experiential intelligence, and contextual intelligence.
Emotional intelligence	The expression emotional intelligence indicates a kind of intelligence or skill that involves the ability to perceive, assess and positively influence one's own and other people's emotions.
Heredity	Heredity is the transfer of characteristics from parent to offspring through their genes.
Validity	The extent to which a test measures what it is intended to measure is called validity.
IQ test	An IQ test is a standardized test developed to measure a person's cognitive abilities ("intelligence") in relation to their age group.
Creativity	Creativity is the ability to think about something in novel and unusual ways and come up with unique solutions to problems. It involves divergent thinking, having many solutions or views to a problem.
Society	The social sciences use the term society to mean a group of people that form a semi-closed (or semi-open) social system, in which most interactions are with other individuals belonging to the group.
Individual differences	Individual differences psychology studies the ways in which individual people differ in their behavior. This is distinguished from other aspects of psychology in that although psychology is ostensibly a study of individuals, modern psychologists invariably study groups.
Psychological testing	Psychological testing is a field characterized by the use of small samples of behavior in order to infer larger generalizations about a given individual. The technical term for psychological testing is psychometrics.
Stages	Stages represent relatively discrete periods of time in which functioning is qualitatively different from functioning at other periods.
Galton	Galton was one of the first experimental psychologists, and the founder of the field of Differential Psychology, which concerns itself with individual differences rather than on common trends. He created the statistical methods correlation and regression.
Evolutionary theory	Evolutionary theory is concerned with heritable variability rather than behavioral variations. Natural selection requirements: (1) natural variability within a species must exist, (2) only some individual differences are heritable, and (3) natural selection only takes place when there is an interaction between the inborn attributes of organisms and the environment in which they live.
Darwin	Darwin achieved lasting fame as originator of the theory of evolution through natural selection. His book Expression of Emotions in Man and Animals is generally considered the first text on comparative psychology.
Nurture	Nurture refers to the environmental influences on behavior due to nutrition, culture,

	socioeconomic status, and learning.
Species	Species refers to a reproductively isolated breeding population.
Extinction	In operant extinction, if no reinforcement is delivered after the response, gradually the behavior will no longer occur in the presence of the stimulus. The process is more rapid following continuous reinforcement rather than after partial reinforcement. In Classical Conditioning, repeated presentations of the CS without being followed by the US results in the extinction of the CS.
Goddard	Goddard is known especially for his 1912 work, The Kallikak Family: A Study in the Heredity of Feeble-Mindedness and for being the first to translate the Binet intelligence test into English in 1908.
Terman	Terman revised the Stanford-Binet Intelligence Scale in 1916, commonly used to measure intelligence (or I.Q.) in the United States. William Stern's suggestion that mental age/chronological age times 100 (to get rid of the decimal) be made the "intelligence quotient" or I.Q. This apparent mathematization of the measurement gave it an air of scientific accuracy and detachment which contributed greatly to its acceptance among educators and the broad public.
Reliability	Reliability means the extent to which a test produces a consistent , reproducible score .
Correlation	A statistical technique for determining the degree of association between two or more variables is referred to as correlation.
Correlation coefficient	Correlation coefficient refers to a number from +1.00 to -1.00 that expresses the direction and extent of the relationship between two variables. The closer to 1, the stronger the relationship. The sign, + or -, indicates the direction.
Scheme	According to Piaget, a hypothetical mental structure that permits the classification and organization of new information is called a scheme.
Coding	In senation, coding is the process by which information about the quality and quantity of a stimulus is preserved in the pattern of action potentials sent through sensory neurons to the central nervous system.
Trait	An enduring personality characteristic that tends to lead to certain behaviors is called a trait. The term trait also means a genetically inherited feature of an organism.
Construct validity	The extent to which there is evidence that a test measures a particular hypothetical construct is referred to as construct validity.
Face validity	Condition of testing in which test items appear plausible for their intended purposes is called face validity.
Psychiatrist	A psychiatrist is a physician who specializes in the diagnosis and treatment of psychological disorders.
Predictive validity	Predictive validity refers to the relation between test scores and the student 's future performance .
Construct	A generalized concept, such as anxiety or gravity, is a construct.
Norms	In testing, standards of test performance that permit the comparison of one person's score on the test to the scores of others who have taken the same test are referred to as norms.
Depression	In everyday language depression refers to any downturn in mood, which may be relatively transitory and perhaps due to something trivial. This is differentiated from Clinical depression which is marked by symptoms that last two weeks or more and are so severe that they interfere with daily living.

Social class	Social class describes the relationships between people in hierarchical societies or cultures. Those with more power usually subordinate those with less power.
Intelligence test	An intelligence test is a standardized means of assessing a person's current mental ability, for example, the Stanford-Binet test and the Wechsler Adult Intelligence Scale.
Developmentally disabled	developmentally disabled is a term for a pattern of persistently slow learning of basic motor and language skills during childhood, and a significantly below-normal global intellectual capacity as an adult.
Alfred Binet	Alfred Binet published the first modern intelligence test, the Binet-Simon intelligence scale, in 1905. Binet stressed that the core of intelligence consists of complex cognitive processes, such as memory, imagery, comprehension, and judgment; and, that these developed over time in the individual.
Yerkes	Yerkes worked in the field of comparative psychology. He is best known for studying the intelligence and social behavior of gorillas and chimpanzees. Joining with John D. Dodson, he developed the Yerkes-Dodson law relating arousal to performance.
Wechsler Scales	The Wechsler Scales are two well-known intelligence scales, namely the Wechsler Adult Intelligence Scale and the Wechsler Intelligence Scale for Children.
Stanford-Binet	Terman released the "Stanford Revision of the Binet-Simon Scale" or the Stanford-Binet for short. Using validation experiments, he removed several of the Binet-Simon test items and added new ones. In 1985 it was revised to analyze an individual's responses in four content areas: verbal reasoning, quantitative reasoning, abstract reasoning, and short-term memory.
Intelligence quotient	An intelligence quotient is a score derived from a set of standardized tests that were developed with the purpose of measuring a person's cognitive abilities ("intelligence") in relation to their age group.
Clinical psychology	Clinical psychology is involved in the diagnosis, assessment, and treatment of patients with mental or behavioral disorders, and conducts research in these various areas.
Chronological age	Chronological age refers to the number of years that have elapsed since a person's birth.
William Stern	William Stern developed the original formula for the Intelligence Quotient (IQ) after studying the scores on Binet's intelligence test.
Mental age	The mental age refers to the accumulated months of credit that a person earns on the Stanford-Binet Intelligence Scale.
Thorndike	Thorndike worked in animal behavior and the learning process leading to the theory of connectionism. Among his most famous contributions were his research on cats escaping from puzzle boxes, and his formulation of the Law of Effect.
David Wechsler	David Wechsler developed two well-known intelligence scales, namely the Wechsler Adult Intelligence Scale and the Wechsler Intelligence Scale for Children. He held the view that human intelligence is not a single thing, but a mixture of many distinct -- and separately measurable -- human capabilities.
Wechsler Preschool and Primary Scale of Intelligence	The Wechsler Preschool and Primary Scale of intelligence is an IQ test for young children that measures a range of performance, verbal, and preverbal abilities for children from 3 to
Mental retardation	Mental retardation refers to having significantly below-average intellectual functioning and limitations in at least two areas of adaptive functioning. Many categorize retardation as mild, moderate, severe, or profound.

Acquisition	Acquisition is the process of adapting to the environment, learning or becoming conditioned. In classical conditoning terms, it is the initial learning of the stimulus response link, which involves a neutral stimulus being associated with a unconditioned stimulus and becoming a conditioned stimulus.
Social skills	Social skills are skills used to interact and communicate with others to assist status in the social structure and other motivations.
Learning disorder	A disorder characterized by a discrepancy between one's academic achievement and one's intellectual ability is referred to as a learning disorder.
Motivation	In psychology, motivation is the driving force (desire) behind all actions of an organism.
Clinician	A health professional authorized to provide services to people suffering from one or more pathologies is a clinician.
Personality	Personality refers to the pattern of enduring characteristics that differentiates a person, the patterns of behaviors that make each individual unique.
Independent variable	A condition in a scientific study that is manipulated (assigned different values by a researcher) so that the effects of the manipulation may be observed is called an independent variable.
Factor analysis	Factor analysis is a statistical technique that originated in psychometrics. The objective is to explain the most of the variability among a number of observable random variables in terms of a smaller number of unobservable random variables called factors.
Charles Spearman	Charles Spearman is known for his work in statistics, as a pioneer of factor analysis, and for his rank correlation coefficient. He also did seminal work on models for human intelligence, including discovering that disparate cognitive test scores reflect a single general factor and coining the term g factor.
Fluid intelligence	Mental flexibility in the ability to reason abstractly is called fluid intelligence. Fluid intelligence tends to decline around middle adulthood.
Raymond Cattell	Raymond Cattell proposed that 16 factors underlie human personality. He called these 16 factors source traits because he believed that they provide the underlying source for the surface behaviors that we think of as personality.
Crystallized intelligence	One's lifetime of intellectual achievement, as and shown largely through vocabulary and knowledge of world affairs is called crystallized intelligence.
Spatial visualization	An aspect of spatial cognition that involves the mental manipulations of visual stimuli, such as performing mental rotation or solving embedded-figures problems is referred to as spatial visualization.
Convergent production	Convergent production is the deductive generation of the best single answer to a set problem, usually where there is a compelling inference.
Divergent production	Divergent production is the creative generation of multiple answers to a set problem.
Cognition	The intellectual processes through which information is obtained, transformed, stored, retrieved, and otherwise used is cognition.
Learning	Learning is a relatively permanent change in behavior that results from experience. Thus, to attribute a behavioral change to learning, the change must be relatively permanent and must result from experience.
Guilford	Guilford observed that most individuals display a preference for either convergent or divergent thinking. Scientists and engineers typically prefer the former and artists and

	performers, the latter.
Analytical intelligence	Analytical intelligence involves the ability to analyze, judge, evaluate, compare, and contrast.
Information processing	Information processing is an approach to the goal of understanding human thinking. The essence of the approach is to see cognition as being essentially computational in nature, with mind being the software and the brain being the hardware.
Anagram	An anagram is a type of word play, the result of rearranging the letters of a word or phrase to produce other words, using all the original letters exactly once.
Practical intelligence	Practical intelligence focuses on the ability to use, apply, implement, and put into practice.
Variable	A variable refers to a measurable factor, characteristic, or attribute of an individual or a system.
Howard Gardner	Howard Gardner is best known for his theory of multiple intelligences. He outlined seven dimensions of intelligence: Visual / Spatial Intelligence, Musical Intelligence, Verbal Intelligence, Logical/Mathematical Intelligence, Interpersonal Intelligence, Intrapersonal Intelligence, and Bodily / Kinesthetic Intelligence. Since the publication of Frames of Mind, he has additionally identified the 8th and 9th dimensions of intelligence: Naturalist Intelligence and Existentialist Intelligence.
Individualistic	Cultures have been classified as individualistic, which means having a set of values that give priority to personal goals rather than group goals.
Collectivist	A person who defines the self in terms of relationships to other people and groups and gives priority to group goals is called collectivist.
Timbre	The distinctive quality of a sound that distinguishes it from other sounds of the same pitch and loudness is called timbre.
Pitch	Pitch is the psychological interpretation of a sound or musical tone corresponding to its physical frequency
Perception	Perception is the process of acquiring, interpreting, selecting, and organizing sensory information.
Temperament	Temperament refers to a basic, innate disposition to change behavior. The activity level is an important dimension of temperament.
Intrapersonal	Intrapersonal is the ability to recognize, define, and pursue inner feelings and thoughts, as in poetry and self-knowledge.
Hypothesis	A specific statement about behavior or mental processes that is testable through research is a hypothesis.
Control group	A group that does not receive the treatment effect in an experiment is referred to as the control group or sometimes as the comparison group.
Innate	Innate behavior is not learned or influenced by the environment, rather, it is present or predisposed at birth.
Moron	Moron, was originally a scientific term, coined by psychologist Henry Goddard from a Greek word meaning "foolish", and used to describe a person with a genetically determined mental age between 8 and 12 on the Binet scale.
Alcoholism	A disorder that involves long-term, repeated, uncontrolled, compulsive, and excessive use of alcoholic beverages and that impairs the drinker's health and work and social relationships is called alcoholism.

Eugenics	The field concerned with improving the hereditary qualities of the human race through social control of mating and reproduction is called eugenics.
Gene	A gene is an ultramicroscopic area of the chromosome. It is the smallest physical unit of the DNA molecule that carries a piece of hereditary information.
Fraternal twins	Fraternal twins usually occur when two fertilized eggs are implanted in the uterine wall at the same time. The two eggs form two zygotes, and these twins are therefore also known as dizygotic. Dizygotic twins are no more similar genetically than any siblings.
Identical twins	Identical twins occur when a single egg is fertilized to form one zygote (monozygotic) but the zygote then divides into two separate embryos. The two embryos develop into foetuses sharing the same womb. Monozygotic twins are genetically identical unless there has been a mutation in development, and they are almost always the same gender.
Monozygotic	Identical twins occur when a single egg is fertilized to form one zygote, calld monozygotic, but the zygote then divides into two separate embryos. The two embryos develop into foetuses sharing the same womb. Monozygotic twins are genetically identical unless there has been a mutation in development, and they are almost always the same gender.
Dizygotic	Fraternal twins (commonly known as "non-identical twins") usually occur when two fertilized eggs are implanted in the uterine wall at the same time. The two eggs form two zygotes, and these twins are therefore also known as dizygotic.
Heritability	Heritability It is that proportion of the observed variation in a particular phenotype within a particular population, that can be attributed to the contribution of genotype. In other words: it measures the extent to which differences between individuals in a population are due their being different genetically.
Variability	Statistically, variability refers to how much the scores in a distribution spread out, away from the mean.
Population	Population refers to all members of a well-defined group of organisms, events, or things.
Variance	The degree to which scores differ among individuals in a distribution of scores is the variance.
Life span	Life span refers to the upper boundary of life, the maximum number of years an individual can live. The maximum life span of human beings is about 120 years of age. Females live an average of 6 years longer than males.
Ethnic group	An ethnic group is a culture or subculture whose members are readily distinguishable by outsiders based on traits originating from a common racial, national, linguistic, or religious source. Members of an ethnic group are often presumed to be culturally or biologically similar, although this is not in fact necessarily the case.
Relative size	Relative size is a monocular cue where an an automobile that is close to us seems larger than one that is far away. The visual system exploits the relative size of similar (or familiar) objects to judge distance.
Stimulus	A change in an environmental condition that elicits a response is a stimulus.
Affect	A subjective feeling or emotional tone often accompanied by bodily expressions noticeable to others is called affect.
Low birth weight	Low birth weight is a fetus that weighs less than 2500 g (5 lb 8 oz) regardless of gestational age.
Empirical	Empirical means the use of working hypotheses which are capable of being disproved using observation or experiment.

Early Intervention	Early intervention is a process used to recognize warning signs for mental health problems and to take early action against factors that put individuals at risk.
Role model	A person who serves as a positive example of desirable behavior is referred to as a role model.
Attention	Attention is the cognitive process of selectively concentrating on one thing while ignoring other things. Psychologists have labeled three types of attention: sustained attention, selective attention, and divided attention.
Motives	Needs or desires that energize and direct behavior toward a goal are motives.
Stereotype vulnerability	Stereotype vulnerability refers to the tendency to focus on a conventional, negative belief about one's group, such that the individual risks behaving in a way that confirms that belief.
Stereotype	A stereotype is considered to be a group concept, held by one social group about another.They are often used in a negative or prejudicial sense and are frequently used to justify certain discriminatory behaviors. This allows powerful social groups to legitimize and protect their dominant position
Aronson	Aronson is credited with refining the theory of cognitive dissonance, which posits that when attitudes and behaviors are inconsistent with one another that psychological discomfort results. This discomfort motivates the person experiencing it to either change their behavior or attitude so that consonance is restored.
Stereotype threat	A stereotype threat is perceived by persons who believe that they will be evaluated in terms of stereotypes. This is a potential influence on test performance, the resulting anxiety that one's behavior might confirm a negative stereotype about one's group.
Gender difference	A gender difference is a disparity between genders involving quality or quantity. Though some gender differences are controversial, they are not to be confused with sexist stereotypes.
Cultural bias	Cultural bias is interpreting and judging phenomena in terms particular to one's own culture. This is a danger in any field of knowledge that claims objectivity and universality.
Divergent thinking	A thought process that attempts to generate multiple solutions to problems is called divergent thinking.
Graham	Graham has conducted a number of studies that reveal stronger socioeconomic-status influences rather than ethnic influences in achievement.
Intrinsic motivation	Intrinsic motivation causes people to engage in an activity for its own sake. They are subjective factors and include self-determination, curiosity, challenge, effort, and others.
Bipolar disorder	Bipolar Disorder is a mood disorder typically characterized by fluctuations between manic and depressive states; and, more generally, atypical mood regulation and mood instability.
Kraepelin	Kraepelin postulated that there is a specific brain or other biological pathology underlying each of the major psychiatric disorders. Just as his laboratory discovered the pathologic basis of what is now known as Alzheimers disease, Kraepelin was confident that it would someday be possible to identify the pathologic basis of each of the major psychiatric disorders.
Insanity	A legal status indicating that a person cannot be held responsible for his or her actions because of mental illness is called insanity.
Plato	According to Plato, people must come equipped with most of their knowledge and need only hints and contemplation to complete it. Plato suggested that the brain is the mechanism of mental processes and that one gained knowledge by reflecting on the contents of one's mind.

Mania	Mania is a medical condition characterized by severely elevated mood. Mania is most usually associated with bipolar disorder, where episodes of mania may cyclically alternate with episodes of depression.
Shaping	The concept of reinforcing successive, increasingly accurate approximations to a target behavior is called shaping. The target behavior is broken down into a hierarchy of elemental steps, each step more sophisticated then the last. By successively reinforcing each of the the elemental steps, a form of differential reinforcement, until that step is learned while extinguishing the step below, the target behavior is gradually achieved.
Achievement test	A test designed to determine a person's level of knowledge in a given subject area is referred to as an achievement test.
Maladjustment	Maladjustment is the condition of being unable to adapt properly to your environment with resulting emotional instability.
Pathology	Pathology is the study of the processes underlying disease and other forms of illness, harmful abnormality, or dysfunction.
Standardized test	An oral or written assessment for which an individual receives a score indicating how the individual reponded relative to a previously tested large sample of others is referred to as a standardized test.
Insight	Insight refers to a sudden awareness of the relationships among various elements that had previously appeared to be independent of one another.

Acquisition — Acquisition is the process of adapting to the environment, learning or becoming conditioned. In classical conditoning terms, it is the initial learning of the stimulus response link, which involves a neutral stimulus being associated with a unconditioned stimulus and becoming a conditioned stimulus.

Reasoning — Reasoning is the act of using reason to derive a conclusion from certain premises. There are two main methods to reach a conclusion,deductive reasoning and inductive reasoning.

Kohlberg — Kohlberg believed that people progressed in their moral reasoning through a series of developmental stages.

Stages — Stages represent relatively discrete periods of time in which functioning is qualitatively different from functioning at other periods.

Human nature — Human nature is the fundamental nature and substance of humans, as well as the range of human behavior that is believed to be invariant over long periods of time and across very different cultural contexts.

Premise — A premise is a statement presumed true within the context of a discourse, especially of a logical argument.

Life span — Life span refers to the upper boundary of life, the maximum number of years an individual can live. The maximum life span of human beings is about 120 years of age. Females live an average of 6 years longer than males.

Bronfenbrenner — Bronfenbrenner was a co-founder of the U.S. national Head Start program and founder of the Ecological Theory of Development.

Normative — The term normative is used to describe the effects of those structures of culture which regulate the function of social activity.

Chronological age — Chronological age refers to the number of years that have elapsed since a person's birth.

Norms — In testing, standards of test performance that permit the comparison of one person's score on the test to the scores of others who have taken the same test are referred to as norms.

Developmental psychologist — A psychologist interested in human growth and development from conception until death is referred to as a developmental psychologist.

Research design — A research design tests a hypothesis. The basic typess are: descriptive, correlational, and experimental.

Longitudinal design — A research design in which investigators observe one group of subjects repeatedly over a period of time is called a longitudinal design.

Individual differences — Individual differences psychology studies the ways in which individual people differ in their behavior. This is distinguished from other aspects of psychology in that although psychology is ostensibly a study of individuals, modern psychologists invariably study groups.

Longitudinal research — Research that studies the same subjects over an extended period of time, usually several years or more, is called longitudinal research.

Socioeconomic — Socioeconomic pertains to the study of the social and economic impacts of any product or service offering, market intervention or other activity on an economy as a whole and on the companies, organization and individuals who are its main economic actors.

Generalization — In conditioning, the tendency for a conditioned response to be evoked by stimuli that are similar to the stimulus to which the response was conditioned is a generalization. The greater the similarity among the stimuli, the greater the probability of generalization.

Cohort — A cohort is a group of individuals defined by their date of birth.

Cross-sectional design	A research design in which investigators compare groups of subjects of differing age on some variable is a cross-sectional design.
Social support	Social Support is the physical and emotional comfort given by family, friends, co-workers and others. Research has identified three main types of social support: emotional, practical, sharing points of view.
Chromosome	The DNA which carries genetic information in biological cells is normally packaged in the form of one or more large macromolecules called a chromosome. Humans normally have 46.
Prenatal	Prenatal period refers to the time from conception to birth.
Zygote	A zygote is a cell that is the result of fertilization. That is, two haploid cells—usually (but not always) a sperm cell from a male and an ovum from a female—merge into a single diploid cell called the zygote.
Embryo	A developed zygote that has a rudimentary heart, brain, and other organs is referred to as an embryo.
Fetus	A fetus develops from the end of the 8th week of pregnancy (when the major structures have formed), until birth.
Malnutrition	Malnutrition is a general term for the medical condition in a person or animal caused by an unbalanced diet—either too little or too much food, or a diet missing one or more important nutrients.
Dendrite	A dendrite is a slender, typically branched projection of a nerve cell, or "neuron," which conducts the electrical stimulation received from other cells to the body or soma of the cell from which it projects. This stimulation arrives through synapses, which typically are located near the tips of the dendrites and away from the soma.
Neuron	The neuron is the primary cell of the nervous system. They are found in the brain, the spinal cord, in the nerves and ganglia of the peripheral nervous system. It is a specialized cell that conducts impulses through the nervous system and contains three major parts: cell body, dendrites, and an axon. It can have many dendrites but only one axon.
Brain	The brain controls and coordinates most movement, behavior and homeostatic body functions such as heartbeat, blood pressure, fluid balance and body temperature. Functions of the brain are responsible for cognition, emotion, memory, motor learning and other sorts of learning. The brain is primarily made up of two types of cells: glia and neurons.
Cowan	Cowan regards working memory not as a separate system, but as a part of long-term memory. Representations in working memory are a subset of the representations in long-term memory.
Axon	An axon, or "nerve fiber," is a long slender projection of a nerve cell, or "neuron," which conducts electrical impulses away from the neuron's cell body or soma.
Sensitive period	A sensitive period is a developmental window in which a predisposed behavior is most likely to develop given appropriate stimulation. In linguistic theory, the period from about 18 months to puberty is when the brain is thought to be primed for learning language because of plasticity of the brain.
Placenta	A membrane that permits the exchange of nutrients and waste products between the mother and her developing child but does not allow the maternal and fetal bloodstreams to mix is the placenta.
Cocaine	Cocaine is a crystalline tropane alkaloid that is obtained from the leaves of the coca plant. It is a stimulant of the central nervous system and an appetite suppressant, creating what has been described as a euphoric sense of happiness and increased energy.
Affect	A subjective feeling or emotional tone often accompanied by bodily expressions noticeable to

	others is called affect.
Deprivation	Deprivation, is the loss or withholding of normal stimulation, nutrition, comfort, love, and so forth; a condition of lacking. The level of stimulation is less than what is required.
Behaviorism	The school of psychology that defines psychology as the study of observable behavior and studies relationships between stimuli and responses is called behaviorism. Behaviorism relied heavily on animal research and stated the same principles governed the behavior of both nonhumans and humans.
John Watson	John Watson, the father of behaviorism, developed the term "Behaviorism" as a name for his proposal to revolutionize the study of human psychology in order to put it on a firm experimental footing.
Senses	The senses are systems that consist of a sensory cell type that respond to a specific kind of physical energy, and that correspond to a defined region within the brain where the signals are received and interpreted.
Spence	Spence attributed improvement in performance to motivational factors rather than habit factors. His Discrimination Learning Theory argued that reinforcement combined with frustration or inhibitors facilitates finding a correct stimulus among a cluster which includes incorrect ones.
Rooting reflex	The rooting reflex is a newborn's built-in reaction that occurs when the infant's cheek is stroked or the side of the mouth is touched. In response, the infant turns its head toward the side that was touched in an apparent effort to find something to suck.
Visual acuity	Visual acuity is the eye's ability to detect fine details and is the quantitative measure of the eye's ability to see an in-focus image at a certain distance.
Discrimination	In Learning theory, discrimination refers the ability to distinguish between a conditioned stimulus and other stimuli. It can be brought about by extensive training or differential reinforcement. In social terms, it is the denial of privileges to a person or a group on the basis of prejudice.
Photoreceptor	Photoreceptor cells are contained in the retina and are responsible for transducing, or converting, light into signals that can be ultimately transmitted to the brain via the optic nerve. A photoreceptor cell contains a membranous protein called an opsin which contains a pigment molecule called retinal.
Visual cortex	The visual cortex is the general term applied to both the primary visual cortex and the visual association area. Anatomically, the visual cortex occupies the entire occipital lobe, the inferior temporal lobe (IT), posterior parts of the parietal lobe, and a few small regions in the frontal lobe.
Visual cliff	An apparatus used to test depth perception in infants and young animals is the visual cliff. Infants, 6-14 months, were placed on the edge of the visual cliff, a small cliff with a drop-off covered by glass, to see if they would crawl over the edge. Most infants refused to crawl out on the glass signifying that they could perceive depth and that depth perception is not learned.
Maturation	The orderly unfolding of traits, as regulated by the genetic code is called maturation.
Species	Species refers to a reproductively isolated breeding population.
Adolescence	The period of life bounded by puberty and the assumption of adult responsibilities is adolescence.
Growth hormone	Growth hormone is a polypeptide hormone synthesised and secreted by the anterior pituitary gland which stimulates growth and cell reproduction in humans and other vertebrate animals.

Puberty	Puberty refers to the process of physical changes by which a child's body becomes an adult body capable of reproduction.
Menarche	Menarche is the first menstrual period as a girl's body progresses through the changes of puberty. Menarche usually occurs about two years after the first changes of breast development.
Frontal lobe	The frontal lobe comprises four major folds of cortical tissue: the precentral gyrus, superior gyrus and the middle gyrus of the frontal gyri, the inferior frontal gyrus. It has been found to play a part in impulse control, judgement, language, memory, motor function, problem solving, sexual behavior, socialization and spontaneity.
Emotion	An emotion is a mental states that arise spontaneously, rather than through conscious effort. They are often accompanied by physiological changes.
Dark adaptation	Dark adaptation is the tendency for the peak sensitivity of the human eye to shift toward the blue end of the color spectrum at low illumination levels.
Late adulthood	The developmental period that lasts from about 60 to 70 years of age until death is referred to as late adulthood.
Menopause	Menopause is a stage of the human female reproductive cycle that occurs as the ovaries stop producing estrogen, causing the reproductive system to gradually shut down.
Ovulation	Ovulation is the process in the menstrual cycle by which a mature ovarian follicle ruptures and discharges an ovum (also known as an oocyte, female gamete, or casually, an egg) that participates in reproduction.
Aerobic exercise	Aerobic exercise is a type of exercise in which muscles draw on oxygen in the blood as well as fats and glucose, that increase cardiovascular endurance.
Cognitive development	The process by which a child's understanding of the world changes as a function of age and experience is called cognitive development.
Attention	Attention is the cognitive process of selectively concentrating on one thing while ignoring other things. Psychologists have labeled three types of attention: sustained attention, selective attention, and divided attention.
Nurture	Nurture refers to the environmental influences on behavior due to nutrition, culture, socioeconomic status, and learning.
Tabula rasa	In Locke's philosophy, Tabula rasa is the notion that individual human beings are born "blank" (with no built-in mental content), and that their identity is defined entirely by events after birth.
Learning	Learning is a relatively permanent change in behavior that results from experience. Thus, to attribute a behavioral change to learning, the change must be relatively permanent and must result from experience.
Empiricism	Empiricism is generally regarded as being at the heart of the modern scientific method, that our theories should be based on our observations of the world rather than on intuition, or deductive logic.
Rousseau	Rousseau rejected the idea of the blank slate. He believed that learning was a natural consequence of human existence. Further, he thought socialization unimportant in development. Because of his insistence that childhood was different than adulthood and his creation of stages of development, he is known as the father of developmental psychology.
Innate	Innate behavior is not learned or influenced by the environment, rather, it is present or predisposed at birth.

Theories	Theories are logically self-consistent models or frameworks describing the behavior of a certain natural or social phenomenon. They are broad explanations and predictions concerning phenomena of interest.
Insight	Insight refers to a sudden awareness of the relationships among various elements that had previously appeared to be independent of one another.
Piaget	Piaget argued that young children's answers were qualitatively different than older children rather than quantitative. There are two major aspects to his theory: the process of coming to know and the stages we move through as we gradually acquire this ability.
Scheme	According to Piaget, a hypothetical mental structure that permits the classification and organization of new information is called a scheme.
Sensorimotor	The first of Piaget's stages is the Sensorimotor stage. This stage typically ranges from birth to 2 years. In this stage, children experience the world through their senses. During this stage, object permanence and stranger anxiety develop.
Accommodation	Piaget's developmental process of accommodation is the modification of currently held schemes or new schemes so that new information inconsistent with the existing schemes can be integrated and understood.
Assimilation	According to Piaget, assimilation is the process of the organism interacting with the environment given the organism's cognitive structure. Assimilation is reuse of schemas to fit new information.
Reflex	A simple, involuntary response to a stimulus is referred to as reflex. Reflex actions originate at the spinal cord rather than the brain.
Object permanence	Object permanence is the term used to describe the awareness that objects continue to exist even when they are no longer visible. According to Piaget, object permance for the infant develops once the sensorimotor stage is complete.
Egocentrism	The inability to distinguish between one's own perspective and someone else's is referred to as egocentrism.
Concrete operations	In Piaget's theory, the third major stage of cognitive development, in which children can decenter their perception, are less egocentric, and can think logically about concrete objects is called concrete operations.
Conservation	Conservation refers to the recognition that basic properties of substances such as weight and mass remain the same even when transformations merely alter their appearance.
Mental Representation	Stage six of the sensorimotor substages, Mental representation, 18 months to 2 years, marks the beginnings of insight, or true creativity. This marks the passage into unique thought in Piaget's later three areas of development.
Infancy	The developmental period that extends from birth to 18 or 24 months is called infancy.
Preoperational stage	The Preoperational stage is the second stage of development in Piaget's theory. By observing sequences of play, Piaget was able to demonstrate that towards the end of the second year a qualitatively quite new kind of functioning occurs. Operation in Piagetian theory is any procedure for mentally acting on objects.
Concrete operations stage	Concrete operations stage is Piaget's third stage of cognitive development, during which a child acquires the concepts of reversibility and conservation and is able to apply logical thinking to concrete objects.
Reversibility	Reversibility according to Piaget, is recognition that processes can be undone, that things can be made as they were.

Formal operations	Formal operations in Piaget's theory is the final stage of cognitive development, in which children are able to apply abstract logical rules. Not everyone reaches the formal operations stage of development.
Research method	The scope of the research method is to produce some new knowledge. This, in principle, can take three main forms: Exploratory research; Constructive research; and Empirical research.
Habituation	In habituation there is a progressive reduction in the response probability with continued repetition of a stimulus.
Stimulus	A change in an environmental condition that elicits a response is a stimulus.
Theory of mind	A theory of mind considers the nature of mind, and its structure and processes
Perception	Perception is the process of acquiring, interpreting, selecting, and organizing sensory information.
Vygotsky	The Vygotsky model of human development has been termed as a sociocultural approach. The individual's development is a result of his or her culture.
Internalization	The developmental change from behavior that is externally controlled to behavior that is controlled by internal standards and principles is referred to as internalization.
Cognition	The intellectual processes through which information is obtained, transformed, stored, retrieved, and otherwise used is cognition.
Cross-cultural studies	Cross-cultural studies are comparisons of a culture with one or more other cultures, which provides information about the degree to which behavior is similar across cultures or the degree to which it is culture specific .
Schematic representation	The representation of objects in terms of real or potential interactions with other objects is called a schematic representation.
Stereotype	A stereotype is considered to be a group concept, held by one social group about another.They are often used in a negative or prejudicial sense and are frequently used to justify certain discriminatory behaviors. This allows powerful social groups to legitimize and protect their dominant position
Population	Population refers to all members of a well-defined group of organisms, events, or things.
Crystallized intelligence	One's lifetime of intellectual achievement, as and shown largely through vocabulary and knowledge of world affairs is called crystallized intelligence.
Fluid intelligence	Mental flexibility in the ability to reason abstractly is called fluid intelligence. Fluid intelligence tends to decline around middle adulthood.
Baltes	Baltes describes the life-span perspective as one that sees hurman development as lifelong, multidimensional, multidirectional, plastic, contextual, and multidisciplinary, and as involving growth, maintenance, and regulation.
Control group	A group that does not receive the treatment effect in an experiment is referred to as the control group or sometimes as the comparison group.
Paired associate	Paired associate is a method where subjects learn pairs of items so that when they are shown one member of the pair, they can respond with the other.
Disuse	Disuse refers to theory that memory traces weaken when memories are not periodically used or retrieved.
Compensation	In personaility, compensation, according to Adler, is an effort to overcome imagined or real inferiorities by developing one's abilities.
Memory trace	A memory trace is the postulated assumed change in the nervous system that reflects the

	impression made by a stimulus. They are said to be held in sensory registers.
American Sign Language	The American Sign Language is a language of hand gestures used by deaf and hearing impaired persons.
Phoneme	In oral language, a phoneme is the theoretical basic unit of sound that can be used to distinguish words or morphemes; in sign language, it is a similarly basic unit of hand shape, motion, position, or facial expression.
Phonology	Phonology is a subfield of linguistics closely associated with phonetics. Whereas phonetics is about the physical production and perception of sounds of speech, phonology describes the way sounds function - within a given language or across languages.
Phonetics	Phonetics is the study of sounds (voice). It is concerned with the actual properties of speech sounds (phones) as well as those of non-speech sounds, and their production, audition and perception.
Syntax	Syntax can be described as the study of the rules, or "patterned relations" that govern the way the words in a sentence come together.
Morpheme	A morpheme is the smallest language unit that carries a semantic interpretation. They are, generally, a distinctive collocation of phonemes (as the free form pin or the bound form -s of pins) having no smaller meaningful members.
Semantics	Semantics is a subfield of linguistics that is traditionally defined as the study of meaning of words, phrases, sentences, and texts.
Pragmatics	Pragmatics is generally the study of natural language understanding, and specifically the study of how context influences the interpretation of meanings. It is a subfield of linguistics.
Child-directed speech	Baby talk, motherese, parentese, caretaker, or child-directed speech is a nonstandard form of speech used by adults, particularly mothers, in talking to children.
Intonation	The use of pitches of varying levels to help communicate meaning is called intonation.
Chomsky	Chomsky has greatly influenced the field of theoretical linguistics with his work on the theory of generative grammar. Accordingly, humans are biologically prewired to learn language at a certain time and in a certain way.
Predisposition	Predisposition refers to an inclination or diathesis to respond in a certain way, either inborn or acquired. In abnormal psychology, it is a factor that lowers the ability to withstand stress and inclines the individual toward pathology.
Telegraphic speech	Telegraphic speech refers to the use of short and precise words to communicate. Young children's two- and three-word utterances characteristically are telegraphic.
Toddler	A toddler is a child between the ages of one and three years old. During this period, the child learns a great deal about social roles and develops motor skills; to toddle is to walk unsteadily.
Overregulari-ation	Overregularization is the application of regular grammatical rules for forming inflections to irregular verbs and nouns.
Social development	The person's developing capacity for social relationships and the effects of those relationships on further development is referred to as social development.
Social policy	Social policy is the study of the welfare state, and the range of responses to social need.
Erik Erikson	Erik Erikson conceived eight stages of development, each confronting the individual with its own psychosocial demands, that continued into old age. Personality development, according to Erikson, takes place through a series of crises that must be overcome and internalized by the

	individual in preparation for the next developmental stage. Such crisis are not catastrophes but vulnerabilities.
Psychosocial stages	Erikson's eight developmental stages through the life span, each defined by a conflict that must be resolved satisfactorily in order for healthy personality development to occur are called psychosocial stages.
Sigmund Freud	Sigmund Freud was the founder of the psychoanalytic school, based on his theory that unconscious motives control much behavior, that particular kinds of unconscious thoughts and memories are the source of neurosis, and that neurosis could be treated through bringing these unconscious thoughts and memories to consciousness in psychoanalytic treatment.
Anna Freud	Anna Freud was a pioneer of child psychoanalysis. She popularized the notion that adolescence is a period that includes rapid mood fluctuation with enormous uncertainty about self.
Attachment	Attachment is the tendency to seek closeness to another person and feel secure when that person is present.
Anxiety	Anxiety is a complex combination of the feeling of fear, apprehension and worry often accompanied by physical sensations such as palpitations, chest pain and/or shortness of breath.
Society	The social sciences use the term society to mean a group of people that form a semi-closed (or semi-open) social system, in which most interactions are with other individuals belonging to the group.
Autonomy	Autonomy is the condition of something that does not depend on anything else.
Guilt	Guilt describes many concepts related to a negative emotion or condition caused by actions which are believed to be, morally wrong. According to Freud, the avoidance of guilt is the basis for moral behavior.
Social skills	Social skills are skills used to interact and communicate with others to assist status in the social structure and other motivations.
Life stages	Widely recognized periods of life corresponding to broad phases of development are called life stages. They may cross-culturally or socially defined.
Self-image	A person's self-image is the mental picture, generally of a kind that is quite resistant to change, that depicts not only details that are potentially available to objective investigation by others, but also items that have been learned by that person about himself or herself.
Generativity	Generativity refers to an adult's concern for and commitment to the well-being of future generations.
Socialization	Social rules and social relations are created, communicated, and changed in verbal and nonverbal ways creating social complexity useful in identifying outsiders and intelligent breeding partners. The process of learning these skills is called socialization.
Attitude	An enduring mental representation of a person, place, or thing that evokes an emotional response and related behavior is called attitude.
Motives	Needs or desires that energize and direct behavior toward a goal are motives.
Critical period	A period of time when an innate response can be elicited by a particular stimulus is referred to as the critical period.
Imprinting	Imprinting describes any kind of critical period sensitive learning (learning occurring at a particular age or a particular life stage) that is rapid and apparently independent of the consequences of behavior.

Automaticity	The ability to process information with little or no effort is referred to as automaticity.
Lorenz	Lorenz demonstrated how incubator-hatched geese would imprint on the first suitable moving stimulus they saw within what he called a "critical period" of about 36 hours shortly after hatching. Most famously, the goslings would imprint on Lorenz himself .
Bowlby	Bowlby, a developmental psychologist of the psychoanalytic tradition, was responsible for much of the early research conducted on attachment in humans. He identified three stages of separation: protest, despair, and detachment.
Strange situation test	Strange situation test is a procedure used to study attachment. An infant is placed in a novel environment and is observed reacting to it in the presence and then absence of a caregiver.
Insecure attachment	Insecure attachment occurs when infants either avoid the caregiver or show considerable resistance or ambivalence toward the caregiver.
Strange situation	An observational measure of infant attachment that requires the infant to move through a series of introductions, separations, and reunions with the caregiver and an adult stranger in a prescribed order is called Ainsworth's strange situation.
Memory structure	Patterns of associations among bits of information stored in memory is a memory structure.
Schema	Schema refers to a way of mentally representing the world, such as a belief or an expectation, that can influence perception of persons, objects, and situations.
Secure attachment	With secure attachment, the infant uses a caregiver as a secure base from which to explore the environment. Ainsworth believes that secure attachment in the first year of life provides an important foundation for psychological development later in life.
Temperament	Temperament refers to a basic, innate disposition to change behavior. The activity level is an important dimension of temperament.
Individuality	According to Cooper, individuality consists of two dimensions: self-assertion and separateness.
Primary caregiver	Primary caregiver refers to a person primarily responsible for the care of an infant, usually the infant's mother or father.
Harlow	Harlow and his famous wire and cloth surrogate mother monkey studies demonstrated that the need for affection created a stronger bond between mother and infant than did physical needs. He also found that the more discrimination problems the monkeys solved, the better they became at solving them.
Contact comfort	A hypothethetical primary drive to seek physical comfort through contact with another is called contact comfort.
Empathy	Empathy is the recognition and understanding of the states of mind, including beliefs, desires and particularly emotions of others without injecting your own.
Child abuse	Child abuse is the physical or psychological maltreatment of a child.
Longitudinal study	Longitudinal study is a type of developmental study in which the same group of participants is followed and measured for an extended period of time, often years.
Hyperactivity	Hyperactivity can be described as a state in which a individual is abnormally easily excitable and exuberant. Strong emotional reactions and a very short span of attention is also typical for the individual.
Maladjustment	Maladjustment is the condition of being unable to adapt properly to your environment with resulting emotional instability.

Suicide	Suicide behavior is rare in childhood but escalates in adolescence. The suicide rate increases in a linear fashion from adolescence through late adulthood.
Hartup	According to Hartup, the single best childhood predictor of adult adaptation is not school grades, and not classroom behavior, but rather, the adequacy with which the child gets along with other children.
Friendship	The essentials of friendship are reciprocity and commitment between individuals who see themselves more or less as equals. Interaction between friends rests on a more equal power base than the interaction between children and adults.
Reflection	Reflection is the process of rephrasing or repeating thoughts and feelings expressed, making the person more aware of what they are saying or thinking.
Gender role	A cluster of behaviors that characterizes traditional female or male behaviors within a cultural setting is a gender role.
Maslow	Maslow is mostly noted today for his proposal of a hierarchy of human needs which he often presented as a pyramid. Maslow was an instrumental player in the formation of the humanistic movement, also known as the third force in psychology.
Affective	Affective is the way people react emotionally, their ability to feel another living thing's pain or joy.
Homosexual	Homosexual refers to a sexual orientation characterized by aesthetic attraction, romantic love, and sexual desire exclusively for members of the same sex or gender identity.
Personality	Personality refers to the pattern of enduring characteristics that differentiates a person, the patterns of behaviors that make each individual unique.
Ageism	Ageism is bias against a person or group on the grounds of age. When that bias is the primary motivation behind acts of discrimination against that person or group, then those acts constitute age discrimination..
Survey	A method of scientific investigation in which a large sample of people answer questions about their attitudes or behavior is referred to as a survey.
Social role	Social role refers to expected behavior patterns associated with particular social positions.
Gender identity	Gender identity describes the gender with which a person identifies, but can also be used to refer to the gender that other people attribute to the individual on the basis of what they know from gender role indications.
Moral development	Development regarding rules and conventions about what people should do in their interactions with other people is called moral development.
Moral reasoning	Moral reasoning involves concepts of justice, whereas social conventional judgments are concepts of social organization.
Moral judgment	Making decisions about which actions are right and which are wrong is a moral judgment.
Carol Gilligan	Carol Gilligan is best known for her work on the ethics of care, a theory that contrasts ethics of care to so-called ethics of justice. She claimed that the results of Kohlberg were biased because the participants in the basic study were largely male, and that the scoring method subsequently used tended to favor a principled way of reasoning that was more common to boys, over a moral argumentation concentrating on relations, which would be more amenable to girls.
Gender difference	A gender difference is a disparity between genders involving quality or quantity. Though some gender differences are controversial, they are not to be confused with sexist stereotypes.
Concrete	According to Piaget, the period from 7 to 12 years of age, which is characterized by logical

operational	thought and a loss of egocentrism, is referred to as concrete operational stage. Conservation skills are formed - understanding that quantity, length or number of items is unrelated to the appearance of the object or items.
Formal operational	According to Piaget, the period from age 12 to adulthood, which is characterized by abstract thought is referred to as the formal operational stage.
Paradigm	Paradigm refers to the set of practices that defines a scientific discipline during a particular period of time. It provides a framework from which to conduct research, it ensures that a certain range of phenomena, those on which the paradigm focuses, are explored thoroughly. Itmay also blind scientists to other, perhaps more fruitful, ways of dealing with their subject matter.
Personal identity	The portion of the self-concept that pertains to the self as a distinct, separate individual is called personal identity.
Gender stereotypes	Broad categories that reflect our impressions and beliefs about typical females and males are referred to as gender stereotypes.

Motivation	In psychology, motivation is the driving force (desire) behind all actions of an organism.
Motives	Needs or desires that energize and direct behavior toward a goal are motives.
Deprivation	Deprivation, is the loss or withholding of normal stimulation, nutrition, comfort, love, and so forth; a condition of lacking. The level of stimulation is less than what is required.
Motivational state	A motivational state is an internal, reversible condition in an individual that orients the individual toward one or another type of goal. This condition is not observed directly but is inferred from the individual's behavior.
Theories	Theories are logically self-consistent models or frameworks describing the behavior of a certain natural or social phenomenon. They are broad explanations and predictions concerning phenomena of interest.
Species	Species refers to a reproductively isolated breeding population.
Emotion	An emotion is a mental states that arise spontaneously, rather than through conscious effort. They are often accompanied by physiological changes.
Brain	The brain controls and coordinates most movement, behavior and homeostatic body functions such as heartbeat, blood pressure, fluid balance and body temperature. Functions of the brain are responsible for cognition, emotion, memory, motor learning and other sorts of learning. The brain is primarily made up of two types of cells: glia and neurons.
Lungs	The lungs are the essential organs of respiration. Its principal function is to transport oxygen from the atmosphere into the bloodstream, and excrete carbon dioxide from the bloodstream into the atmosphere.
Incentive	An incentive is what is expected once a behavior is performed. An incentive acts as a reinforcer.
Physiological needs	The easiest kinds of motivation to analyse, at least superficially, are those based upon obvious physiological needs. These include hunger, thirst, and escape from pain.
Hull	Hull is best known for the Drive Reduction Theory which postulated that behavior occurs in response to primary drives such as hunger, thirst, sexual interest, etc. When the goal of the drive is attained the drive is reduced. This reduction of drive serves as a reinforcer for learning.
Homeostasis	Homeostasis is the property of an open system, especially living organisms, to regulate its internal environment so as to maintain a stable condition, by means of multiple dynamic equilibrium adjustments controlled by interrelated regulation mechanisms.
Biological needs	Beyond physiological needs for survivial, the next level are motivations that have an obvious biological basis but are not required for the immediate survival of the organism. These biological needs include the powerful motivations for sex, parenting and aggression.
Zimbardo	Zimbardo is best-known for his Stanford prison experiment. The experiment led to theories about the importance of the social situation in individual psychology that are still controversial today.
Berlyne	According to Berlyne, play is exciting and pleasurable in itself because it satisfies the exploratory drive. Play encourages exploratory behavior by offering children the possibilities of novelty, complexity, uncertainty, and surprise.
Harlow	Harlow and his famous wire and cloth surrogate mother monkey studies demonstrated that the need for affection created a stronger bond between mother and infant than did physical needs. He also found that the more discrimination problems the monkeys solved, the better they became at solving them.

Anxiety	Anxiety is a complex combination of the feeling of fear, apprehension and worry often accompanied by physical sensations such as palpitations, chest pain and/or shortness of breath.
Instinct	Instinct is the word used to describe inherent dispositions towards particular actions. They are generally an inherited pattern of responses or reactions to certain kinds of situations.
William James	Functionalism as a psychology developed out of Pragmatism as a philosophy: To find the meaning of an idea, you have to look at its consequences. This led William James and his students towards an emphasis on cause and effect, prediction and control, and observation of environment and behavior, over the careful introspection of the Structuralists.
Death instinct	The death instinct was defined by Sigmund Freud, in Beyond the Pleasure Principle(1920). It speculated on the existence of a fundamental death wish or death instinct, referring to an individual's own need to die.
Sigmund Freud	Sigmund Freud was the founder of the psychoanalytic school, based on his theory that unconscious motives control much behavior, that particular kinds of unconscious thoughts and memories are the source of neurosis, and that neurosis could be treated through bringing these unconscious thoughts and memories to consciousness in psychoanalytic treatment.
Empirical	Empirical means the use of working hypotheses which are capable of being disproved using observation or experiment.
Reinforcement	In operant conditioning, reinforcement is any change in an environment that (a) occurs after the behavior, (b) seems to make that behavior re-occur more often in the future and (c) that reoccurence of behavior must be the result of the change.
Cognition	The intellectual processes through which information is obtained, transformed, stored, retrieved, and otherwise used is cognition.
Cognitive approach	A cognitive approach focuses on the mental processes involved in knowing: how we direct our attention, perceive, remember, think, and solve problems.
Observational learning	The acquisition of knowledge and skills through the observation of others rather than by means of direct experience is observational learning. Four major processes are thought to influence the observational learning: attentional, retentional, behavioral production, and motivational.
Social learning	Social learning is learning that occurs as a function of observing, retaining and replicating behavior observed in others. Although social learning can occur at any stage in life, it is thought to be particularly important during childhood, particularly as authority becomes important.
Rotter	Rotter focused on the application of social learning theory (SLT) to clinical psychology. She introduced the ideas of learning from generalized expectancies of reinforcement and internal/ external locus of control (self-initiated change versus change influenced by others). According to Rotter, health outcomes could be improved by the development of a sense of personal control over one's life.
Fritz Heider	Attribution theory in social psychology was initiated by Fritz Heider in 1958. It concerned how people choose explanations for the behavior of others. It explores how individuals attribute causes to events and how this cognitive perception affects their motivation.
Learning	Learning is a relatively permanent change in behavior that results from experience. Thus, to attribute a behavioral change to learning, the change must be relatively permanent and must result from experience.
Affect	A subjective feeling or emotional tone often accompanied by bodily expressions noticeable to others is called affect.

Evolution	Commonly used to refer to gradual change, evolution is the change in the frequency of alleles within a population from one generation to the next. This change may be caused by different mechanisms, including natural selection, genetic drift, or changes in population (gene flow).
Hypothalamus	The hypothalamus is a region of the brain located below the thalamus, forming the major portion of the ventral region of the diencephalon and functioning to regulate certain metabolic processes and other autonomic activities.
Walter Cannon	Walter Cannon developed the concept of homeostasis, and popularized it in his book The Wisdom of the Body. In 1929, he coined the term fight or flight to describe an animal's response to threats.
Hypothesis	A specific statement about behavior or mental processes that is testable through research is a hypothesis.
Necessary condition	A circumstance required for a particular phenomenon to occur is a necessary condition if and only if the condition does not occur in the absense of the circumstance.
Satiety	Satiety refers to the state of being satisfied; fullness.
Protein	A protein is a complex, high-molecular-weight organic compound that consists of amino acids joined by peptide bonds. It is essential to the structure and function of all living cells and viruses. Many are enzymes or subunits of enzymes.
Lesion	A lesion is a non-specific term referring to abnormal tissue in the body. It can be caused by any disease process including trauma (physical, chemical, electrical), infection, neoplasm, metabolic and autoimmune.
Receptor	A sensory receptor is a structure that recognizes a stimulus in the internal or external environment of an organism. In response to stimuli the sensory receptor initiates sensory transduction by creating graded potentials or action potentials in the same cell or in an adjacent one.
Metabolism	Metabolism is the biochemical modification of chemical compounds in living organisms and cells.
Glucose	Glucose, a simple monosaccharide sugar, is one of the most important carbohydrates and is used as a source of energy in animals and plants. Glucose is one of the main products of photosynthesis and starts respiration.
Neuron	The neuron is the primary cell of the nervous system. They are found in the brain, the spinal cord, in the nerves and ganglia of the peripheral nervous system. It is a specialized cell that conducts impulses through the nervous system and contains three major parts: cell body, dendrites, and an axon. It can have many dendrites but only one axon.
Liver	The liver plays a major role in metabolism and has a number of functions in the body including detoxification, glycogen storage and plasma protein synthesis. It also produces bile, which is important for digestion. The liver converts most carbohydrates, proteing, and fats into glucose.
Perception	Perception is the process of acquiring, interpreting, selecting, and organizing sensory information.
Obesity	The state of being more than 20 percent above the average weight for a person of one's height is called obesity.
Body mass index	The body mass index is a calculated number, used to compare and analyse the health effects of body weight on human bodies of all heights. It is equal to the weight, divided by the square of the height.
Nurture	Nurture refers to the environmental influences on behavior due to nutrition, culture,

	socioeconomic status, and learning.
Schachter	Schachter found that all emotions have approximately the same arousal pattern; variation is only in strength of the impulse and actions are largely dependent on our cognitive appraisal of the situation.
Human genome project	The Human Genome Project (HGP) endeavored to map the human genome down to the nucleotide (or base pair) level and to identify all the genes present in it.
Human genome	The complete sequence or mapping of genes in the human body and their locations is the human genome. It is made up of 23 chromosome pairs with a total of about 3 billion DNA base pairs.
Gene	A gene is an ultramicroscopic area of the chromosome. It is the smallest physical unit of the DNA molecule that carries a piece of hereditary information.
Innate	Innate behavior is not learned or influenced by the environment, rather, it is present or predisposed at birth.
Leptin	Leptin refers to a hormone produced by fat cells that acts in the brain to inhibit hunger and regulate body weight.
Binge	Binge refers to relatively brief episode of uncontrolled, excessive consumption.
Disinhibition	A temporary increase in the strength of an extinguished response caused by an unrelated stimulus event is referred to as disinhibition.
Self-esteem	Self-esteem refers to a person's subjective appraisal of himself or herself as intrinsically positive or negative to some degree.
Baseline	Measure of a particular behavior or process taken before the introduction of the independent variable or treatment is called the baseline.
Eating disorders	Psychological disorders characterized by distortion of the body image and gross disturbances in eating patterns are called eating disorders.
Body image	A person's body image is their perception of their physical appearance. It is more than what a person thinks they will see in a mirror, it is inextricably tied to their self-esteem and acceptance by peers.
Anorexia	Anorexia nervosa is an eating disorder characterized by voluntary starvation and exercise stress.
Bulimia	Bulimia refers to a disorder in which a person binges on incredibly large quantities of food, then purges by vomiting or by using laxatives. Bulimia is often less about food, and more to do with deep psychological issues and profound feelings of lack of control.
Syndrome	The term syndrome is the association of several clinically recognizable features, signs, symptoms, phenomena or characteristics which often occur together, so that the presence of one feature indicates the presence of the others.
Late adolescence	Late adolescence refers to approximately the latter half of the second decade of life. Career interests, dating, and identity exploration are often more pronounced in late adolescence than in early adolescence.
Early adulthood	The developmental period beginning in the late teens or early twenties and lasting into the thirties is called early adulthood; characterized by an increasing self-awareness.
Attention	Attention is the cognitive process of selectively concentrating on one thing while ignoring other things. Psychologists have labeled three types of attention: sustained attention, selective attention, and divided attention.
Society	The social sciences use the term society to mean a group of people that form a semi-closed

	(or semi-open) social system, in which most interactions are with other individuals belonging to the group.
Ethnic group	An ethnic group is a culture or subculture whose members are readily distinguishable by outsiders based on traits originating from a common racial, national, linguistic, or religious source. Members of an ethnic group are often presumed to be culturally or biologically similar, although this is not in fact necessarily the case.
Physiology	The study of the functions and activities of living cells, tissues, and organs and of the physical and chemical phenomena involved is referred to as physiology.
Reinforcer	In operant conditioning, a reinforcer is any stimulus that increases the probability that a preceding behavior will occur again. In Classical Conditioning, the unconditioned stimulus (US) is the reinforcer.
Norms	In testing, standards of test performance that permit the comparison of one person's score on the test to the scores of others who have taken the same test are referred to as norms.
Primary motivation	Instinctive or biologically motivated behavior is referred to as primary motivation.
Pituitary gland	The pituitary gland is an endocrine gland about the size of a pea that sits in the small, bony cavity at the base of the brain. The pituitary gland secretes hormones regulating a wide variety of bodily activities, including trophic hormones that stimulate other endocrine glands.
Hormone	A hormone is a chemical messenger from one cell (or group of cells) to another. The best known are those produced by endocrine glands, but they are produced by nearly every organ system. The function of hormones is to serve as a signal to the target cells; the action of the hormone is determined by the pattern of secretion and the signal transduction of the receiving tissue.
Gonads	The gonads are the organs that make gametes. Gametes are haploid germ cells. For example, sperm and egg cells are gametes. In the male the gonads are the testicles, and in the female the gonads are the ovaries.
Androgen	Androgen is the generic term for any natural or synthetic compound, usually a steroid hormone, that stimulates or controls the development and maintenance of masculine characteristics in vertebrates by binding to androgen receptors.
Estrogen	Estrogen is a group of steroid compounds that function as the primary female sex hormone. They are produced primarily by developing follicles in the ovaries, the corpus luteum and the placenta.
Stimulant	A stimulant is a drug which increases the activity of the sympathetic nervous system and produces a sense of euphoria or awakeness.
Physiological changes	Alterations in heart rate, blood pressure, perspiration, and other involuntary responses are physiological changes.
Testes	Testes are the male reproductive glands or gonads; this is where sperm develop and are stored.
Ovulation	Ovulation is the process in the menstrual cycle by which a mature ovarian follicle ruptures and discharges an ovum (also known as an oocyte, female gamete, or casually, an egg) that participates in reproduction.
Testosterone	Testosterone is a steroid hormone from the androgen group. It is the principal male sex hormone and the "original" anabolic steroid.
Sexual response	Masters and Johnson's model of the sexual response cycle consists of four stages or phases:

cycle	excitement, plateau, orgasmic, resolution.
Excitement phase	The excitement phase refers to the first phase of the sexual response cycle, characterized by muscle tension, increases in the heart rate, and erection in the male and vaginal lubrication in the female.
Attitude	An enduring mental representation of a person, place, or thing that evokes an emotional response and related behavior is called attitude.
Variable	A variable refers to a measurable factor, characteristic, or attribute of an individual or a system.
Penis	The penis is the external male copulatory organ and the external male organ of urination. In humans, the penis is homologous to the female clitoris, as it develops from the same embryonic structure. It is capable of erection for use in copulation.
Clitoris	Clitoris refers to an external female sex organ that is highly sensitive to sexual stimulation.
Plateau phase	The plateau phase is the second phase of the sexual cycle. Further increases in circulation and heart rate occur in both sexes, sexual pleasure increases with increased stimulation, muscle tension increases further.
Orgasm phase	The orgasm phase is the stage of sexual activity involving ejaculation in men and vaginal wall contractions in women. Women are able to experience orgasm again immediately while men are unable to form an erection for a time interval called a refractory period.
Ejaculation	Ejaculation is the process of ejecting semen from the penis, and is usually accompanied by orgasm as a result of sexual stimulation.
Semen	Semen is a fluid that contains spermatozoa. It is secreted by the gonads of males for the fertilization of female ova.
Resolution phase	The resolution phase refers to the fourth phase of the sexual response cycle. The resolution phase occurs after orgasm and allows the muscles to relax, blood pressure to drop and the body to slow down from its excited state.
Refractory period	Refractory period refers to a phase following firing during which a neuron is less sensitive to messages from other neurons and will not fire. In the sexual response cycle, it is a period of time following orgasm during which an individual is not responsive to sexual stimulation.
Masters and Johnson	Masters and Johnson produced the four stage model of sexual response, which they described as the human sexual response cycle. They defined the four stages of this cycle as: excitement phase, plateau phase, orgasm, and resolution phase.
Guilt	Guilt describes many concepts related to a negative emotion or condition caused by actions which are believed to be, morally wrong. According to Freud, the avoidance of guilt is the basis for moral behavior.
Evolutionary theory	Evolutionary theory is concerned with heritable variability rather than behavioral variations. Natural selection requirements: (1) natural variability within a species must exist, (2) only some individual differences are heritable, and (3) natural selection only takes place when there is an interaction between the inborn attributes of organisms and the environment in which they live.
Variability	Statistically, variability refers to how much the scores in a distribution spread out, away from the mean.
Alfred Kinsey	Alfred Kinsey researched human sexuality and profoundly influenced social and cultural values in the United States especially in the 1960s and was an important influence on the sexual

	revolution
Script	A schema, or behavioral sequence, for an event is called a script. It is a form of schematic organization, with real-world events organized in terms of temporal and causal relations between component acts.
Sexual script	A sexual script is a stereotyped pattern of role prescriptions for how individuals should behave sexually.
Social norm	A social norm, is a rule that is socially enforced. In social situations, such as meetings, they are unwritten and often unstated rules that govern individuals' behavior. A social norm is most evident when not followed or broken.
Sexually Transmitted Disease	Sexually transmitted disease is commonly transmitted between partners through some form of sexual activity, most commonly vaginal intercourse, oral sex, or anal sex.
Rape	Rape is a crime where the victim is forced into sexual activity, in particular sexual penetration, against his or her will.
Fisher	Fisher was a eugenicist, evolutionary biologist, geneticist and statistician. He has been described as "The greatest of Darwin's successors", and a genius who almost single-handedly created the foundations for modern statistical science inventing the techniques of maximum likelihood and analysis of variance.
Date rape	Date rape refers to non-consensual sexual activity between people who are already acquainted, or who know each other socially where it is alleged that consent for sexual activity was not given, or was given under duress.
Homosexuality	Homosexuality refers to a sexual orientation characterized by aesthetic attraction, romantic love, and sexual desire exclusively for members of the same sex or gender identity.
Homosexual	Homosexual refers to a sexual orientation characterized by aesthetic attraction, romantic love, and sexual desire exclusively for members of the same sex or gender identity.
Concordance	Concordance as used in genetics means the presence of the same trait in both members of a pair of twins, or in sets of individuals. A twin study examines the concordance rates of twins having the same trait, especially a disease, which can help determine how much the disease is affected by genetics versus environment.
Monozygotic	Identical twins occur when a single egg is fertilized to form one zygote, calld monozygotic, but the zygote then divides into two separate embryos. The two embryos develop into foetuses sharing the same womb. Monozygotic twins are genetically identical unless there has been a mutation in development, and they are almost always the same gender.
Dizygotic	Fraternal twins (commonly known as "non-identical twins") usually occur when two fertilized eggs are implanted in the uterine wall at the same time. The two eggs form two zygotes, and these twins are therefore also known as dizygotic.
Sexual orientation	Sexual orientation refers to the sex or gender of people who are the focus of a person's amorous or erotic desires, fantasies, and spontaneous feelings, the gender(s) toward which one is primarily "oriented".
Lesbian	A lesbian is a homosexual woman. They are women who are sexually and romantically attracted to other women.
Bem	Bem is the originator of the self-perception theory of attitude change. According to the self-perception account, people infer their attitudes about others from their own behavior and its causes.
Heterosexuality	Sexual attraction and behavior directed to the opposite sex is heterosexuality.

Homophobia	An intense, irrational hostility toward or fear of homosexuals is referred to as homophobia.
Survey	A method of scientific investigation in which a large sample of people answer questions about their attitudes or behavior is referred to as a survey.
American Psychological Association	The American Psychological Association is a professional organization representing psychology in the US. The mission statement is to "advance psychology as a science and profession and as a means of promoting health, education , and human welfare".
Psychological disorder	Mental processes and/or behavior patterns that cause emotional distress and/or substantial impairment in functioning is a psychological disorder.
Need for achievement	Need for Achievement is a term introduced by David McClelland into the field of psychology, referring to an individual's desire for significant accomplishment, mastering of skills, control, or high standards.
Construct	A generalized concept, such as anxiety or gravity, is a construct.
Henry Murray	Henry Murray believed that personality could be better understood by investigating the unconscious mind. He is most famous for the development of the Thematic Apperception Test (TAT), a widely used projective measure of personality.
Achievement motivation	The psychological need in humans for success is called achievement motivation.
McClelland	McClelland asserts that human motivation comprises three dominant needs: the need for achievement (N-Ach), the need for power (N-Pow) and the need for affiliation (N-Affil). The subjective importance of each need varies from individual to individual and depends also on an individual's cultural background.
Apperception	A newly experienced sensation is related to past experiences to form an understood situation. For Wundt, consciousness is composed of two "stages:" There is a large capacity working memory called the Blickfeld and the narrower consciousness called Apperception, or selective attention.
Reflection	Reflection is the process of rephrasing or repeating thoughts and feelings expressed, making the person more aware of what they are saying or thinking.
Individual differences	Individual differences psychology studies the ways in which individual people differ in their behavior. This is distinguished from other aspects of psychology in that although psychology is ostensibly a study of individuals, modern psychologists invariably study groups.
Feedback	Feedback refers to information returned to a person about the effects a response has had.
Positive correlation	A relationship between two variables in which both vary in the same direction is called a positive correlation.
Attribution theory	Attribution theory is concerned with the ways in which people explain the behavior of others. It explores how individuals "attribute" causes to events and how this cognitive perception affects their motivation.
Attributional style	One's tendency to attribute one's behavior to internal or external factors, stable or unstable factors, and so on is their attributional style.
Locus of control	The place to which an individual attributes control over the receiving of reinforcers -either inside or outside the self is referred to as locus of control.
Depression	In everyday language depression refers to any downturn in mood, which may be relatively transitory and perhaps due to something trivial. This is differentiated from Clinical depression which is marked by symptoms that last two weeks or more and are so severe that they interfere with daily living.

Generalization	In conditioning, the tendency for a conditioned response to be evoked by stimuli that are similar to the stimulus to which the response was conditioned is a generalization. The greater the similarity among the stimuli, the greater the probability of generalization.
Experimental group	Experimental group refers to any group receiving a treatment effect in an experiment.
Control group	A group that does not receive the treatment effect in an experiment is referred to as the control group or sometimes as the comparison group.
Job satisfaction	A person's attitudes and feelings about his or her job and facets of the job is called job satisfaction.
Socialization	Social rules and social relations are created, communicated, and changed in verbal and nonverbal ways creating social complexity useful in identifying outsiders and intelligent breeding partners. The process of learning these skills is called socialization.
Expectancy theory	According to the expectancy theory the amount of effort people exert on a specific task depends on their expectations of the outcome.
Equity theory	Equity theory suggests that people are most satisfied with a relationship when the ratio between benefits and contributions is similar.
Counselor	A counselor is a mental health professional who specializes in helping people with problems not involving serious mental disorders.
Agreeableness	Agreeableness, one of the big-five personality traits, reflects individual differences in concern with cooperation and social harmony. It is the degree individuals value getting along with others.
Vroom	Vroom proposed the Expectancy theory of motivation. The three main factors of this theory are Valence, Expectancy, and Instrumentality. These three factors result in motivation. If any one of these factors doesn't exist then motivation vanishes.
Instrumentality	In expectancy theory, the belief that performance will lead to rewards is called instrumentality.
Valence	In expectancy theory, the value or worth a person gives to an outcome is called the valence.
Hierarchy of needs	Maslow's hierarchy of needs is often depicted as a pyramid consisting of five levels: the four lower levels are grouped together as deficiency needs, while the top level is termed being needs. While our deficiency needs must be met, our being needs are continually shaping our behavior.
Attachment	Attachment is the tendency to seek closeness to another person and feel secure when that person is present.
Self-actualizing	Self-actualizing is the need of a human to make the most of their unique abilities.
Maslow	Maslow is mostly noted today for his proposal of a hierarchy of human needs which he often presented as a pyramid. Maslow was an instrumental player in the formation of the humanistic movement, also known as the third force in psychology.
Drive Theory	Drive Theory states that due to the unpredictable nature of people, a person performing a task rarely knows for certain what others are going to do in response. This creates a state of arousal that in some cases will facilitate performance, while in other cases it will inhibit performance.
Instinct theory	The notion that human behavior is motivated by certain innate tendencies, or instincts, shared by all individuals is an instinct theory.
Evolutionary	A perspective that focuses on how humans have evolved and adapted behaviors required for

perspective	survival against various environmental pressures over the long course is called the evolutionary perspective.
Genetics	Genetics is the science of genes, heredity, and the variation of organisms.

Emotion	An emotion is a mental states that arise spontaneously, rather than through conscious effort. They are often accompanied by physiological changes.
Darwin	Darwin achieved lasting fame as originator of the theory of evolution through natural selection. His book Expression of Emotions in Man and Animals is generally considered the first text on comparative psychology.
Species	Species refers to a reproductively isolated breeding population.
Evolutionary perspective	A perspective that focuses on how humans have evolved and adapted behaviors required for survival against various environmental pressures over the long course is called the evolutionary perspective.
Affective	Affective is the way people react emotionally, their ability to feel another living thing's pain or joy.
Innate	Innate behavior is not learned or influenced by the environment, rather, it is present or predisposed at birth.
Ekman	Ekman found that at least some facial expressions and their corresponding emotions are not culturally determined, and thus presumably biological in origin. Expressions he found to be universal included anger, disgust, fear, joy, sadness and surprise.
Basic emotions	Basic emotions are those found in all cultures, as evidinced by the same facial expressions. They include: fear, anger, disgust, surprise, happiness, and distress.
Population	Population refers to all members of a well-defined group of organisms, events, or things.
Evolution	Commonly used to refer to gradual change, evolution is the change in the frequency of alleles within a population from one generation to the next. This change may be caused by different mechanisms, including natural selection, genetic drift, or changes in population (gene flow).
Brain	The brain controls and coordinates most movement, behavior and homeostatic body functions such as heartbeat, blood pressure, fluid balance and body temperature. Functions of the brain are responsible for cognition, emotion, memory, motor learning and other sorts of learning. The brain is primarily made up of two types of cells: glia and neurons.
Society	The social sciences use the term society to mean a group of people that form a semi-closed (or semi-open) social system, in which most interactions are with other individuals belonging to the group.
Suicide	Suicide behavior is rare in childhood but escalates in adolescence. The suicide rate increases in a linear fashion from adolescence through late adulthood.
Norms	In testing, standards of test performance that permit the comparison of one person's score on the test to the scores of others who have taken the same test are referred to as norms.
Pitch	Pitch is the psychological interpretation of a sound or musical tone corresponding to its physical frequency
Affect	A subjective feeling or emotional tone often accompanied by bodily expressions noticeable to others is called affect.
Individualistic	Cultures have been classified as individualistic, which means having a set of values that give priority to personal goals rather than group goals.
Collectivist	A person who defines the self in terms of relationships to other people and groups and gives priority to group goals is called collectivist.
Reasoning	Reasoning is the act of using reason to derive a conclusion from certain premises. There are two main methods to reach a conclusion,deductive reasoning and inductive reasoning.

Theories	Theories are logically self-consistent models or frameworks describing the behavior of a certain natural or social phenomenon. They are broad explanations and predictions concerning phenomena of interest.
Autonomic nervous system	A division of the peripheral nervous system, the autonomic nervous system, regulates glands and activities such as heartbeat, respiration, digestion, and dilation of the pupils. It is responsible for homeostasis, maintaining a relatively constant internal environment .
Parasympathetic	The parasympathetic nervous system is one of two divisions of the autonomic nervous system. It conserves energy as it slows the heart rate, increases intestinal and gland activity, and relaxes sphincter muscles. In another words, it acts to reverse the effects of the Sympathetic nervous system.
Sympathetic	The sympathetic nervous system activates what is often termed the "fight or flight response". It is an automatic regulation system, that is, one that operates without the intervention of conscious thought.
Nervous system	The body's electrochemical communication circuitry, made up of billions of neurons is a nervous system.
Hormone	A hormone is a chemical messenger from one cell (or group of cells) to another. The best known are those produced by endocrine glands, but they are produced by nearly every organ system. The function of hormones is to serve as a signal to the target cells; the action of the hormone is determined by the pattern of secretion and the signal transduction of the receiving tissue.
Central nervous system	The vertebrate central nervous system consists of the brain and spinal cord.
Limbic system	The limbic system is a group of brain structures that are involved in various emotions such as aggression, fear, pleasure and also in the formation of memory. The limbic system affects the endocrine system and the autonomic nervous system. It consists of several subcortical structures located around the thalamus.
Hypothalamus	The hypothalamus is a region of the brain located below the thalamus, forming the major portion of the ventral region of the diencephalon and functioning to regulate certain metabolic processes and other autonomic activities.
Neuroanatomy	Neuroanatomy is the study of the anatomy of the central nervous system.
Amygdala	Located in the brain's medial temporal lobe, the almond-shaped amygdala is believed to play a key role in the emotions. It forms part of the limbic system and is linked to both fear responses and pleasure. Its size is positively correlated with aggressive behavior across species.
Senses	The senses are systems that consist of a sensory cell type that respond to a specific kind of physical energy, and that correspond to a defined region within the brain where the signals are received and interpreted.
Neurotransmitter	A neurotransmitter is a chemical that is used to relay, amplify and modulate electrical signals between a neurons and another cell.
Serotonin	Serotonin, a neurotransmitter, is believed to play an important part of the biochemistry of depression, bipolar disorder and anxiety. It is also believed to be influential on sexuality and appetite.
Gene	A gene is an ultramicroscopic area of the chromosome. It is the smallest physical unit of the DNA molecule that carries a piece of hereditary information.
Neural network	A clusters of neurons that is interconnected to process information is referred to as a

	neural network.
Brain circuits	Neurotransmitter currents or neural pathways in the brain are referred to as brain circuits.
William James	Functionalism as a psychology developed out of Pragmatism as a philosophy: To find the meaning of an idea, you have to look at its consequences. This led William James and his students towards an emphasis on cause and effect, prediction and control, and observation of environment and behavior, over the careful introspection of the Structuralists.
James-Lange	The James-Lange theory concerns the origin and nature of emotions as developed independently by two 19th-century scholars. As a response to experiences in the world, the autonomic nervous system creates physiological events. Emotions are feelings which come about as a result of these physiological changes, rather than being their cause.
Aristotle	Aristotle can be credited with the development of the first theory of learning. He concluded that ideas were generated in consciousness based on four principlesof association: contiguity, similarity, contrast, and succession. In contrast to Plato, he believed that knowledge derived from sensory experience and was not inherited.
Stimulus	A change in an environmental condition that elicits a response is a stimulus.
Lange	Lange along with William James, independently developed the James-Lange theory of emotion. Unlike James, Lange specifically stated that vasomotor changes are emotions. Lange also noted the psychotropic effects of lithium, although his work in this area was forgotten and independently rediscovered much later.
Cognitive appraisal	Lazarus' term for individuals' interpretation of events in their lives as threatening, harmful, or challenging and their determination of whether they have the resources to effectively cope with the events is referred to as cognitive appraisal.
Viscera	The internal organs of the body are called viscera.
Thalamus	An area near the center of the brain involved in the relay of sensory information to the cortex and in the functions of sleep and attention is the thalamus.
Schachter	Schachter found that all emotions have approximately the same arousal pattern; variation is only in strength of the impulse and actions are largely dependent on our cognitive appraisal of the situation.
Creativity	Creativity is the ability to think about something in novel and unusual ways and come up with unique solutions to problems. It involves divergent thinking, having many solutions or views to a problem.
Independent variable	A condition in a scientific study that is manipulated (assigned different values by a researcher) so that the effects of the manipulation may be observed is called an independent variable.
Mere exposure effect	The mere exposure effect is a psychological artifact well known to advertisers: people express undue liking for things merely because they are familiar with them. This effect has been nicknamed the "familiarity breeds liking" effect.
Zimbardo	Zimbardo is best-known for his Stanford prison experiment. The experiment led to theories about the importance of the social situation in individual psychology that are still controversial today.
Zajonc	Zajonc is best known for his decades of work on the mere exposure effect, the phenomenon that repeated exposure to a stimulus brings about an attitude change in relation to the stimulus.
Motivation	In psychology, motivation is the driving force (desire) behind all actions of an organism.
Attention	Attention is the cognitive process of selectively concentrating on one thing while ignoring

	other things. Psychologists have labeled three types of attention: sustained attention, selective attention, and divided attention.
Epilepsy	Epilepsy is a chronic neurological condition characterized by recurrent unprovoked neural discharges. It is commonly controlled with medication, although surgical methods are used as well.
Seizure	A seizure is a temporary alteration in brain function expressed as a changed mental state, tonic or clonic movements and various other symptoms. They are due to temporary abnormal electrical activity of a group of brain cells.
Learning	Learning is a relatively permanent change in behavior that results from experience. Thus, to attribute a behavioral change to learning, the change must be relatively permanent and must result from experience.
Information processing	Information processing is an approach to the goal of understanding human thinking. The essence of the approach is to see cognition as being essentially computational in nature, with mind being the software and the brain being the hardware.
Genetics	Genetics is the science of genes, heredity, and the variation of organisms.
Life span	Life span refers to the upper boundary of life, the maximum number of years an individual can live. The maximum life span of human beings is about 120 years of age. Females live an average of 6 years longer than males.
Baseline	Measure of a particular behavior or process taken before the introduction of the independent variable or treatment is called the baseline.
Analogy	An analogy is a comparison between two different things, in order to highlight some form of similarity. Analogy is the cognitive process of transferring information from a particular subject to another particular subject.
Hypothesis	A specific statement about behavior or mental processes that is testable through research is a hypothesis.
Control group	A group that does not receive the treatment effect in an experiment is referred to as the control group or sometimes as the comparison group.
Self-efficacy	Self-efficacy is the belief that one has the capabilities to execute the courses of actions required to manage prospective situations.
Self-concept	Self-concept refers to domain-specific evaluations of the self where a domain may be academics, athletics, etc.
Self-esteem	Self-esteem refers to a person's subjective appraisal of himself or herself as intrinsically positive or negative to some degree.
Chronic	Chronic refers to a relatively long duration, usually more than a few months.
Maladaptive	In psychology, a behavior or trait is adaptive when it helps an individual adjust and function well within their social environment. A maladaptive behavior or trait is counterproductive to the individual.
Walter Cannon	Walter Cannon developed the concept of homeostasis, and popularized it in his book The Wisdom of the Body. In 1929, he coined the term fight or flight to describe an animal's response to threats.
Acute	Acute means sudden, sharp, and abrupt. Usually short in duration.
Pituitary gland	The pituitary gland is an endocrine gland about the size of a pea that sits in the small, bony cavity at the base of the brain. The pituitary gland secretes hormones regulating a wide variety of bodily activities, including trophic hormones that stimulate other endocrine

	glands.
Lungs	The lungs are the essential organs of respiration. Its principal function is to transport oxygen from the atmosphere into the bloodstream, and excrete carbon dioxide from the bloodstream into the atmosphere.
Adrenaline	Adrenaline refers to a hormone produced by the adrenal medulla that stimulates sympathetic ANS activity and generally arouses people and heightens their emotional responsiveness.
Adrenal medulla	Composed mainly of hormone-producing chromaffin cells, the adrenal medulla is the principal site of the conversion of the amino acid tyrosine into the catecholamines epinephrine and norepinephrine (also called adrenaline and noradrenaline, respectively).
Adrenal glands	The adrenal glands sit atop the kidneys. They are chiefly responsible for regulating the stress response through the synthesis of corticosteroids and catecholamines, including cortisol and adrenalin.
Epinephrine	Epinephrine is a hormone and a neurotransmitter. Epinephrine plays a central role in the short-term stress reaction—the physiological response to threatening or exciting conditions. It is secreted by the adrenal medulla. When released into the bloodstream, epinephrine binds to multiple receptors and has numerous effects throughout the body.
Spleen	The spleen is a ductless gland that is not necessary for life but is closely associated with the circulatory system, where it functions in the destruction of old red blood cells and removal of other debris from the bloodstream, and also in holding a reservoir of blood.
Liver	The liver plays a major role in metabolism and has a number of functions in the body including detoxification, glycogen storage and plasma protein synthesis. It also produces bile, which is important for digestion. The liver converts most carbohydrates, proteing, and fats into glucose.
Thyroid Gland	The thyroid gland is an endocrine gland. It is situated on the front side of the neck just below the Adam's apple. The primary function of the thyroid is production of hormones such as thyroxine.
Adrenal cortex	Adrenal cortex refers to the outer layer of the adrenal glands, which produces hormones that affect salt intake, reactions to stress, and sexual development.
Fight-or-flight	The fight-or-flight response, also called the "acute stress response", was first described by Walter Cannon. Animals react to threats with a general discharge of the sympathetic nervous system. In layman's terms, an animal has two options when faced with danger. They can either face the threat, or they can avoid the threat.
Physiological changes	Alterations in heart rate, blood pressure, perspiration, and other involuntary responses are physiological changes.
Ciliary muscle	The ciliary muscle is a smooth muscle that affects zonules in the eye (fibers that suspend the lens in position during accommodation), enabling changes in lens shape for light focusing.
Adaptation	Adaptation is a lowering of sensitivity to a stimulus following prolonged exposure to that stimulus. Behavioral adaptations are special ways a particular organism behaves to survive in its natural habitat.
Selye	Selye did much important theoretical work on the non-specific response of the organism to stress. Selye discovered and documented that stress differs from other physical responses in that stress is stressful whether the one receives good or bad news, whether the impulse is positive or negative. He called negative stress distress and positive stress eustress.
Trauma	Trauma refers to a severe physical injury or wound to the body caused by an external force,

	or a psychological shock having a lasting effect on mental life.
Homeostasis	Homeostasis is the property of an open system, especially living organisms, to regulate its internal environment so as to maintain a stable condition, by means of multiple dynamic equilibrium adjustments controlled by interrelated regulation mechanisms.
Alarm reaction	The first stage of the general adaptation syndrome, which is triggered by the impact of a stressor and characterized by sympathetic activity is called the alarm reaction.
Stages	Stages represent relatively discrete periods of time in which functioning is qualitatively different from functioning at other periods.
Stress hormones	Group of hormones including cortico steroids, that are involved in the body's physiological stress response are referred to as stress hormones.
Immune system	The most important function of the human immune system occurs at the cellular level of the blood and tissues. The lymphatic and blood circulation systems are highways for specialized white blood cells. These cells include B cells, T cells, natural killer cells, and macrophages. All function with the primary objective of recognizing, attacking and destroying bacteria, viruses, cancer cells, and all substances seen as foreign.
Social readjustment rating scale	Holmes and Rahe's social readjustment rating scale ranks 43 life events from most to least stressful and assigns a point value to each.
Health psychology	The field of psychology that studies the relationships between psychological factors and the prevention and treatment of physical illness is called health psychology.
Rape	Rape is a crime where the victim is forced into sexual activity, in particular sexual penetration, against his or her will.
Stress disorder	A significant emotional disturbance caused by stresses outside the range of normal human experience is referred to as stress disorder.
Nightmare	Nightmare was the original term for the state later known as waking dream, and more currently as sleep paralysis, associated with rapid eye movement (REM) periods of sleep.
Survey	A method of scientific investigation in which a large sample of people answer questions about their attitudes or behavior is referred to as a survey.
Anxiety	Anxiety is a complex combination of the feeling of fear, apprehension and worry often accompanied by physical sensations such as palpitations, chest pain and/or shortness of breath.
Clinical depression	Although nearly any mood with some element of sadness may colloquially be termed a depression, clinical depression is more than just a temporary state of sadness. Symptoms lasting two weeks or longer in duration, and of a severity that they begin to interfere with daily living.
Positive correlation	A relationship between two variables in which both vary in the same direction is called a positive correlation.
Immune response	The body's defensive reaction to invasion by bacteria, viral agents, or other foreign substances is called the immune response.
Primary appraisal	A primary appraisal is an evaluation of the significance of a potentially stressful event according to how it will affect one's well-being-whether it is perceived as irrelevant or as involving harm or loss, threat, or challenge.
Moderator variable	A variable that affects the relation between two other variables is called the moderator variable.

Variable	A variable refers to a measurable factor, characteristic, or attribute of an individual or a system.
Emotion-focused coping	Lazarus' emotion-focused coping describes individuals' response to stress demonstrated in an emotional manner, especially using defensive methods.
Resilient children	Resilient children weather adverse circumstances, function well despite challenges or threats, or bounce back from traumatic events.
Cognition	The intellectual processes through which information is obtained, transformed, stored, retrieved, and otherwise used is cognition.
Social anxiety	A feeling of apprehension in the presence of others is social anxiety.
Stress inoculation	Use of positive coping statements to control fear and anxiety is a form of stress inoculation.
Adaptive behavior	An adaptive behavior increases the probability of the individual or organism to survive or exist within its environment.
Subjective experience	Subjective experience refers to reality as it is perceived and interpreted, not as it exists objectively.
Physical therapy	Physical therapy is a health profession concerned with the assessment, diagnosis, and treatment of disease and disability through physical means. It is based upon principles of medical science, and is generally held to be within the sphere of conventional medicine.
Social support	Social Support is the physical and emotional comfort given by family, friends, co-workers and others. Research has identified three main types of social support: emotional, practical, sharing points of view.
Feedback	Feedback refers to information returned to a person about the effects a response has had.
Biopsychosocial	The biopsychosocial model is a way of looking at the mind and body of a patient as two important systems that are interlinked. The biopsychosocial model draws a distinction between the actual pathological processes that cause disease, and the patient's perception of their health and the effects on it, called the illness.
Psyche	Psyche is the soul, spirit, or mind as distinguished from the body. In psychoanalytic theory, it is the totality of the id, ego, and superego, including both conscious and unconscious components.
Biomedical model	The biomedical model has been around for centuries as the predominant model used by physicians in the diagnosis of disease. This model focuses on the physical processes, such as the pathology, the biochemistry and the physiology of a disease. It does not take into account the role of a person's mind or society in the cause and treatment.
Asymptomatic	A disease is asymptomatic when it is at a stage where the patient does not experience symptoms. By their nature, asymptomatic diseases are not usually discovered until the patient undergoes medical tests (X-rays or other investigations). Some diseases remain asymptomatic for a remarkably long time, including some forms of cancer.
Measles	Measles, also known as rubeola, is a common disease caused by a virus of the genus Morbillivirus. Complications with measles are relatively common, ranging from relatively common and less serious diarrhea, to pneumonia and encephalitis. Complications are usually more severe amongst infants and adults who catch the virus.
Personality	Personality refers to the pattern of enduring characteristics that differentiates a person, the patterns of behaviors that make each individual unique.
Sensation	A generalized preference for high or low levels of sensory stimulation is referred to as

seeking	sensation seeking.
Personality type	A persistent style of complex behaviors defined by a group of related traits is referred to as a personality type. Myer Friedman and his co-workers first defined personality types in the 1950s. Friedman classified people into 2 categories, Type A and Type B.
Cholesterol	Cholesterol is a steroid, a lipid, and an alcohol, found in the cell membranes of all body tissues, and transported in the blood plasma of all animals. Cholesterol is an important component of the membranes of cells, providing stability; it makes the membrane's fluidity stable over a bigger temperature interval.
Friendship	The essentials of friendship are reciprocity and commitment between individuals who see themselves more or less as equals. Interaction between friends rests on a more equal power base than the interaction between children and adults.
Nicotine	Nicotine is an organic compound, an alkaloid found naturally throughout the tobacco plant, with a high concentration in the leaves. It is a potent nerve poison and is included in many insecticides. In lower concentrations, the substance is a stimulant and is one of the main factors leading to the pleasure and habit-forming qualities of tobacco smoking.
Acquired immune deficiency syndrome	Acquired Immune Deficiency Syndrome is defined as a collection of symptoms and infections resulting from the depletion of the immune system caused by infection with the human immunodeficiency virus, commonly called HIV.
Human immunodefici-ncy virus	The human immunodeficiency virus is a retrovirus that primarily infects vital components of the human immune system. It is transmitted through penetrative and oral sex; blood transfusion; the sharing of contaminated needles in health care settings and through drug injection; and, between mother and infant, during pregnancy, childbirth and breastfeeding.
Lymphocyte	A lymphocyte is a type of white blood cell involved in the human body's immune system. There are two broad categories, namely T cells and B cells. The lymphocyte play an important and integral part of the body's defenses.
Meningitis	Meningitis is inflammation of the membranes covering the brain and the spinal cord. Although the most common causes are infection (bacterial, viral, fungal or parasitic), chemical agents and even tumor cells may cause meningitis.
Semen	Semen is a fluid that contains spermatozoa. It is secreted by the gonads of males for the fertilization of female ova.
Hemophilia	Hemophilia is the name of any of several hereditary genetic illnesses that impair the body's ability to control bleeding. Genetic deficiencies cause lowered plasma clotting factor activity so as to compromise blood-clotting; when a blood vessel is injured, a scab will not form and the vessel can continue to bleed excessively for a very long period of time.
Applied psychology	The basic premise of applied psychology is the use of psychological principles and theories to overcome practical problems.
Attitude	An enduring mental representation of a person, place, or thing that evokes an emotional response and related behavior is called attitude.
Individual differences	Individual differences psychology studies the ways in which individual people differ in their behavior. This is distinguished from other aspects of psychology in that although psychology is ostensibly a study of individuals, modern psychologists invariably study groups.
Social norm	A social norm, is a rule that is socially enforced. In social situations, such as meetings, they are unwritten and often unstated rules that govern individuals' behavior. A social norm is most evident when not followed or broken.
Biofeedback	Biofeedback is the process of measuring and quantifying an aspect of a subject's physiology,

	analyzing the data, and then feeding back the information to the subject in a form that allows the subject to enact physiological change.
Meditation	Meditation usually refers to a state in which the body is consciously relaxed and the mind is allowed to become calm and focused.
Self-Regulatory	Bandura proposes that self-regulatory systems mediate external influences and provide a basis for purposeful action, allowing people to have personal control over their own thoughts, feelings, motivations, and actions.
Neal Miller	Neal Miller introduced the concepts of the approach gradient and avoidance gradient. Whether organisms drive toward or away from a positive stimulus or a negative stimulus is a function of the distance that it is from that stimulus.
Psychoneuroi-munology	Psychoneuroimmunology is a specialist field of research that studies the connection between the brain, or mental states, and the immunal and hormonal systems of the human body.
Conditioning	Conditioning describes the process by which behaviors can be learned or modified through interaction with the environment.
Insight	Insight refers to a sudden awareness of the relationships among various elements that had previously appeared to be independent of one another.
Rheumatoid arthritis	Rheumatoid arthritis is a chronic, inflammatory autoimmune disorder that causes the immune system to attack the joints. It is a disabling and painful inflammatory condition, which can lead to substantial loss of mobility due to pain and joint destruction.
Coronary heart disease	Coronary heart disease is the end result of the accumulation of atheromatous plaques within the walls of the arteries that supply the myocardium (the muscle of the heart).
Personality trait	According to the Diagnostic and Statistical Manual of the American Psychiatric Association, a personality trait is a "prominent aspect of personality that is exhibited in a wide range of important social and personal contexts. ...".
Depersonaliz-tion	Depersonalization is the experience of feelings of loss of a sense of reality. A sufferer feels that they have changed and the world has become less real — it is vague, dreamlike, or lacking in significance.
Syndrome	The term syndrome is the association of several clinically recognizable features, signs, symptoms, phenomena or characteristics which often occur together, so that the presence of one feature indicates the presence of the others.
Psychosomatic	A psychosomatic illness is one with physical manifestations and perhaps a supposed psychological cause. It is often diagnosed when any known or identifiable physical cause was excluded by medical examination.

Humanistic theories	Humanistic theories focus attention on the whole, unique person, especially on the person's conscious understanding of his or her self and the world.
Cognitive theories	Cognitive theories emphasize thinking, reasoning, problem solving, and language. Contributions include an emphasis on the active construction of understanding and developmental changes in thinking. Criticisms include giving too little attention to individual variations and underrating the unconscious aspects of thought.
Projective test	A projective test is a personality test designed to let a person respond to ambiguous stimuli, presumably revealing hidden emotions and internal conflicts. This is different from an "objective test" in which responses are analyzed according to a universal standard rather than an individual psychiatrist's judgement.
Self-concept	Self-concept refers to domain-specific evaluations of the self where a domain may be academics, athletics, etc.
Personality	Personality refers to the pattern of enduring characteristics that differentiates a person, the patterns of behaviors that make each individual unique.
Self-esteem	Self-esteem refers to a person's subjective appraisal of himself or herself as intrinsically positive or negative to some degree.
Theories	Theories are logically self-consistent models or frameworks describing the behavior of a certain natural or social phenomenon. They are broad explanations and predictions concerning phenomena of interest.
Bandura	Bandura is best known for his work on social learning theory or Social Cognitivism. His famous Bobo doll experiment illustrated that people learn from observing others.
Mischel	Mischel is known for his cognitive social learning model of personality that focuses on the specific cognitive variables that mediate the manner in which new experiences affect the individual.
Trait	An enduring personality characteristic that tends to lead to certain behaviors is called a trait. The term trait also means a genetically inherited feature of an organism.
Personality type	A persistent style of complex behaviors defined by a group of related traits is referred to as a personality type. Myer Friedman and his co-workers first defined personality types in the 1950s. Friedman classified people into 2 categories, Type A and Type B.
All-or-none	All-or-none indicates a situation in which there are two possibilities (a binary choice set), one of which is 100% and one of which is 0%. It is a phrase commonly used to describe action potentials of neurons, which, if they fire at all, propagate from the beginning to the end of the axonal process.
Hippocrates	Hippocrates was an ancient Greek physician, commonly regarded as one of the most outstanding figures in medicine of all time; he has been called "the father of medicine."
Temperament	Temperament refers to a basic, innate disposition to change behavior. The activity level is an important dimension of temperament.
William Sheldon	William Sheldon is known for his categories of somatotypes. He assigned people into three categories of body types: endomorphic, mesomorphic, and ectomorphic. He also assigned personality traits to the body types as well.
Hans Eysenck	Hans Eysenck using Factor Analysis concluded that all human traits can be broken down into two distinct categories: 1. Extroversion-Introversion, 2. Neuroticism. He called these categories Supertraits.
Trait theory	According to trait theory, personality can be broken down into a limited number of traits, which are present in each individual to a greater or lesser degree. This approach is highly

	compatible with the quantitative psychometric approach to personality testing.
Darwin	Darwin achieved lasting fame as originator of the theory of evolution through natural selection. His book Expression of Emotions in Man and Animals is generally considered the first text on comparative psychology.
Attachment	Attachment is the tendency to seek closeness to another person and feel secure when that person is present.
Attention	Attention is the cognitive process of selectively concentrating on one thing while ignoring other things. Psychologists have labeled three types of attention: sustained attention, selective attention, and divided attention.
Openness to Experience	Openness to Experience, one of the big-five traits, describes a dimension of cognitive style that distinguishes imaginative, creative people from down-to-earth, conventional people.
Individuality	According to Cooper, individuality consists of two dimensions: self-assertion and separateness.
Allport	Allport was a trait theorist. Those traits he believed to predominate a person's personality were called central traits. Traits such that one could be indentifed by the trait, were referred to as cardinal traits. Central traits and cardinal traits are influenced by environmental factors.
Intervening variables	Hull developed a version of behaviorism based on Tolman's intervening variables concept, in which the stimulus (S) affects the organism (O) and the resulting response (R) depends upon characteristics of both O and S. Hull was interested in studying intervening variables that affected behavior such as initial drive, incentives, inhibitors, and prior training (habit strength).
Cardinal trait	A cardinal trait is Gordon Allport's name for a personal quality that is so strong a part of a person's personality, that he or she may become identified with that trait.
Central trait	Gordon Allport delineated different kinds of traits, which he also called dispositions. A Central trait is basic to an individual's personality, while secondary traits are more peripheral. Common traits are those recognized within a culture and thus may vary from culture to culture. Cardinal traits are those by which an individual may be strongly recognized.
Personality test	A personality test aims to describe aspects of a person's character that remain stable across situations.
Source traits	Cattell's name for the traits that make up the most basic personality structure and causes of behavior is source traits.
Five-factor model	The five-factor model of personality proposes that there are five universal dimensions of personality: Neuroticism, Extraversion, Openness, Conscientiousness, and Agreeableness.
Questionnaire	A self-report method of data collection or clinical assessment method in which the individual being studied checks off items on a printed list, answers multiple-choice questions, or writes out answers to essay questions aimed at producing a selfdescription is called questionnaire.
Extraversion	Extraversion, one of the big-five personailty traits, is marked by pronounced engagement with the external world. They are people who enjoy being with people, are full of energy, and often experience positive emotions.
Amygdala	Located in the brain's medial temporal lobe, the almond-shaped amygdala is believed to play a key role in the emotions. It forms part of the limbic system and is linked to both fear responses and pleasure. Its size is positively correlated with aggressive behavior across

	species.
Brain	The brain controls and coordinates most movement, behavior and homeostatic body functions such as heartbeat, blood pressure, fluid balance and body temperature. Functions of the brain are responsible for cognition, emotion, memory, motor learning and other sorts of learning. The brain is primarily made up of two types of cells: glia and neurons.
Individual differences	Individual differences psychology studies the ways in which individual people differ in their behavior. This is distinguished from other aspects of psychology in that although psychology is ostensibly a study of individuals, modern psychologists invariably study groups.
Evolution	Commonly used to refer to gradual change, evolution is the change in the frequency of alleles within a population from one generation to the next. This change may be caused by different mechanisms, including natural selection, genetic drift, or changes in population (gene flow).
Positive correlation	A relationship between two variables in which both vary in the same direction is called a positive correlation.
Heritability	Heritability It is that proportion of the observed variation in a particular phenotype within a particular population, that can be attributed to the contribution of genotype. In other words: it measures the extent to which differences between individuals in a population are due their being different genetically.
Personality trait	According to the Diagnostic and Statistical Manual of the American Psychiatric Association, a personality trait is a "prominent aspect of personality that is exhibited in a wide range of important social and personal contexts. ...".
Behavioral genetics	Behavioral genetics is the field of biology that studies the role of genetics in behavior.
Genetics	Genetics is the science of genes, heredity, and the variation of organisms.
Gene	A gene is an ultramicroscopic area of the chromosome. It is the smallest physical unit of the DNA molecule that carries a piece of hereditary information.
Identical twins	Identical twins occur when a single egg is fertilized to form one zygote (monozygotic) but the zygote then divides into two separate embryos. The two embryos develop into foetuses sharing the same womb. Monozygotic twins are genetically identical unless there has been a mutation in development, and they are almost always the same gender.
Monozygotic	Identical twins occur when a single egg is fertilized to form one zygote, calld monozygotic, but the zygote then divides into two separate embryos. The two embryos develop into foetuses sharing the same womb. Monozygotic twins are genetically identical unless there has been a mutation in development, and they are almost always the same gender.
Dizygotic	Fraternal twins (commonly known as "non-identical twins") usually occur when two fertilized eggs are implanted in the uterine wall at the same time. The two eggs form two zygotes, and these twins are therefore also known as dizygotic.
Adoption studies	Research studies that assess hereditary influence by examining the resemblance between adopted children and both their biological and their adoptive parents are referred to as adoption studies. The studies have been inconclusive about the relative importance of heredity in intelligence.
Correlation	A statistical technique for determining the degree of association between two or more variables is referred to as correlation.
Self-Regulatory	Bandura proposes that self-regulatory systems mediate external influences and provide a basis for purposeful action, allowing people to have personal control over their own thoughts, feelings, motivations, and actions.

Zimbardo	Zimbardo is best-known for his Stanford prison experiment. The experiment led to theories about the importance of the social situation in individual psychology that are still controversial today.
Shyness	A tendency to avoid others plus uneasiness and strain when socializing is called shyness.
Chronic	Chronic refers to a relatively long duration, usually more than a few months.
Kagan	The work of Kagan supports the concept of an inborn, biologically based temperamental predisposition to severe anxiety.
Psychodynamic	Most psychodynamic approaches are centered around the idea of a maladapted function developed early in life (usually childhood) which are at least in part unconscious. This maladapted function (a.k.a. defense mechanism) does not do well in place of a normal/healthy one.
Sigmund Freud	Sigmund Freud was the founder of the psychoanalytic school, based on his theory that unconscious motives control much behavior, that particular kinds of unconscious thoughts and memories are the source of neurosis, and that neurosis could be treated through bringing these unconscious thoughts and memories to consciousness in psychoanalytic treatment.
Ernest Jones	Ernest Jones was arguably the best-known follower of Freud. His writings on the subject of psychoanalysis prompted him to launch The International Journal of Psychoanalysis in 1920.
Habit	A habit is a response that has become completely separated from its eliciting stimulus. Early learning theorists used the term to describe S-R associations, however not all S-R associations become a habit, rather many are extinguished after reinforcement is withdrawn.
Meditation	Meditation usually refers to a state in which the body is consciously relaxed and the mind is allowed to become calm and focused.
Psychoanalysis	Psychoanalysis refers to the school of psychology that emphasizes the importance of unconscious motives and conflicts as determinants of human behavior. It was Freud's method of exploring human personality.
Psychoanalytic	Freud's theory that unconscious forces act as determinants of personality is called psychoanalytic theory. The theory is a developmental theory characterized by critical stages of development.
Motivation	In psychology, motivation is the driving force (desire) behind all actions of an organism.
Motives	Needs or desires that energize and direct behavior toward a goal are motives.
Psychosexual development	In psychodynamic theory, the process by which libidinal energy is expressed through different erogenous zones during different stages of development is called psychosexual development.
Neurologist	A physician who studies the nervous system, especially its structure, functions, and abnormalities is referred to as neurologist.
Instinct	Instinct is the word used to describe inherent dispositions towards particular actions. They are generally an inherited pattern of responses or reactions to certain kinds of situations.
Species	Species refers to a reproductively isolated breeding population.
Eros	In Freudian psychology, Eros is the life instinct innate in all humans. It is the desire to create life and favours productivity and construction. Eros battles against the destructive death instinct of Thanatos.
Death instinct	The death instinct was defined by Sigmund Freud, in Beyond the Pleasure Principle(1920). It speculated on the existence of a fundamental death wish or death instinct, referring to an individual's own need to die.
Thanatos	In psychoanalytical theory, Thanatos is the death instinct, which opposes Eros. The "death

	instinct" identified by Sigmund Freud, which signals a desire to give up the struggle of life and return to quiescence and the grave.
Puberty	Puberty refers to the process of physical changes by which a child's body becomes an adult body capable of reproduction.
Erogenous zone	An erogenous zone is an area of the human body that has heightened sensitivity and stimulation normally results in sexual response.
Genitals	Genitals refers to the internal and external reproductive organs.
Phallic stage	The phallic stage is the 3rd of Freud's psychosexual stages, when awareness of and manipulation of the genitals is supposed to be a primary source of pleasure. In this stage the child deals with the Oedipus complex, if male, or the Electra Complex, if female.
Oedipus complex	The Oedipus complex is a concept developed by Sigmund Freud to explain the maturation of the infant boy through identification with the father and desire for the mother.
Innate	Innate behavior is not learned or influenced by the environment, rather, it is present or predisposed at birth.
Fixation	Fixation in abnormal psychology is the state where an individual becomes obsessed with an attachment to another human, animal or inanimate object. Fixation in vision refers to maintaining the gaze in a constant direction. .
Determinism	Determinism is the philosophical proposition that every event, including human cognition and action, is causally determined by an unbroken chain of prior occurrences.
Manifest content	In psychodynamic theory, the reported content of dreams is referred to as manifest content.
Latent content	In psychodynamic theory, the symbolized or underlying content of dreams is called latent content.
Information processing	Information processing is an approach to the goal of understanding human thinking. The essence of the approach is to see cognition as being essentially computational in nature, with mind being the software and the brain being the hardware.
Freudian slip	The Freudian slip is named after Sigmund Freud, who described the phenomenon he called faulty action in his 1901 book The Psychopathology of Everyday Life. The Freudian slip is an error in human action, speech or memory that is believed to be caused by the unconscious mind.
Superego	Frued's third psychic structure, which functions as a moral guardian and sets forth high standards for behavior is the superego.
Ego	In Freud's view the Ego serves to balance our primitive needs and our moral beliefs and taboos. Relying on experience, a healthy Ego provides the ability to adapt to reality and interact with the outside world.
Mental processes	The thoughts, feelings, and motives that each of us experiences privately but that cannot be observed directly are called mental processes.
Pleasure principle	The pleasure principle is the tendency to seek pleasure and avoid pain. In Freud's theory, this principle rules the Id, but is at least partly repressed by the reality principle.
Attitude	An enduring mental representation of a person, place, or thing that evokes an emotional response and related behavior is called attitude.
Society	The social sciences use the term society to mean a group of people that form a semi-closed (or semi-open) social system, in which most interactions are with other individuals belonging to the group.
Ego ideal	The component of the superego that involves ideal standards approved by parents is called ego

	ideal. The ego ideal rewards the child by conveying a sense of pride and personal value when the child acts according to ideal standards.
Reality principle	The reality principle tells us to subordinate pleasure to what needs to be done. Subordinating the pleasure principle to the reality principle is done through a psychological process Freud calls sublimation, where you take desires that can't be fulfilled, or shouldn't be fulfilled, and turn their energy into something useful and productive.
Repression	A defense mechanism, repression involves moving thoughts unacceptable to the ego into the unconscious, where they cannot be easily accessed.
Anxiety	Anxiety is a complex combination of the feeling of fear, apprehension and worry often accompanied by physical sensations such as palpitations, chest pain and/or shortness of breath.
Guilt	Guilt describes many concepts related to a negative emotion or condition caused by actions which are believed to be, morally wrong. According to Freud, the avoidance of guilt is the basis for moral behavior.
Consciousness	The awareness of the sensations, thoughts, and feelings being experienced at a given moment is called consciousness.
Self-image	A person's self-image is the mental picture, generally of a kind that is quite resistant to change, that depicts not only details that are potentially available to objective investigation by others, but also items that have been learned by that person about himself or herself.
Empirical	Empirical means the use of working hypotheses which are capable of being disproved using observation or experiment.
Hypothesis	A specific statement about behavior or mental processes that is testable through research is a hypothesis.
Collective unconscious	Collective unconscious is a term of analytical psychology, originally coined by Carl Jung. It refers to that part of a person's unconscious which is common to all human beings. It contains archetypes, which are forms or symbols that are manifested by all people in all cultures.
Creativity	Creativity is the ability to think about something in novel and unusual ways and come up with unique solutions to problems. It involves divergent thinking, having many solutions or views to a problem.
Jung	Jung was in some aspects a response to Sigmund Freud's psychoanalysis. He proposed and developed the concepts of the extroverted and introverted personality, archetypes, and the collective unconscious. His work has been influential in psychiatry and in the study of religion, literature, and related fields.
Variable	A variable refers to a measurable factor, characteristic, or attribute of an individual or a system.
Shaping	The concept of reinforcing successive, increasingly accurate approximations to a target behavior is called shaping. The target behavior is broken down into a hierarchy of elemental steps, each step more sophisticated then the last. By successively reinforcing each of the the elemental steps, a form of differential reinforcement, until that step is learned while extinguishing the step below, the target behavior is gradually achieved.
Life span	Life span refers to the upper boundary of life, the maximum number of years an individual can live. The maximum life span of human beings is about 120 years of age. Females live an average of 6 years longer than males.

Adler	Adler argued that human personality could be explained teleologically, separate strands dominated by the guiding purpose of the individual's unconscious self ideal to convert feelings of inferiority to superiority (or rather completeness). The desires of the self ideal were countered by social and ethical demands.
Karen Horney	Karen Horney, a neo-Freudian, deviated from orthodox Freudian analysis by emphasizing environmental and cultural, rather than biological, factors in neurosis.
Archetype	The archetype is a concept of psychologist Carl Jung. They are innate prototypes for ideas, which may subsequently become involved in the interpretation of observed phenomena. A group of memories and interpretations closely associated with an archetype is called a complex.
Anima	Anima, according to Carl Jung, is the feminine side of a man's personal unconscious. It can be identified as all the unconscious feminine psychological qualities that a man possesses.
Libido	Sigmund Freud suggested that libido is the instinctual energy or force that can come into conflict with the conventions of civilized behavior. Jung, condidered the libido as the free creative, or psychic, energy an individual has to put toward personal development, or individuation.
Humanistic	Humanistic refers to any system of thought focused on subjective experience and human problems and potentials.
Self-actualization	Self-actualization (a term originated by Kurt Goldstein) is the instinctual need of a human to make the most of their unique abilities. Maslow described it as follows: Self Actualization is the intrinsic growth of what is already in the organism, or more accurately, of what the organism is.
Carl Rogers	Carl Rogers was instrumental in the development of non-directive psychotherapy, also known as "client-centered" psychotherapy. Rogers' basic tenets were unconditional positive regard, genuineness, and empathic understanding, with each demonstrated by the counselor.
Maslow	Maslow is mostly noted today for his proposal of a hierarchy of human needs which he often presented as a pyramid. Maslow was an instrumental player in the formation of the humanistic movement, also known as the third force in psychology.
Hierarchy of needs	Maslow's hierarchy of needs is often depicted as a pyramid consisting of five levels: the four lower levels are grouped together as deficiency needs, while the top level is termed being needs. While our deficiency needs must be met, our being needs are continually shaping our behavior.
Unconditional positive regard	Unqualified caring and nonjudgmental acceptance of another is called unconditional positive regard.
Humanistic psychology	Humanistic psychology refers to the school of psychology that focuses on the uniqueness of human beings and their capacity for choice, growth, and psychological health.
Basic anxiety	Basic anxiety is a child's insecurity and doubt when a parent is indifferent, unloving, or disparaging. This anxiety, according to Horney, leads the child to a basic hostility toward his or her parents. The child may then become neurotic as an adult.
Humanistic therapy	The aim of much humanistic therapy is to give a holistic description of the person. By using phenomenological, intersubjective and first-person categories, the humanistic psychologist hopes to get a glimpse of the whole person and not just the fragmented parts of the personality.
Human nature	Human nature is the fundamental nature and substance of humans, as well as the range of human behavior that is believed to be invariant over long periods of time and across very different cultural contexts.

Trauma	Trauma refers to a severe physical injury or wound to the body caused by an external force, or a psychological shock having a lasting effect on mental life.
Construct	A generalized concept, such as anxiety or gravity, is a construct.
Learning	Learning is a relatively permanent change in behavior that results from experience. Thus, to attribute a behavioral change to learning, the change must be relatively permanent and must result from experience.
Reinforcement	In operant conditioning, reinforcement is any change in an environment that (a) occurs after the behavior, (b) seems to make that behavior re-occur more often in the future and (c) that reoccurence of behavior must be the result of the change.
Perception	Perception is the process of acquiring, interpreting, selecting, and organizing sensory information.
Sensation	Sensation is the first stage in the chain of biochemical and neurologic events that begins with the impinging of a stimulus upon the receptor cells of a sensory organ, which then leads to perception, the mental state that is reflected in statements like "I see a uniformly blue wall."
Psychological situation	A psychological situation refers to situation as it is perceived and interpreted by an individual, not necessarily as it exists objectively.
Counselor	A counselor is a mental health professional who specializes in helping people with problems not involving serious mental disorders.
Emotion	An emotion is a mental states that arise spontaneously, rather than through conscious effort. They are often accompanied by physiological changes.
Affective	Affective is the way people react emotionally, their ability to feel another living thing's pain or joy.
Feedback	Feedback refers to information returned to a person about the effects a response has had.
Observational learning	The acquisition of knowledge and skills through the observation of others rather than by means of direct experience is observational learning. Four major processes are thought to influence the observational learning: attentional, retentional, behavioral production, and motivational.
Reciprocal Determinism	Bandura's term for the social-cognitive view that people influence their environment just as their environment influences them is reciprocal determinism.
Self-efficacy	Self-efficacy is the belief that one has the capabilities to execute the courses of actions required to manage prospective situations.
Problem solving	An attempt to find an appropriate way of attaining a goal when the goal is not readily available is called problem solving.
Affect	A subjective feeling or emotional tone often accompanied by bodily expressions noticeable to others is called affect.
Intrapersonal	Intrapersonal is the ability to recognize, define, and pursue inner feelings and thoughts, as in poetry and self-knowledge.
Generalization	In conditioning, the tendency for a conditioned response to be evoked by stimuli that are similar to the stimulus to which the response was conditioned is a generalization. The greater the similarity among the stimuli, the greater the probability of generalization.
Schema	Schema refers to a way of mentally representing the world, such as a belief or an expectation, that can influence perception of persons, objects, and situations.

Interdependence	Interdependence is a dynamic of being mutually responsible to and dependent on others.
Individualistic	Cultures have been classified as individualistic, which means having a set of values that give priority to personal goals rather than group goals.
Collectivist	A person who defines the self in terms of relationships to other people and groups and gives priority to group goals is called collectivist.
Social identity	Social identity is the way we define ourselves in terms of group membership.
Survey	A method of scientific investigation in which a large sample of people answer questions about their attitudes or behavior is referred to as a survey.
Nature versus nurture	Nature versus nurture is a shorthand expression for debates about the relative importance of an individual's innate makeup versus personal experiences in determining or causing physical and behavioral traits.
Heredity	Heredity is the transfer of characteristics from parent to offspring through their genes.
Social support	Social Support is the physical and emotional comfort given by family, friends, co-workers and others. Research has identified three main types of social support: emotional, practical, sharing points of view.
Homosexuality	Homosexuality refers to a sexual orientation characterized by aesthetic attraction, romantic love, and sexual desire exclusively for members of the same sex or gender identity.
Self-disclosure	The process of revealing private thoughts, feelings, and one's personal history to others is referred to as self-disclosure.
Adaptive behavior	An adaptive behavior increases the probability of the individual or organism to survive or exist within its environment.
Reid	Reid was the founder of the Scottish School of Common Sense, and played an integral role in the Scottish Enlightenment. He advocated direct realism, or common sense realism, and argued strongly against the Theory of Ideas advocated by John Locke and René Descartes.
Reliability	Reliability means the extent to which a test produces a consistent , reproducible score .
Validity	The extent to which a test measures what it is intended to measure is called validity.
Maladjustment	Maladjustment is the condition of being unable to adapt properly to your environment with resulting emotional instability.
Normative	The term normative is used to describe the effects of those structures of culture which regulate the function of social activity.
Personality inventory	A self-report questionnaire by which an examinee indicates whether statements assessing habitual tendencies apply to him or her is referred to as a personality inventory.
Population	Population refers to all members of a well-defined group of organisms, events, or things.
Psychiatrist	A psychiatrist is a physician who specializes in the diagnosis and treatment of psychological disorders.
Schizophrenia	Schizophrenia is characterized by persistent defects in the perception or expression of reality. A person suffering from untreated schizophrenia typically demonstrates grossly disorganized thinking, and may also experience delusions or auditory hallucinations
Norms	In testing, standards of test performance that permit the comparison of one person's score on the test to the scores of others who have taken the same test are referred to as norms.
Psychopathology	Psychopathology refers to the field concerned with the nature and development of mental disorders.

Heterogeneous	A heterogeneous compound, mixture, or other such object is one that consists of many different items, which are often not easily sorted or separated, though they are clearly distinct.
Ethnic group	An ethnic group is a culture or subculture whose members are readily distinguishable by outsiders based on traits originating from a common racial, national, linguistic, or religious source. Members of an ethnic group are often presumed to be culturally or biologically similar, although this is not in fact necessarily the case.
Clinician	A health professional authorized to provide services to people suffering from one or more pathologies is a clinician.
Standardized score	A score that is expressed in terms of the number of standard deviations the original score is from the mean of the original scores is a standardized score.
Conscientiou-ness	Conscientiousness is one of the dimensions of the five-factor model of personality and individual differences involving being organized, thorough, and reliable as opposed to careless, negligent, and unreliable.
Agreeableness	Agreeableness, one of the big-five personality traits, reflects individual differences in concern with cooperation and social harmony. It is the degree individuals value getting along with others.
Neuroticism	Eysenck's use of the term neuroticism (or Emotional Stability) was proposed as the dimension describing individual differences in the predisposition towards neurotic disorder.
Depression	In everyday language depression refers to any downturn in mood, which may be relatively transitory and perhaps due to something trivial. This is differentiated from Clinical depression which is marked by symptoms that last two weeks or more and are so severe that they interfere with daily living.
Big five	The big five factors of personality are Openness to experience, Conscientiousness, Extraversion, Agreeableness, and Emotional Stability.
Psychometric	Psychometric study is concerned with the theory and technique of psychological measurement, which includes the measurement of knowledge, abilities, attitudes, and personality traits. The field is primarily concerned with the study of differences between individuals
Social psychology	Social psychology is the study of the nature and causes of human social behavior, with an emphasis on how people think towards each other and how they relate to each other.
Psychoanalyst	A psychoanalyst is a specially trained therapist who attempts to treat the individual by uncovering and revealing to the individual otherwise subconscious factors that are contributing to some undesirable behavor.
Apperception	A newly experienced sensation is related to past experiences to form an understood situation. For Wundt, consciousness is composed of two "stages:" There is a large capacity working memory called the Blickfeld and the narrower consciousness called Apperception, or selective attention.
Super-ego	The Super-ego stands in opposition to the desires of the Id. The Super-ego is based upon the internalization of the world view, norms and mores a child absorbs from parents and the surrounding environment at a young age. As the conscience, it includes our sense of right and wrong, maintaining taboos specific to a child's internalization of parental culture.
Defense mechanism	A Defense mechanism is a set of unconscious ways to protect one's personality from unpleasant thoughts and realities which may otherwise cause anxiety. The notion is an integral part of the psychoanalytic theory.
Ambiguous	Patterns that allow more than one perceptual organization are called ambiguous stimuli.

stimuli

Rorschach

The Rorschach inkblot test is a method of psychological evaluation. It is a projective test associated with the Freudian school of thought. Psychologists use this test to try to probe the unconscious minds of their patients.

Schizophrenia	Schizophrenia is characterized by persistent defects in the perception or expression of reality. A person suffering from untreated schizophrenia typically demonstrates grossly disorganized thinking, and may also experience delusions or auditory hallucinations
Nurture	Nurture refers to the environmental influences on behavior due to nutrition, culture, socioeconomic status, and learning.
Psychological disorder	Mental processes and/or behavior patterns that cause emotional distress and/or substantial impairment in functioning is a psychological disorder.
Abnormal psychology	The scientific study whose objectives are to describe, explain, predict, and control behaviors that are considered strange or unusual is referred to as abnormal psychology.
Mental disorder	Mental disorder refers to a disturbance in a person's emotions, drives, thought processes, or behavior that involves serious and relatively prolonged distress and/or impairment in ability to function, is not simply a normal response to some event or set of events in the person's environment.
Mental illness	Mental illness is the term formerly used to mean psychological disorder but less preferred because it implies that the causes of the disorder can be found in a medical disease process.
Society	The social sciences use the term society to mean a group of people that form a semi-closed (or semi-open) social system, in which most interactions are with other individuals belonging to the group.
Maladaptive	In psychology, a behavior or trait is adaptive when it helps an individual adjust and function well within their social environment. A maladaptive behavior or trait is counterproductive to the individual.
Norms	In testing, standards of test performance that permit the comparison of one person's score on the test to the scores of others who have taken the same test are referred to as norms.
Hallucination	A hallucination is a sensory perception experienced in the absence of an external stimulus, as distinct from an illusion, which is a misperception of an external stimulus. They may occur in any sensory modality - visual, auditory, olfactory, gustatory, tactile, or mixed.
Necessary condition	A circumstance required for a particular phenomenon to occur is a necessary condition if and only if the condition does not occur in the absense of the circumstance.
Mania	Mania is a medical condition characterized by severely elevated mood. Mania is most usually associated with bipolar disorder, where episodes of mania may cyclically alternate with episodes of depression.
Paranoid	The term paranoid is typically used in a general sense to signify any self-referential delusion, or more specifically, to signify a delusion involving the fear of persecution.
Psychiatrist	A psychiatrist is a physician who specializes in the diagnosis and treatment of psychological disorders.
Social norm	A social norm, is a rule that is socially enforced. In social situations, such as meetings, they are unwritten and often unstated rules that govern individuals' behavior. A social norm is most evident when not followed or broken.
Szasz	Szasz is a critic of the moral and scientific foundations of psychiatry. He argues that the belief that mental illness is a real illness has hurt many more people than it has helped. He is well known for his books The Myth of Mental Illness and The Manufacture of Madness: A Comparative Study of the Inquisition and the Mental Health Movement.
Abnormal behavior	An action, thought, or feeling that is harmful to the person or to others is called abnormal behavior.

Attitude — An enduring mental representation of a person, place, or thing that evokes an emotional response and related behavior is called attitude.

Hysteria — Hysteria is a diagnostic label applied to a state of mind, one of unmanageable fear or emotional excesses. The fear is often centered on a body part, most often on an imagined problem with that body part.

Affect — A subjective feeling or emotional tone often accompanied by bodily expressions noticeable to others is called affect.

Uterus — The uterus or womb is the major female reproductive organ. The main function of the uterus is to accept a fertilized ovum which becomes implanted into the endometrium, and derives nourishment from blood vessels which develop exclusively for this purpose.

Sensation — Sensation is the first stage in the chain of biochemical and neurologic events that begins with the impinging of a stimulus upon the receptor cells of a sensory organ, which then leads to perception, the mental state that is reflected in statements like "I see a uniformly blue wall."

Medical model — The medical model views abnormal behavior as a disease.

Clinician — A health professional authorized to provide services to people suffering from one or more pathologies is a clinician.

Pinel — Pinel is regarded as the father of modern psychiatry. He was a clinician believing that medical truth derived from clinical experience. While at Bicêtre, Pinel did away with bleeding, purging, and blistering in favor a therapy that involved close contact with and careful observation of patients.

Kraepelin — Kraepelin postulated that there is a specific brain or other biological pathology underlying each of the major psychiatric disorders. Just as his laboratory discovered the pathologic basis of what is now known as Alzheimers disease, Kraepelin was confident that it would someday be possible to identify the pathologic basis of each of the major psychiatric disorders.

Animal magnetism — Animal magnetism is both a synonym for Mesmerism as well as the 18th century term for the supposed ethereal medium postulated by Franz Mesmer as a therapeutic agent. Its existence was examined by a French royal commission in 1784, and the commission concluded there was no evidence of its existence.

Mesmer — Mesmer discovered what he called animal magnetism and others often called mesmerism. The evolution of Mesmer's ideas and practices led James Braid to develop hypnosis in 1842.

Hypnosis — Hypnosis is a psychological state whose existence and effects are strongly debated. Some believe that it is a state under which the subject's mind becomes so suggestible that the hypnotist, the one who induces the state, can establish communication with the subconscious mind of the subject and command behavior that the subject would not choose to perform in a conscious state.

Sigmund Freud — Sigmund Freud was the founder of the psychoanalytic school, based on his theory that unconscious motives control much behavior, that particular kinds of unconscious thoughts and memories are the source of neurosis, and that neurosis could be treated through bringing these unconscious thoughts and memories to consciousness in psychoanalytic treatment.

Charcot — Charcot took an interest in the malady then called hysteria. It seemed to be a mental disorder with physical manifestations, of immediate interest to a neurologist. He believed that hysteria was the result of a weak neurological system which was hereditary.

Psychopathology — Psychopathology refers to the field concerned with the nature and development of mental disorders.

Psychodynamic	Most psychodynamic approaches are centered around the idea of a maladapted function developed early in life (usually childhood) which are at least in part unconscious. This maladapted function (a.k.a. defense mechanism) does not do well in place of a normal/healthy one.
Personality	Personality refers to the pattern of enduring characteristics that differentiates a person, the patterns of behaviors that make each individual unique.
Theories	Theories are logically self-consistent models or frameworks describing the behavior of a certain natural or social phenomenon. They are broad explanations and predictions concerning phenomena of interest.
Etiology	Etiology is the study of causation. The term is used in philosophy, physics and biology in reference to the causes of various phenomena. It is generally the study of why things occur, or even the reasons behind the way that things act.
Brain	The brain controls and coordinates most movement, behavior and homeostatic body functions such as heartbeat, blood pressure, fluid balance and body temperature. Functions of the brain are responsible for cognition, emotion, memory, motor learning and other sorts of learning. The brain is primarily made up of two types of cells: glia and neurons.
Behavioral genetics	Behavioral genetics is the field of biology that studies the role of genetics in behavior.
Gene	A gene is an ultramicroscopic area of the chromosome. It is the smallest physical unit of the DNA molecule that carries a piece of hereditary information.
Early childhood	Early childhood refers to the developmental period extending from the end of infancy to about 5 or 6 years of age; sometimes called the preschool years.
Anxiety	Anxiety is a complex combination of the feeling of fear, apprehension and worry often accompanied by physical sensations such as palpitations, chest pain and/or shortness of breath.
Superego	Frued's third psychic structure, which functions as a moral guardian and sets forth high standards for behavior is the superego.
Ego	In Freud's view the Ego serves to balance our primitive needs and our moral beliefs and taboos. Relying on experience, a healthy Ego provides the ability to adapt to reality and interact with the outside world.
Defense mechanism	A Defense mechanism is a set of unconscious ways to protect one's personality from unpleasant thoughts and realities which may otherwise cause anxiety. The notion is an integral part of the psychoanalytic theory.
Repression	A defense mechanism, repression involves moving thoughts unacceptable to the ego into the unconscious, where they cannot be easily accessed.
Motives	Needs or desires that energize and direct behavior toward a goal are motives.
Denial	Denial is a psychological defense mechanism in which a person faced with a fact that is uncomfortable or painful to accept rejects it instead, insisting that it is not true despite what may be overwhelming evidence.
Operant Conditioning	A simple form of learning in which an organism learns to engage in behavior because it is reinforced is referred to as operant conditioning. The consequences of a behavior produce changes in the probability of the behavior's occurence.
Reinforcer	In operant conditioning, a reinforcer is any stimulus that increases the probability that a preceding behavior will occur again. In Classical Conditioning, the unconditioned stimulus (US) is the reinforcer.

Stimulus	A change in an environmental condition that elicits a response is a stimulus.
Variable	A variable refers to a measurable factor, characteristic, or attribute of an individual or a system.
Cognitive approach	A cognitive approach focuses on the mental processes involved in knowing: how we direct our attention, perceive, remember, think, and solve problems.
Problem solving	An attempt to find an appropriate way of attaining a goal when the goal is not readily available is called problem solving.
Perception	Perception is the process of acquiring, interpreting, selecting, and organizing sensory information.
Reasoning	Reasoning is the act of using reason to derive a conclusion from certain premises. There are two main methods to reach a conclusion,deductive reasoning and inductive reasoning.
Sociocultural perspective	The view that focuses on the roles of ethnicity, gender, culture, and socioeconomic status in personality formation, behavior, and mental processes is a sociocultural perspective.
Depression	In everyday language depression refers to any downturn in mood, which may be relatively transitory and perhaps due to something trivial. This is differentiated from Clinical depression which is marked by symptoms that last two weeks or more and are so severe that they interfere with daily living.
Scheme	According to Piaget, a hypothetical mental structure that permits the classification and organization of new information is called a scheme.
Diagnostic and Statistical Manual of Mental Disorders	The Diagnostic and Statistical Manual of Mental Disorders, published by the American Psychiatric Association, is the handbook used most often in diagnosing mental disorders in the United States and internationally.
Variability	Statistically, variability refers to how much the scores in a distribution spread out, away from the mean.
Adolescence	The period of life bounded by puberty and the assumption of adult responsibilities is adolescence.
Infancy	The developmental period that extends from birth to 18 or 24 months is called infancy.
Mental retardation	Mental retardation refers to having significantly below-average intellectual functioning and limitations in at least two areas of adaptive functioning. Many categorize retardation as mild, moderate, severe, or profound.
Personality disorder	A mental disorder characterized by a set of inflexible, maladaptive personality traits that keep a person from functioning properly in society is referred to as a personality disorder.
Diabetes	Diabetes is a medical disorder characterized by varying or persistent elevated blood sugar levels, especially after eating. All types of diabetes share similar symptoms and complications at advanced stages: dehydration and ketoacidosis, cardiovascular disease, chronic renal failure, retinal damage which can lead to blindness, nerve damage which can lead to erectile dysfunction, gangrene with risk of amputation of toes, feet, and even legs.
Prognosis	A forecast about the probable course of an illess is referred to as prognosis.
Evolution	Commonly used to refer to gradual change, evolution is the change in the frequency of alleles within a population from one generation to the next. This change may be caused by different mechanisms, including natural selection, genetic drift, or changes in population (gene flow).
Psychotic	A psychotic behavior is a severe psychological disorder characterized by hallucinations and

behavior	loss of contact with reality.
Homosexuality	Homosexuality refers to a sexual orientation characterized by aesthetic attraction, romantic love, and sexual desire exclusively for members of the same sex or gender identity.
Lesbian	A lesbian is a homosexual woman. They are women who are sexually and romantically attracted to other women.
Sexual orientation	Sexual orientation refers to the sex or gender of people who are the focus of a person's amorous or erotic desires, fantasies, and spontaneous feelings, the gender(s) toward which one is primarily "oriented".
Insanity	A legal status indicating that a person cannot be held responsible for his or her actions because of mental illness is called insanity.
Delusion	A false belief, not generally shared by others, and that cannot be changed despite strong evidence to the contrary is a delusion.
Obsession	An obsession is a thought or idea that the sufferer cannot stop thinking about. Common examples include fears of acquiring disease, getting hurt, or causing harm to someone. They are typically automatic, frequent, distressing, and difficult to control or put an end to by themselves.
Attention	Attention is the cognitive process of selectively concentrating on one thing while ignoring other things. Psychologists have labeled three types of attention: sustained attention, selective attention, and divided attention.
Penis	The penis is the external male copulatory organ and the external male organ of urination. In humans, the penis is homologous to the female clitoris, as it develops from the same embryonic structure. It is capable of erection for use in copulation.
Comorbidity	Comorbidity refers to the presence of more than one mental disorder occurring in an individual at the same time.
Anxiety disorder	Anxiety disorder is a blanket term covering several different forms of abnormal anxiety, fear, phobia and nervous condition, that come on suddenly and prevent pursuing normal daily routines.
Panic disorder	A panic attack is a period of intense fear or discomfort, typically with an abrupt onset and usually lasting no more than thirty minutes. The disorder is strikingly different from other types of anxiety, in that panic attacks are very sudden, appear to be unprovoked, and are often disabling. People who have repeated attacks, or feel severe anxiety about having another attack are said to have panic disorder.
Panic attack	An attack of overwhelming anxiety, fear, or terror is called panic attack.
Chronic	Chronic refers to a relatively long duration, usually more than a few months.
Hyperactivity	Hyperactivity can be described as a state in which a individual is abnormally easily excitable and exuberant. Strong emotional reactions and a very short span of attention is also typical for the individual.
Agoraphobia	An irrational fear of open, crowded places is called agoraphobia. Many people suffering from agoraphobia, however, are not afraid of the open spaces themselves, but of situations often associated with these spaces, such as social gatherings.
Phobia	A persistent, irrational fear of an object, situation, or activity that the person feels compelled to avoid is referred to as a phobia.
Social phobia	An irrational, excessive fear of public scrutiny is referred to as social phobia.
Self-fulfilling	A self-fulfilling prophecy is a prediction that, in being made, actually causes itself to

prophecy	become true.
Specific phobia	A specific phobia is a generic term for anxiety disorders that amount to unreasonable or irrational fear or anxiety related with exposure to specific objects or situations. As a result, the affected persons tend to actively avoid these objects or situations.
Obsessive-compulsive disorder	Obsessive-compulsive disorder is an anxiety disorder manifested in a variety of forms, but is most commonly characterized by a subject's obsessive drive to perform a particular task or set of tasks, compulsions commonly termed rituals.
Senses	The senses are systems that consist of a sensory cell type that respond to a specific kind of physical energy, and that correspond to a defined region within the brain where the signals are received and interpreted.
Consciousness	The awareness of the sensations, thoughts, and feelings being experienced at a given moment is called consciousness.
Compulsion	An apparently irresistible urge to repeat an act or engage in ritualistic behavior such as hand washing is referred to as a compulsion.
Stress disorder	A significant emotional disturbance caused by stresses outside the range of normal human experience is referred to as stress disorder.
Rape	Rape is a crime where the victim is forced into sexual activity, in particular sexual penetration, against his or her will.
Trauma	Trauma refers to a severe physical injury or wound to the body caused by an external force, or a psychological shock having a lasting effect on mental life.
Sexual dysfunction	Sexual dysfunction or sexual malfunction is difficulty during any stage of the sexual act (which includes desire, arousal, orgasm, and resolution) that prevents the individual or couple from enjoying sexual activity.
Major depression	Major depression is characterized by a severely depressed mood that persists for at least two weeks. Episodes of depression may start suddenly or slowly and can occur several times through a person's life. The disorder may be categorized as "single episode" or "recurrent" depending on whether previous episodes have been experienced before.
Population	Population refers to all members of a well-defined group of organisms, events, or things.
Gender difference	A gender difference is a disparity between genders involving quality or quantity. Though some gender differences are controversial, they are not to be confused with sexist stereotypes.
Predisposition	Predisposition refers to an inclination or diathesis to respond in a certain way, either inborn or acquired. In abnormal psychology, it is a factor that lowers the ability to withstand stress and inclines the individual toward pathology.
Nerve	A nerve is an enclosed, cable-like bundle of nerve fibers or axons, which includes the glia that ensheath the axons in myelin. Neurons are sometimes called nerve cells, though this term is technically imprecise since many neurons do not form nerves.
Fraternal twins	Fraternal twins usually occur when two fertilized eggs are implanted in the uterine wall at the same time. The two eggs form two zygotes, and these twins are therefore also known as dizygotic. Dizygotic twins are no more similar genetically than any siblings.
Identical twins	Identical twins occur when a single egg is fertilized to form one zygote (monozygotic) but the zygote then divides into two separate embryos. The two embryos develop into foetuses sharing the same womb. Monozygotic twins are genetically identical unless there has been a mutation in development, and they are almost always the same gender.
Personality	According to the Diagnostic and Statistical Manual of the American Psychiatric Association, a

trait	personality trait is a "prominent aspect of personality that is exhibited in a wide range of important social and personal contexts. ...".
Mood disorder	A mood disorder is a condition where the prevailing emotional mood is distorted or inappropriate to the circumstances.
Clinical depression	Although nearly any mood with some element of sadness may colloquially be termed a depression, clinical depression is more than just a temporary state of sadness. Symptoms lasting two weeks or longer in duration, and of a severity that they begin to interfere with daily living.
Hypersomnia	Hypersomnia is an excessive amount of sleepiness, resulting in an inability to stay awake. A person is considered to have hypersomnia if he or she sleeps more than 10 hours per day on a regular basis for at least two weeks.
Major depressive disorder	The diagnosis of a major depressive disorder occurs when an individual experiences a major depressive episode and depressed characteristics, such as lethargy and depression, last for 2 weeks or longer and daily functioning becomes impaired.
Bipolar disorder	Bipolar Disorder is a mood disorder typically characterized by fluctuations between manic and depressive states; and, more generally, atypical mood regulation and mood instability.
Manic episode	A manic episode is a period of unusually high energy, sometimes including uncontrollable excitement. Such episodes most commonly occur as part of bipolar disorder. In extreme cases, the person may need to be hospitalized.
Self-esteem	Self-esteem refers to a person's subjective appraisal of himself or herself as intrinsically positive or negative to some degree.
Guilt	Guilt describes many concepts related to a negative emotion or condition caused by actions which are believed to be, morally wrong. According to Freud, the avoidance of guilt is the basis for moral behavior.
Neurotransmitter	A neurotransmitter is a chemical that is used to relay, amplify and modulate electrical signals between a neurons and another cell.
Norepinephrine	Norepinephrine is released from the adrenal glands as a hormone into the blood, but it is also a neurotransmitter in the nervous system. As a stress hormone, it affects parts of the human brain where attention and impulsivity are controlled. Along with epinephrine, this compound effects the fight-or-flight response, activating the sympathetic nervous system to directly increase heart rate, release energy from fat, and increase muscle readiness.
Serotonin	Serotonin, a neurotransmitter, is believed to play an important part of the biochemistry of depression, bipolar disorder and anxiety. It is also believed to be influential on sexuality and appetite.
Affective	Affective is the way people react emotionally, their ability to feel another living thing's pain or joy.
Experimental group	Experimental group refers to any group receiving a treatment effect in an experiment.
Brain imaging	Brain imaging is a fairly recent discipline within medicine and neuroscience. Brain imaging falls into two broad categories -- structural imaging and functional imaging.
Prefrontal cortex	The prefrontal cortex is the anterior part of the frontal lobes of the brain, lying in front of the motor and associative areas. It has been implicated in planning complex cognitive behaviors, personality expression and moderating correct social behavior. The prefrontal cortex continues to develop until around age 6.
Positive	In positive reinforcement, a stimulus is added and the rate of responding increases.

reinforcement	
Punishment	Punishment is the addtion of a stimulus that reduces the frequency of a response, or the removal of a stimulus that results in a reduction of the response.
Negative feedback	In negative feedback, the output of a system is added back into the input, so as to reverse the direction of change. This tends to keep the output from changing, so it is stabilizing and attempts to maintain homeostasis.
Positive feedback	When a change in a variable occurs in a system, the system responds. In the case of positive feedback the response of the system is to cause that variable to increase in the same direction.
Aaron Beck	Aaron Beck was initially trained as a psychoanalyst and conducted research on the psychoanalytic treatment of depression. With out the strong ability to collect data to this end, he began exploring cognitive approaches to treatment and originated cognitive behavior therapy.
Cognition	The intellectual processes through which information is obtained, transformed, stored, retrieved, and otherwise used is cognition.
Species	Species refers to a reproductively isolated breeding population.
Learned helplessness	Learned helplessness is a description of the effect of inescapable positive punishment (such as electrical shock) on animal (and by extension, human) behavior.
Learning	Learning is a relatively permanent change in behavior that results from experience. Thus, to attribute a behavioral change to learning, the change must be relatively permanent and must result from experience.
Questionnaire	A self-report method of data collection or clinical assessment method in which the individual being studied checks off items on a printed list, answers multiple-choice questions, or writes out answers to essay questions aimed at producing a selfdescription is called questionnaire.
Cognitive theories	Cognitive theories emphasize thinking, reasoning, problem solving, and language. Contributions include an emphasis on the active construction of understanding and developmental changes in thinking. Criticisms include giving too little attention to individual variations and underrating the unconscious aspects of thought.
Insight	Insight refers to a sudden awareness of the relationships among various elements that had previously appeared to be independent of one another.
Primary caregiver	Primary caregiver refers to a person primarily responsible for the care of an infant, usually the infant's mother or father.
Sexual abuse	Sexual abuse is a term used to describe non- consentual sexual relations between two or more parties which are considered criminally and/or morally offensive.
Suicide	Suicide behavior is rare in childhood but escalates in adolescence. The suicide rate increases in a linear fashion from adolescence through late adulthood.
Life span	Life span refers to the upper boundary of life, the maximum number of years an individual can live. The maximum life span of human beings is about 120 years of age. Females live an average of 6 years longer than males.
Survey	A method of scientific investigation in which a large sample of people answer questions about their attitudes or behavior is referred to as a survey.
Anti-social	Anti-social behavior is lacking in judgement and consideration for others, ranging from careless negligence to deliberately damaging activity, vandalism and graffiti for example.

Correlation	A statistical technique for determining the degree of association between two or more variables is referred to as correlation.
Causation	Causation concerns the time order relationship between two or more objects such that if a specific antecendent condition occurs the same consequent must always follow.
Trait	An enduring personality characteristic that tends to lead to certain behaviors is called a trait. The term trait also means a genetically inherited feature of an organism.
Dissociative disorder	Psychological dysfunctions characterized by the separation of critical personality facets that are normally integrated, allowing stress avoidance by escape is a dissociative disorder.
Emotion	An emotion is a mental states that arise spontaneously, rather than through conscious effort. They are often accompanied by physiological changes.
Dissociative identity disorder	Dissociative identity disorder refers to a disorder in which a person appears to have two or more distinct identities or personalities that may alternately emerge. Previously termed multiple personality.
Dissociation	Dissociation is a psychological state or condition in which certain thoughts, emotions, sensations, or memories are separated from the rest.
Autistic disorder	An autistic disorder is a neurodevelopmental disorder that manifests itself in markedly abnormal social interaction, communication ability, patterns of interests, and patterns of behavior.
Theory of mind	A theory of mind considers the nature of mind, and its structure and processes
Heritability	Heritability It is that proportion of the observed variation in a particular phenotype within a particular population, that can be attributed to the contribution of genotype. In other words: it measures the extent to which differences between individuals in a population are due their being different genetically.
Monozygotic	Identical twins occur when a single egg is fertilized to form one zygote, calld monozygotic, but the zygote then divides into two separate embryos. The two embryos develop into foetuses sharing the same womb. Monozygotic twins are genetically identical unless there has been a mutation in development, and they are almost always the same gender.
Dizygotic	Fraternal twins (commonly known as "non-identical twins") usually occur when two fertilized eggs are implanted in the uterine wall at the same time. The two eggs form two zygotes, and these twins are therefore also known as dizygotic.
Genotype	The genotype is the specific genetic makeup of an individual, usually in the form of DNA. It codes for the phenotype of that individual. Any given gene will usually cause an observable change in an organism, known as the phenotype.
Human genome	The complete sequence or mapping of genes in the human body and their locations is the human genome. It is made up of 23 chromosome pairs with a total of about 3 billion DNA base pairs.
Acute	Acute means sudden, sharp, and abrupt. Usually short in duration.
Zimbardo	Zimbardo is best-known for his Stanford prison experiment. The experiment led to theories about the importance of the social situation in individual psychology that are still controversial today.
Delusions of grandeur	Delusions of grandeur are a false belief that one is a famous person or a person who has some great knowledge, ability, or authority.
Paranoid schizophrenia	Paranoid schizophrenia is a type of schizophrenia characterized primarily by delusions-commonly of persecution-and by vivid hallucinations .
Thought disorder	Thought disorder describes a persistent underlying disturbance to conscious thought and is

	classified largely by its effects on speech and writing. Affected persons may show pressure of speech, derailment or flight of ideas, thought blocking, rhyming, punning, or word salad.
Genetics	Genetics is the science of genes, heredity, and the variation of organisms.
Diathesis-stress	In the diathesis-stress model, an inborn and genetic vulnerability or predisposition interacts with the environment and life events to trigger behaviors or psychological disorders.
Hypothesis	A specific statement about behavior or mental processes that is testable through research is a hypothesis.
Heredity	Heredity is the transfer of characteristics from parent to offspring through their genes.
Confederate	Someone who is posing as a participant in an experiment but is actually assisting the experimenter is a confederate.
Human nature	Human nature is the fundamental nature and substance of humans, as well as the range of human behavior that is believed to be invariant over long periods of time and across very different cultural contexts.
Personal identity	The portion of the self-concept that pertains to the self as a distinct, separate individual is called personal identity.

Client-Centered Therapy	Client-Centered Therapy was developed by Carl Rogers. It is based on the principal of talking therapy and is a non-directive approach. The therapist encourages the patient to express their feelings and does not suggest how the person might wish to change, but by listening and then mirroring back what the patient reveals to them, helps them to explore and understand their feelings for themselves.
Contingency management	Providing a supply of reinforcers to promote and maintain desired behaviors, and the prompt removal of reinforcers that maintain undesired behaviors is called contingency management.
Behavior modification	Behavior Modification is a technique of altering an individual's reactions to stimuli through positive reinforcement and the extinction of maladaptive behavior.
Countercondi-ioning	The process of eliminating a classically conditioned response by pairing the CS with an unconditioned stimulus for a response that is stronger than the conditioned response and that cannot occur at the same time as the CR is called counterconditioning.
Gestalt therapy	Gestalt therapy is a form of psychotherapy, based on the experiential ideal of "here and now," and relationships with others and the world. By focusing the individual on their self-awareness as part of present reality, new insights can be made into their behavior, and they can engage in self-healing.
Mental illness	Mental illness is the term formerly used to mean psychological disorder but less preferred because it implies that the causes of the disorder can be found in a medical disease process.
Family therapy	Family therapy is a branch of psychotherapy that treats family problems. Family therapists consider the family as a system of interacting members; as such, the problems in the family are seen to arise as an emergent property of the interactions in the system, rather than ascribed exclusively to the "faults" or psychological problems of individual members.
Generalization	In conditioning, the tendency for a conditioned response to be evoked by stimuli that are similar to the stimulus to which the response was conditioned is a generalization. The greater the similarity among the stimuli, the greater the probability of generalization.
Psychosurgery	Psychosurgery is a term for surgeries of the brain or autonomic nervous system involving the severance of neural pathways to effect a change in behavior, usually to treat or alleviate severe mental illness. The procedures typically considered psychosurgery are now almost universally shunned as inappropriate, due in part to the emergence of less-invasive methods of treatment such as psychiatric medication.
Humanistic	Humanistic refers to any system of thought focused on subjective experience and human problems and potentials.
Brain	The brain controls and coordinates most movement, behavior and homeostatic body functions such as heartbeat, blood pressure, fluid balance and body temperature. Functions of the brain are responsible for cognition, emotion, memory, motor learning and other sorts of learning. The brain is primarily made up of two types of cells: glia and neurons.
Mental disorder	Mental disorder refers to a disturbance in a person's emotions, drives, thought processes, or behavior that involves serious and relatively prolonged distress and/or impairment in ability to function, is not simply a normal response to some event or set of events in the person's environment.
Presenting problem	The presenting problem is the original complaint reported by the client to the therapist. The actual treated problem may sometimes be a modification derived from the presenting problem or entirely different..
Etiology	Etiology is the study of causation. The term is used in philosophy, physics and biology in reference to the causes of various phenomena. It is generally the study of why things occur, or even the reasons behind the way that things act.

Prognosis	A forecast about the probable course of an illess is referred to as prognosis.
Central nervous system	The vertebrate central nervous system consists of the brain and spinal cord.
Psychiatrist	A psychiatrist is a physician who specializes in the diagnosis and treatment of psychological disorders.
Psychotherapy	Psychotherapy is a set of techniques based on psychological principles intended to improve mental health, emotional or behavioral issues.
Feedback	Feedback refers to information returned to a person about the effects a response has had.
Psychodynamic	Most psychodynamic approaches are centered around the idea of a maladapted function developed early in life (usually childhood) which are at least in part unconscious. This maladapted function (a.k.a. defense mechanism) does not do well in place of a normal/healthy one.
Trauma	Trauma refers to a severe physical injury or wound to the body caused by an external force, or a psychological shock having a lasting effect on mental life.
Insight	Insight refers to a sudden awareness of the relationships among various elements that had previously appeared to be independent of one another.
Behavior therapy	Behavior therapy refers to the systematic application of the principles of learning to direct modification of a client's problem behaviors.
Reinforcement contingencies	The circumstances or rules that determine whether responses lead to the presentation of reinforcers are referred to as reinforcement contingencies. Skinner defined culture as a set of reinforcement contingencies.
Conditioned response	A conditioned response is the response to a stimulus that occurs when an animal has learned to associate the stimulus with a certain positive or negative effect.
Problem solving	An attempt to find an appropriate way of attaining a goal when the goal is not readily available is called problem solving.
Cognitive therapy	Cognitive therapy is a kind of psychotherapy used to treat depression, anxiety disorders, phobias, and other forms of mental disorder. It involves recognizing distorted thinking and learning how to replace it with more realistic thoughts and actions.
Cognition	The intellectual processes through which information is obtained, transformed, stored, retrieved, and otherwise used is cognition.
Counselor	A counselor is a mental health professional who specializes in helping people with problems not involving serious mental disorders.
Society	The social sciences use the term society to mean a group of people that form a semi-closed (or semi-open) social system, in which most interactions are with other individuals belonging to the group.
Clinical psychologist	A psychologist, usually with a Ph.D, whose training is in the diagnosis, treatment, or research of psychological and behavioral disorders is a clinical psychologist.
Psychological disorder	Mental processes and/or behavior patterns that cause emotional distress and/or substantial impairment in functioning is a psychological disorder.
Counseling psychologist	A doctoral level mental health professional whose training is similar to that of a clinical psychologist, though usually with less emphasis on research and serious psychopathology is referred to as a counseling psychologist.
Psychoanalyst	A psychoanalyst is a specially trained therapist who attempts to treat the individual by uncovering and revealing to the individual otherwise subconscious factors that are

	contributing to some undesirable behavor.
Therapeutic alliance	A therapeutic alliance refers to a caring relationship that unites a therapist and a client in working to solve the client's problems.
Population	Population refers to all members of a well-defined group of organisms, events, or things.
Perception	Perception is the process of acquiring, interpreting, selecting, and organizing sensory information.
Bedlam	Bedlam is the world's oldest psychiatric hospital. It became famous and afterwards infamous for the brutal ill-treatment meted out to the insane.
Punishment	Punishment is the addtion of a stimulus that reduces the frequency of a response, or the removal of a stimulus that results in a reduction of the response.
Pinel	Pinel is regarded as the father of modern psychiatry. He was a clinician believing that medical truth derived from clinical experience. While at Bicêtre, Pinel did away with bleeding, purging, and blistering in favor a therapy that involved close contact with and careful observation of patients.
Insanity	A legal status indicating that a person cannot be held responsible for his or her actions because of mental illness is called insanity.
Humors	The four humors were four fluids that were thought to permeate the body and influence its health. The concept was developed by ancient Greek thinkers around 400 BC and was directly linked with another popular theory of the four elements. Paired qualities were associated with each humour and its season.
Asylums	Asylums are hospitals specializing in the treatment of persons with mental illness. Psychiatric wards differ only in that they are a unit of a larger hospital.
Demonology	Demonology refers to the doctrine that a person's abnormal behavior is caused by an autonomous evil spirit.
Consciousness	The awareness of the sensations, thoughts, and feelings being experienced at a given moment is called consciousness.
Dissociation	Dissociation is a psychological state or condition in which certain thoughts, emotions, sensations, or memories are separated from the rest.
Social support	Social Support is the physical and emotional comfort given by family, friends, co-workers and others. Research has identified three main types of social support: emotional, practical, sharing points of view.
Psychoanalysis	Psychoanalysis refers to the school of psychology that emphasizes the importance of unconscious motives and conflicts as determinants of human behavior. It was Freud's method of exploring human personality.
Sigmund Freud	Sigmund Freud was the founder of the psychoanalytic school, based on his theory that unconscious motives control much behavior, that particular kinds of unconscious thoughts and memories are the source of neurosis, and that neurosis could be treated through bringing these unconscious thoughts and memories to consciousness in psychoanalytic treatment.
Motivation	In psychology, motivation is the driving force (desire) behind all actions of an organism.
Anxiety	Anxiety is a complex combination of the feeling of fear, apprehension and worry often accompanied by physical sensations such as palpitations, chest pain and/or shortness of breath.
Superego	Frued's third psychic structure, which functions as a moral guardian and sets forth high standards for behavior is the superego.

Ego	In Freud's view the Ego serves to balance our primitive needs and our moral beliefs and taboos. Relying on experience, a healthy Ego provides the ability to adapt to reality and interact with the outside world.
Repression	A defense mechanism, repression involves moving thoughts unacceptable to the ego into the unconscious, where they cannot be easily accessed.
Psychodynamic therapy	Psychodynamic therapy uses a range of different techniques, applied to the client considering his or her needs. Most approaches are centered around the idea of a maladapted function developed early in life which are at least in part unconscious.
Insight therapy	Insight therapy encourages self-awareness. They include the psychodynamic and humanistic therapies.
Countertrans-erence	Feelings that the psychoanalyst unconsciously directs to the analysis, stemming from his or her own emotional vulnerabilities and unresolved conflicts are countertransference effects.
Free association	In psychoanalysis, the uncensored uttering of all thoughts that come to mind is called free association.
Dream analysis	Dream analysis is a part of psychoanalysis that intends to look beneath the manifest content of a dream, i.e., what we perceive in the dream, to the latent content of a dream, i.e., the meaning of the dream and the reason we dreamt it.
Transference	Transference is a phenomenon in psychology characterized by unconscious redirection of feelings from one person to another.
Catharsis	Catharsis has been adopted by modern psychotherapy as the act of giving expression to deep emotions often associated with events in the individuals past which have never before been adequately expressed.
Motives	Needs or desires that energize and direct behavior toward a goal are motives.
Attitude	An enduring mental representation of a person, place, or thing that evokes an emotional response and related behavior is called attitude.
Sexual abuse	Sexual abuse is a term used to describe non- consentual sexual relations between two or more parties which are considered criminally and/or morally offensive.
Clinician	A health professional authorized to provide services to people suffering from one or more pathologies is a clinician.
Melanie Klein	Melanie Klein built on the work of Sigmund Freud and was one of the theoretical cofounders of object relations theory. Her insistence on regarding aggression as an important force in its own right when analyzing children brought her into conflict with Anna Freud.
Sullivan	Sullivan developed the Self System, a configuration of the personality traits developed in childhood and reinforced by positive affirmation and the security operations developed in childhood to avoid anxiety and threats to self-esteem.
Oedipus conflict	For Freud, a child's sexual interest in his or her opposite-sex parent, typically resolved through identification with the same-sex parent, is an Oedipus conflict.
Psychopathology	Psychopathology refers to the field concerned with the nature and development of mental disorders.
Symptom substitution	Psychodynamic assertion that if overt problem behavior is treated without eliminating the underlying conflict thought to be causing it, that conflict will reemerge in the form of new, perhaps worse, symptoms is symptom substitution.
Abnormal behavior	An action, thought, or feeling that is harmful to the person or to others is called abnormal behavior.

Conditioning	Conditioning describes the process by which behaviors can be learned or modified through interaction with the environment.
Learning	Learning is a relatively permanent change in behavior that results from experience. Thus, to attribute a behavioral change to learning, the change must be relatively permanent and must result from experience.
Reinforcement	In operant conditioning, reinforcement is any change in an environment that (a) occurs after the behavior, (b) seems to make that behavior re-occur more often in the future and (c) that reoccurence of behavior must be the result of the change.
Compulsion	An apparently irresistible urge to repeat an act or engage in ritualistic behavior such as hand washing is referred to as a compulsion.
Depression	In everyday language depression refers to any downturn in mood, which may be relatively transitory and perhaps due to something trivial. This is differentiated from Clinical depression which is marked by symptoms that last two weeks or more and are so severe that they interfere with daily living.
Addiction	Addiction is an uncontrollable compulsion to repeat a behavior regardless of its consequences. Many drugs or behaviors can precipitate a pattern of conditions recognized as addiction, which include a craving for more of the drug or behavior, increased physiological tolerance to exposure, and withdrawal symptoms in the absence of the stimulus.
Phobia	A persistent, irrational fear of an object, situation, or activity that the person feels compelled to avoid is referred to as a phobia.
Empirical	Empirical means the use of working hypotheses which are capable of being disproved using observation or experiment.
Theories	Theories are logically self-consistent models or frameworks describing the behavior of a certain natural or social phenomenon. They are broad explanations and predictions concerning phenomena of interest.
Maladaptive	In psychology, a behavior or trait is adaptive when it helps an individual adjust and function well within their social environment. A maladaptive behavior or trait is counterproductive to the individual.
Relearning	Relearning refers to a measure of retention used in experiments on memory. Material is usually relearned more quickly than it is learned initially.
Mary Cover Jones	Mary Cover Jones stands out as a pioneer of behavior therapy. Her study of unconditioning a fear of rabbits in a three-year-old named Peter is her most often cited work.
Little Albert	The Little Albert experiment was an experiment showing empirical evidence of classical conditioning in children. The actual experiment with Little Albert on conditioned fear involved exposing the child to a loud sound while being presented with a white rat.
Systematic desensitization	Systematic desensitization refers to Wolpe's behavioral fear-reduction technique in which a hierarchy of fear-evoking stimuli are presented while the person remains relaxed. The fear-evoking stimuli thereby become associated with muscle relaxation.
Aversion therapy	Aversion therapy is a now largely discredited form of treatment in which the patient is exposed to a stimulus while simultaneously being hurt or made ill. The theory is that the patient will come to associate the stimulus with unpleasant sensations and will no longer seek it out.
Implosion	A behavioral treatment that attempts to extinguish a fear by having the client imagine the anxiety siituation at its maximum intensity is called implosion.
Flooding	Flooding is a behavioral fear-reduction technique based on principles of classical

	conditioning. Fear-evoking stimuli are presented continuously in the absence of harm so that fear responses are extinguished. However, subjects tend to avoid the stimulus, making extinction difficult.
Exposure therapy	An exposure therapy is any method of treating fears, including flooding and systematic desensitization, that involves exposing the client to the feared object or situation so that the process of extinction or habituation of the fear response can occur.
Wolpe	Wolpe is best known for applying classical conditioning principles to the treatment of phobias, called systematic desensitization. Any "neutral" stimulus, simple or complex that happens to make an impact on an individual at about the time that a fear reaction is evoked acquires the ability to evoke fear subsequently. An acquired CS-CR relationship should be extinguishable.
Stimulus	A change in an environmental condition that elicits a response is a stimulus.
Desensitization	Desensitization refers to the type of sensory or behavioral adaptation in which we become less sensitive to constant stimuli.
Claustrophobia	Claustrophobia is an anxiety disorder that involves the fear of enclosed or confined spaces. It may be accompanied by panic attacks in situations such as being in elevators, trains or aircraft.
Acrophobia	An irrational fear of high places is referred to as acrophobia.
Questionnaire	A self-report method of data collection or clinical assessment method in which the individual being studied checks off items on a printed list, answers multiple-choice questions, or writes out answers to essay questions aimed at producing a selfdescription is called questionnaire.
Obsessive-compulsive disorder	Obsessive-compulsive disorder is an anxiety disorder manifested in a variety of forms, but is most commonly characterized by a subject's obsessive drive to perform a particular task or set of tasks, compulsions commonly termed rituals.
Drug addiction	Drug addiction, or substance dependence is the compulsive use of drugs, to the point where the user has no effective choice but to continue use.
Positive reinforcement	In positive reinforcement, a stimulus is added and the rate of responding increases.
Extinction	In operant extinction, if no reinforcement is delivered after the response, gradually the behavior will no longer occur in the presence of the stimulus. The process is more rapid following continuous reinforcement rather than after partial reinforcement. In Classical Conditioning, repeated presentations of the CS without being followed by the US results in the extinction of the CS.
Reinforcer	In operant conditioning, a reinforcer is any stimulus that increases the probability that a preceding behavior will occur again. In Classical Conditioning, the unconditioned stimulus (US) is the reinforcer.
Attention	Attention is the cognitive process of selectively concentrating on one thing while ignoring other things. Psychologists have labeled three types of attention: sustained attention, selective attention, and divided attention.
Schizophrenia	Schizophrenia is characterized by persistent defects in the perception or expression of reality. A person suffering from untreated schizophrenia typically demonstrates grossly disorganized thinking, and may also experience delusions or auditory hallucinations
Hallucination	A hallucination is a sensory perception experienced in the absence of an external stimulus, as distinct from an illusion, which is a misperception of an external stimulus. They may

	occur in any sensory modality - visual, auditory, olfactory, gustatory, tactile, or mixed.
Participant modeling	A behavior therapy in which an appropriate response is modeled in graduated steps and the client attempts each step, encouraged and supported by the therapist is participant modeling.
Modeling therapy	Modeling therapy is a therapeutic approach to phobias in which the person with the phobia observes a model in the act of coping with, or responding appropriately in the fear-producing situation.
Control group	A group that does not receive the treatment effect in an experiment is referred to as the control group or sometimes as the comparison group.
Social skills	Social skills are skills used to interact and communicate with others to assist status in the social structure and other motivations.
Behavioral rehearsal	Behavior therapy technique in which the client practices coping with troublesome or anxiety arousing situations in a safe and supervised situation is a behavioral rehearsal.
Assertiveness	Assertiveness basically means the ability to express your thoughts and feelings in a way that clearly states your needs and keeps the lines of communication open with the other.
Habit	A habit is a response that has become completely separated from its eliciting stimulus. Early learning theorists used the term to describe S-R associations, however not all S-R associations become a habit, rather many are extinguished after reinforcement is withdrawn.
Pathology	Pathology is the study of the processes underlying disease and other forms of illness, harmful abnormality, or dysfunction.
Social skills training	Social skills training refers to a behavior therapy designed to improve interpersonal skills that emphasizes shaping, modeling, and behavioral rehearsal.
Social isolation	Social isolation refers to a type of loneliness that occurs when a person lacks a sense of integrated involvement. Being deprived of participation in a group or community involving companionship, shared interests, organized activities, and meaningful roles causes a person to feel alone.
Social play	Play that involves social interactions with peers is called social play. It increases affiliation with peers, releases tension, advances cognitive development, and increases exploration.
Socialization	Social rules and social relations are created, communicated, and changed in verbal and nonverbal ways creating social complexity useful in identifying outsiders and intelligent breeding partners. The process of learning these skills is called socialization.
Partial reinforcement	In a partial reinforcement environment, not every correct response is reinforced. Partial reinforcement is usually introduced after a continuous reinforcement schedule has acquired the behavior.
Stages	Stages represent relatively discrete periods of time in which functioning is qualitatively different from functioning at other periods.
Internalization	The developmental change from behavior that is externally controlled to behavior that is controlled by internal standards and principles is referred to as internalization.
Fixation	Fixation in abnormal psychology is the state where an individual becomes obsessed with an attachment to another human, animal or inanimate object. Fixation in vision refers to maintaining the gaze in a constant direction. .
Neo-Freudian	The Neo-Freudian psychologists were those followers of Sigmund Freud who accepted the basic tenets of his theory of psychoanalysis but altered it in some way.
Species	Species refers to a reproductively isolated breeding population.

Adaptive behavior	An adaptive behavior increases the probability of the individual or organism to survive or exist within its environment.
Subjective experience	Subjective experience refers to reality as it is perceived and interpreted, not as it exists objectively.
Cognitive restructuring	Cognitive restructuring refers to any behavior therapy procedure that attempts to alter the manner in which a client thinks about life so that he or she changes overt behavior and emotions.
Aaron Beck	Aaron Beck was initially trained as a psychoanalyst and conducted research on the psychoanalytic treatment of depression. With out the strong ability to collect data to this end, he began exploring cognitive approaches to treatment and originated cognitive behavior therapy.
Albert Ellis	Albert Ellis is a psychologist whose Rational Emotive Behavior Therapy (REBT), is the foundation of all cognitive and cognitive behavior therapies.
Personality	Personality refers to the pattern of enduring characteristics that differentiates a person, the patterns of behaviors that make each individual unique.
Self-worth	In psychology, self-esteem or self-worth refers to a person's subjective appraisal of himself or herself as intrinsically positive or negative to some degree.
Coping statements	Reassuring, self-enhancing statements that are used to stop self-critical thinking are referred to as coping statements.
Self-efficacy	Self-efficacy is the belief that one has the capabilities to execute the courses of actions required to manage prospective situations.
Bandura	Bandura is best known for his work on social learning theory or Social Cognitivism. His famous Bobo doll experiment illustrated that people learn from observing others.
Humanistic theories	Humanistic theories focus attention on the whole, unique person, especially on the person's conscious understanding of his or her self and the world.
Heredity	Heredity is the transfer of characteristics from parent to offspring through their genes.
Self-actualization	Self-actualization (a term originated by Kurt Goldstein) is the instinctual need of a human to make the most of their unique abilities. Maslow described it as follows: Self Actualization is the intrinsic growth of what is already in the organism, or more accurately, of what the organism is.
Individuality	According to Cooper, individuality consists of two dimensions: self-assertion and separateness.
Human nature	Human nature is the fundamental nature and substance of humans, as well as the range of human behavior that is believed to be invariant over long periods of time and across very different cultural contexts.
Syndrome	The term syndrome is the association of several clinically recognizable features, signs, symptoms, phenomena or characteristics which often occur together, so that the presence of one feature indicates the presence of the others.
Carl Rogers	Carl Rogers was instrumental in the development of non-directive psychotherapy, also known as "client-centered" psychotherapy. Rogers' basic tenets were unconditional positive regard, genuineness, and empathic understanding, with each demonstrated by the counselor.
Self-image	A person's self-image is the mental picture, generally of a kind that is quite resistant to change, that depicts not only details that are potentially available to objective investigation by others, but also items that have been learned by that person about himself

or herself.

Self-awareness Realization that one's existence and functioning are separate from those of other people and things is called self-awareness.

Group therapy Group therapy is a form of psychotherapy during which one or several therapists treat a small group of clients together as a group. This may be more cost effective than individual therapy, and possibly even more effective.

Premise A premise is a statement presumed true within the context of a discourse, especially of a logical argument.

Pluralistic ignorance Pluralistic ignorance is involves several members of a group who think that they have different perceptions, beliefs, or attitudes from the rest of the group. While they do not endorse the group norm, the dissenting persons behave like the other group members, because they think that the behavior of the other group members shows that the opinion of the group is unanimous.

Couples therapy Therapy with married or unmarried couples whose major problem is within their relationship is referred to as couples therapy.

Emotion An emotion is a mental states that arise spontaneously, rather than through conscious effort. They are often accompanied by physiological changes.

Alcoholism A disorder that involves long-term, repeated, uncontrolled, compulsive, and excessive use of alcoholic beverages and that impairs the drinker's health and work and social relationships is called alcoholism.

Alcoholic An alcoholic is dependent on alcohol as characterized by craving, loss of control, physical dependence and withdrawal symptoms, and tolerance.

Chronic fatigue syndrome Chronic fatigue syndrome is incapacitating exhaustion following only minimal exertion, accompanied by fever, headaches, muscle and joint pain, depression, and anxiety.

Multiple sclerosis Multiple sclerosis affects neurons, the cells of the brain and spinal cord that carry information, create thought and perception, and allow the brain to control the body. Surrounding and protecting these neurons is a layer of fat, called myelin, which helps neurons carry electrical signals. MS causes gradual destruction of myelin (demyelination) in patches throughout the brain and/or spinal cord, causing various symptoms depending upon which signals are interrupted.

Ecology Ecology refers to the branch of biology that deals with the relationships between living organisms and their environment.

Suicide Suicide behavior is rare in childhood but escalates in adolescence. The suicide rate increases in a linear fashion from adolescence through late adulthood.

Corpus callosum The corpus callosum is the largest white matter structure in the brain. It consists of mostly of contralateral axon projections. The corpus callosum connects the left and right cerebral hemispheres. Most communication between regions in different halves of the brain are carried over the corpus callosum.

Limbic system The limbic system is a group of brain structures that are involved in various emotions such as aggression, fear, pleasure and also in the formation of memory. The limbic system affects the endocrine system and the autonomic nervous system. It consists of several subcortical structures located around the thalamus.

Lobotomy A lobotomy is the intentional severing of the prefrontal cortex from the thalamic region of the brain. The frontal lobe of the brain controls a number of advanced cognitive functions, as well as motor control. Today, lobotomy is very infrequently practised. It may be a

	treatment of last resort for obsessive-compulsive sufferers, and may also be used for people suffering chronic pain.
Epilepsy	Epilepsy is a chronic neurological condition characterized by recurrent unprovoked neural discharges. It is commonly controlled with medication, although surgical methods are used as well.
Seizure	A seizure is a temporary alteration in brain function expressed as a changed mental state, tonic or clonic movements and various other symptoms. They are due to temporary abnormal electrical activity of a group of brain cells.
Diencephalon	The diencephalon is the region of the brain that includes the epithalamus, thalamus, and hypothalamus. It is located above the mesencephalon of the brain stem. Sensory information is relayed between the brain stem and the rest of the brain regions
Frontal lobe	The frontal lobe comprises four major folds of cortical tissue: the precentral gyrus, superior gyrus and the middle gyrus of the frontal gyri, the inferior frontal gyrus. It has been found to play a part in impulse control, judgement, language, memory, motor function, problem solving, sexual behavior, socialization and spontaneity.
Nerve	A nerve is an enclosed, cable-like bundle of nerve fibers or axons, which includes the glia that ensheath the axons in myelin. Neurons are sometimes called nerve cells, though this term is technically imprecise since many neurons do not form nerves.
Neurologist	A physician who studies the nervous system, especially its structure, functions, and abnormalities is referred to as neurologist.
Moniz	Moniz was the inventor of the frontal lobotomy as a surgical approach to the radical treatment of several kinds of mental diseases.
Guilt	Guilt describes many concepts related to a negative emotion or condition caused by actions which are believed to be, morally wrong. According to Freud, the avoidance of guilt is the basis for moral behavior.
Mania	Mania is a medical condition characterized by severely elevated mood. Mania is most usually associated with bipolar disorder, where episodes of mania may cyclically alternate with episodes of depression.
Barbiturate	A barbiturate is a drug that acts as a central nervous system (CNS) depressant, and by virtue of this produces a wide spectrum of effects, from mild sedation to anesthesia.
Amnesia	Amnesia is a condition in which memory is disturbed. The causes of amnesia are organic or functional. Organic causes include damage to the brain, through trauma or disease, or use of certain (generally sedative) drugs.
Major depressive disorder	The diagnosis of a major depressive disorder occurs when an individual experiences a major depressive episode and depressed characteristics, such as lethargy and depression, last for 2 weeks or longer and daily functioning becomes impaired.
Psychopharma-ology	Psychopharmacology refers to the study of the effects of drugs on the mind and on behavior; also known as medication and drug therapy.
Chlorpromazine	Chlorpromazine was the first antipsychotic drug, used during the 1950s and 1960s. Used as chlorpromazine hydrochloride and sold under the tradenames Largactil (the "liquid cosh") and Thorazine, it has sedative, hypotensive and antiemetic properties as well as anticholinergic and antidopaminergic effects. Today, Chlorpromazine is considered a typical antipsychotic.
Neurotransmitter	A neurotransmitter is a chemical that is used to relay, amplify and modulate electrical signals between a neurons and another cell.
Antipsychotic	The term antipsychotic is applied to a group of drugs used to treat psychosis.

Dopamine	Dopamine is critical to the way the brain controls our movements and is a crucial part of the basal ganglia motor loop. It is commonly associated with the 'pleasure system' of the brain, providing feelings of enjoyment and reinforcement to motivate us to do, or continue doing, certain activities.
Delusion	A false belief, not generally shared by others, and that cannot be changed despite strong evidence to the contrary is a delusion.
Haloperidol	Haloperidol is a conventional butyrophenone antipsychotic drug. It posesses a strong activity against delusions and hallucinations, most likely due to an effective dopaminergic receptor blockage in the mesocortex and the limbic system of the brain.
Thorazine	Thorazine is the trade name for chlorpromazine, one of the antipsychotic drugs and a member of the phenothiazine group. It is classified as a low-potency antipsychotic and is used in the treatment of both acute and chronic psychoses, including schizophrenia and the manic phase of manic depression.
Receptor	A sensory receptor is a structure that recognizes a stimulus in the internal or external environment of an organism. In response to stimuli the sensory receptor initiates sensory transduction by creating graded potentials or action potentials in the same cell or in an adjacent one.
Clozapine	Clozapine (trade names Clozaril), was the first of the atypical antipsychotic drugs. Clozapine is the only FDA-approved medication indicated for treatment-resistant schizophrenia and for reducing the risk of suicidal behavior in patients with schizophrenia.
Serotonin	Serotonin, a neurotransmitter, is believed to play an important part of the biochemistry of depression, bipolar disorder and anxiety. It is also believed to be influential on sexuality and appetite.
Tranquilizer	A sedative, or tranquilizer, is a drug that depresses the central nervous system (CNS), which causes calmness, relaxation, reduction of anxiety, sleepiness, slowed breathing, slurred speech, staggering gait, poor judgment, and slow, uncertain reflexes.
Tardive dyskinesia	Tardive dyskinesia is a serious neurological disorder caused by the long-term use of traditional antipsychotic drugs.
Reuptake	Reuptake is the reabsorption of a neurotransmitter by the molecular transporter of a pre-synaptic neuron after it has performed its function of transmitting a neural impulse.
Monoamine oxidase	Monoamine oxidase is an enzyme that catalyzes the oxidation of monoamines. They are found bound to the outer membrane of mitochondria in most cell types in the body. Because of the vital role that it play in the inactivation of neurotransmitters, dysfunction (too much/too little MAO activity) is thought to be responsible for a number of neurological disorders.
Norepinephrine	Norepinephrine is released from the adrenal glands as a hormone into the blood, but it is also a neurotransmitter in the nervous system. As a stress hormone, it affects parts of the human brain where attention and impulsivity are controlled. Along with epinephrine, this compound effects the fight-or-flight response, activating the sympathetic nervous system to directly increase heart rate, release energy from fat, and increase muscle readiness.
Enzyme	An enzyme is a protein that catalyzes, or speeds up, a chemical reaction. Enzymes are essential to sustain life because most chemical reactions in biological cells would occur too slowly, or would lead to different products, without enzymes.
Antidepressant	An antidepressant is a medication used primarily in the treatment of clinical depression. They are not thought to produce tolerance, although sudden withdrawal may produce adverse effects. They create little if any immediate change in mood and require between several days and several weeks to take effect.

Affect	A subjective feeling or emotional tone often accompanied by bodily expressions noticeable to others is called affect.
Tricyclic	Tricyclic antidepressants are a class of antidepressant drugs first used in the 1950s. They are named after the drugs' molecular structure, which contains three rings of atoms.
Bipolar disorder	Bipolar Disorder is a mood disorder typically characterized by fluctuations between manic and depressive states; and, more generally, atypical mood regulation and mood instability.
Lithium	Lithium salts are used as mood stabilizing drugs primarily in the treatment of bipolar disorder, depression, and mania; but also in treating schizophrenia. Lithium is widely distributed in the central nervous system and interacts with a number of neurotransmitters and receptors, decreasing noradrenaline release and increasing serotonin synthesis.
Manic episode	A manic episode is a period of unusually high energy, sometimes including uncontrollable excitement. Such episodes most commonly occur as part of bipolar disorder. In extreme cases, the person may need to be hospitalized.
Antianxiety drugs	Drugs that can reduce a person's level of excitability while increasing feelings of well-being are called antianxiety drugs.
Neuron	The neuron is the primary cell of the nervous system. They are found in the brain, the spinal cord, in the nerves and ganglia of the peripheral nervous system. It is a specialized cell that conducts impulses through the nervous system and contains three major parts: cell body, dendrites, and an axon. It can have many dendrites but only one axon.
Panic disorder	A panic attack is a period of intense fear or discomfort, typically with an abrupt onset and usually lasting no more than thirty minutes. The disorder is strikingly different from other types of anxiety, in that panic attacks are very sudden, appear to be unprovoked, and are often disabling. People who have repeated attacks, or feel severe anxiety about having another attack are said to have panic disorder.
Agoraphobia	An irrational fear of open, crowded places is called agoraphobia. Many people suffering from agoraphobia, however, are not afraid of the open spaces themselves, but of situations often associated with these spaces, such as social gatherings.
Benzodiazepines	The benzodiazepines are a class of drugs with hypnotic, anxiolytic, anticonvulsant, amnestic and muscle relaxant properties. Benzodiazepines are often used for short-term relief of severe, disabling anxiety or insomnia.
Mood disorder	A mood disorder is a condition where the prevailing emotional mood is distorted or inappropriate to the circumstances.
Physical dependence	Physical dependence describes increased tolerance of a drug combined with a physical need of the drug to function. Abrupt cessation of the drug is typically associated with negative physical withdrawal symptoms. Physical dependence is distinguished from addiction. While addiction tends to describe psychological and behavioral attributes, physical dependence is defined primarily using physical and biological concepts.
Placebo effect	The placebo effect is the phenomenon that a patient's symptoms can be alleviated by an otherwise ineffective treatment, apparently because the individual expects or believes that it will work.
Meta-analysis	In statistics, a meta-analysis combines the results of several studies that address a set of related research hypotheses.
Social role	Social role refers to expected behavior patterns associated with particular social positions.
Placebo	Placebo refers to a bogus treatment that has the appearance of being genuine.
Analogy	An analogy is a comparison between two different things, in order to highlight some form of

	similarity. Analogy is the cognitive process of transferring information from a particular subject to another particular subject.
Social phobia	An irrational, excessive fear of public scrutiny is referred to as social phobia.
Amygdala	Located in the brain's medial temporal lobe, the almond-shaped amygdala is believed to play a key role in the emotions. It forms part of the limbic system and is linked to both fear responses and pleasure. Its size is positively correlated with aggressive behavior across species.
Interpersonal therapy	A brief psychotherapy designed to help depressed people better understand and cope with problems relating to their interpersonal relationships is referred to as interpersonal therapy.
Behavioral therapy	The treatment of a mental disorder through the application of basic principles of conditioning and learning is called behavioral therapy.
Paradigm	Paradigm refers to the set of practices that defines a scientific discipline during a particular period of time. It provides a framework from which to conduct research, it ensures that a certain range of phenomena, those on which the paradigm focuses, are explored thoroughly. Itmay also blind scientists to other, perhaps more fruitful, ways of dealing with their subject matter.
Psychoactive substance	A psychoactive substance is a chemical that alters brain function, resulting in temporary changes in perception, mood, consciousness, or behavior. Such drugs are often used for recreational and spiritual purposes, as well as in medicine, especially for treating neurological and psychological illnesses.
Adaptation	Adaptation is a lowering of sensitivity to a stimulus following prolonged exposure to that stimulus. Behavioral adaptations are special ways a particular organism behaves to survive in its natural habitat.
Psychoanalytic	Freud's theory that unconscious forces act as determinants of personality is called psychoanalytic theory. The theory is a developmental theory characterized by critical stages of development.
Operant Conditioning	A simple form of learning in which an organism learns to engage in behavior because it is reinforced is referred to as operant conditioning. The consequences of a behavior produce changes in the probability of the behavior's occurence.
Social-skills training	Behavior therapy procedures for teaching socially unknowledgeable individuals how to meet others, talk to them and maintain eye contact, give and receive criticism, offer and accept compliments, make requests and express feelings is a form of social-skills training.
Antidepressants	Antidepressants are medications used primarily in the treatment of clinical depression. Antidepressants create little if any immediate change in mood and require between several days and several weeks to take effect.

Social psychology	Social psychology is the study of the nature and causes of human social behavior, with an emphasis on how people think towards each other and how they relate to each other.
Perception	Perception is the process of acquiring, interpreting, selecting, and organizing sensory information.
Motives	Needs or desires that energize and direct behavior toward a goal are motives.
Social psychologists	Social psychologists study the nature and causes of human social behavior, emphasizing on how people think and relate towards each other.
Construct	A generalized concept, such as anxiety or gravity, is a construct.
Social perception	A subfield of social psychology that studies the ways in which we form and modify impressions of others is social perception.
Attribution theory	Attribution theory is concerned with the ways in which people explain the behavior of others. It explores how individuals "attribute" causes to events and how this cognitive perception affects their motivation.
Fritz Heider	Attribution theory in social psychology was initiated by Fritz Heider in 1958. It concerned how people choose explanations for the behavior of others. It explores how individuals attribute causes to events and how this cognitive perception affects their motivation.
Variable	A variable refers to a measurable factor, characteristic, or attribute of an individual or a system.
Fundamental attribution error	The fundamental attribution error is the tendency for people to over-emphasize dispositional, or personality-based, explanations for behaviors observed in others while under-emphasizing the role and power of situational influences on the same behavior.
Lee Ross	Lee Ross first coined the term "fundamental attribution error" to explain the effects of a study by Edward E. Jones and Victor Harris, in which people were overly ready to see another person's behavior as revealing a particular attitude even though the person's behavior was a response to situational demands.
Affect	A subjective feeling or emotional tone often accompanied by bodily expressions noticeable to others is called affect.
Self-serving bias	A self-serving bias is the tendency to view one's successes as stemming from internal factors and one's failures as stemming from external factors.
Dispositional causes	Perceived causes of behavior that are based on internal traits or personality factors are dispositional causes.
Friendship	The essentials of friendship are reciprocity and commitment between individuals who see themselves more or less as equals. Interaction between friends rests on a more equal power base than the interaction between children and adults.
Creativity	Creativity is the ability to think about something in novel and unusual ways and come up with unique solutions to problems. It involves divergent thinking, having many solutions or views to a problem.
Normative	The term normative is used to describe the effects of those structures of culture which regulate the function of social activity.
Feedback	Feedback refers to information returned to a person about the effects a response has had.
Pygmalion effect	The Pygmalion effect refers to situations in which students performed better than other students, simply because they were expected to do so.
Hypothesis	A specific statement about behavior or mental processes that is testable through research is

	a hypothesis.
Introversion	A personality trait characterized by intense imagination and a tendency to inhibit impulses is called introversion.
Extraversion	Extraversion, one of the big-five personailty traits, is marked by pronounced engagement with the external world. They are people who enjoy being with people, are full of energy, and often experience positive emotions.
Introvert	Introvert refers to a person whose attention is focused inward; a shy, reserved, timid person.
Motivation	In psychology, motivation is the driving force (desire) behind all actions of an organism.
Personality	Personality refers to the pattern of enduring characteristics that differentiates a person, the patterns of behaviors that make each individual unique.
Stereotype	A stereotype is considered to be a group concept, held by one social group about another.They are often used in a negative or prejudicial sense and are frequently used to justify certain discriminatory behaviors. This allows powerful social groups to legitimize and protect their dominant position
Attitude	An enduring mental representation of a person, place, or thing that evokes an emotional response and related behavior is called attitude.
Obesity	The state of being more than 20 percent above the average weight for a person of one's height is called obesity.
Control group	A group that does not receive the treatment effect in an experiment is referred to as the control group or sometimes as the comparison group.
Correlation	A statistical technique for determining the degree of association between two or more variables is referred to as correlation.
Elaboration	The extensiveness of processing at any given level of memory is called elaboration. The use of elaboration changes developmentally. Adolescents are more likely to use elaboration spontaneously than children.
Mental illness	Mental illness is the term formerly used to mean psychological disorder but less preferred because it implies that the causes of the disorder can be found in a medical disease process.
Affective	Affective is the way people react emotionally, their ability to feel another living thing's pain or joy.
Cognitive dissonance	Cognitive dissonance is a state of opposition between cognitions. Contradicting cognitions serve as a driving force that compel the mind to acquire or invent new thoughts or beliefs, or to modify existing beliefs, so as to minimize the amount of dissonance between cognitions.
Festinger	The theory of social comparison processes, developed by Festinger, suggests that there are large areas of judgment in which reality depends on consensus; it is socially defined. He also developed the cognitive dissonance theory: cognitions that are not in harmony act like drives, motivating actions to resolve dissonance.
Cognition	The intellectual processes through which information is obtained, transformed, stored, retrieved, and otherwise used is cognition.
Self-concept	Self-concept refers to domain-specific evaluations of the self where a domain may be academics, athletics, etc.
Self-perception theory	Self-perception theory is an account of attitude change developed by Daryl Bem. It asserts that we only have that knowledge of our own behavior and its causation that another person can have, and that we develop our attitudes by observing our own behavior and concluding what

	attitudes must have caused them.
Attention	Attention is the cognitive process of selectively concentrating on one thing while ignoring other things. Psychologists have labeled three types of attention: sustained attention, selective attention, and divided attention.
Reciprocity norm	The rule that people should pay back in kind what they receive from others is called the reciprocity norm.
Reciprocity	Reciprocity, in interpersonal attraction, is the tendency to return feelings and attitudes that are expressed about us.
Door-in-the-face	A strategy in which someone makes a large, unreasonable request with the expectation that the person will refuse but will then be more likely to respond favorably to a smaller request at a later time is called the door-in-the-face technique.
Foot-in-the-door	The tendency for a person who has first complied with a small request to be more likely later to fulfill a larger request is called the foot-in-the-door effect.
Prejudice	Prejudice in general, implies coming to a judgment on the subject before learning where the preponderance of the evidence actually lies, or formation of a judgement without direct experience.
Social categorization	Social categorization refers to the tendency to divide the social world into two separate categories: one's in-group and various out-groups.
Random assignment	Assignment of participants to experimental and control groups by chance is called random assignment. Random assigment reduces the likelihood that the results are due to preexisiting systematic differences between the groups.
Discrimination	In Learning theory, discrimination refers the ability to distinguish between a conditioned stimulus and other stimuli. It can be brought about by extensive training or differential reinforcement. In social terms, it is the denial of privileges to a person or a group on the basis of prejudice.
Generalization	In conditioning, the tendency for a conditioned response to be evoked by stimuli that are similar to the stimulus to which the response was conditioned is a generalization. The greater the similarity among the stimuli, the greater the probability of generalization.
Homosexual	Homosexual refers to a sexual orientation characterized by aesthetic attraction, romantic love, and sexual desire exclusively for members of the same sex or gender identity.
Homosexuality	Homosexuality refers to a sexual orientation characterized by aesthetic attraction, romantic love, and sexual desire exclusively for members of the same sex or gender identity.
Society	The social sciences use the term society to mean a group of people that form a semi-closed (or semi-open) social system, in which most interactions are with other individuals belonging to the group.
Muzafer Sherif	Muzafer Sherif studied the origin of prejudice in social groups and conducted the famous Robbers Cave experiment on group hostility.
Interdependence	Interdependence is a dynamic of being mutually responsible to and dependent on others.
Propaganda	Propaganda is a specific type of message presentation directly aimed at influencing the opinions of people, rather than to impartially provide information.
Allport	Allport was a trait theorist. Those traits he believed to predominate a person's personality were called central traits. Traits such that one could be indentifed by the trait, were referred to as cardinal traits. Central traits and cardinal traits are influenced by environmental factors.

Pupil	In the eye, the pupil is the opening in the middle of the iris. It appears black because most of the light entering it is absorbed by the tissues inside the eye. The size of the pupil is controlled by involuntary contraction and dilation of the iris, in order to regulate the intensity of light entering the eye. This is known as the pupillary reflex.
Learning	Learning is a relatively permanent change in behavior that results from experience. Thus, to attribute a behavioral change to learning, the change must be relatively permanent and must result from experience.
Social norm	A social norm, is a rule that is socially enforced. In social situations, such as meetings, they are unwritten and often unstated rules that govern individuals' behavior. A social norm is most evident when not followed or broken.
Interpersonal attraction	Interpersonal attraction is the attraction between people which leads to friendships and romantic relationships. Major variables include propinquity, similarity, familiarity, reciprocal liking, and physical attractiveness.
Physical attractiveness	Physical attractiveness is the perception of an individual as physically beautiful by other people.
Social skills	Social skills are skills used to interact and communicate with others to assist status in the social structure and other motivations.
Individual differences	Individual differences psychology studies the ways in which individual people differ in their behavior. This is distinguished from other aspects of psychology in that although psychology is ostensibly a study of individuals, modern psychologists invariably study groups.
Social development	The person's developing capacity for social relationships and the effects of those relationships on further development is referred to as social development.
Attachment style	Attachment style refers to the way a person typically interacts with significant others.
Attachment	Attachment is the tendency to seek closeness to another person and feel secure when that person is present.
Passionate love	A state of intense absorption includes intense physiological arousal, psychological interest, and caring for the needs of another is referred to as passionate love.
Lange	Lange along with William James, independently developed the James-Lange theory of emotion. Unlike James, Lange specifically stated that vasomotor changes are emotions. Lange also noted the psychotropic effects of lithium, although his work in this area was forgotten and independently rediscovered much later.
Survey	A method of scientific investigation in which a large sample of people answer questions about their attitudes or behavior is referred to as a survey.
Cross-cultural studies	Cross-cultural studies are comparisons of a culture with one or more other cultures, which provides information about the degree to which behavior is similar across cultures or the degree to which it is culture specific .

Evolutionary perspective	A perspective that focuses on how humans have evolved and adapted behaviors required for survival against various environmental pressures over the long course is called the evolutionary perspective.
Individual differences	Individual differences psychology studies the ways in which individual people differ in their behavior. This is distinguished from other aspects of psychology in that although psychology is ostensibly a study of individuals, modern psychologists invariably study groups.
Social norm	A social norm, is a rule that is socially enforced. In social situations, such as meetings, they are unwritten and often unstated rules that govern individuals' behavior. A social norm is most evident when not followed or broken.
Conformity	Conformity is the degree to which members of a group will change their behavior, views and attitudes to fit the views of the group. The group can influence members via unconscious processes or via overt social pressure on individuals.
Obedience	Obedience is the willingness to follow the will of others. Humans have been shown to be surprisingly obedient in the presence of perceived legitimate authority figures, as demonstrated by the Milgram experiment in the 1960s.
Altruism	Altruism is being helpful to other people with little or no interest in being rewarded for one's efforts. This is distinct from merely helping others.
Motives	Needs or desires that energize and direct behavior toward a goal are motives.
Brain	The brain controls and coordinates most movement, behavior and homeostatic body functions such as heartbeat, blood pressure, fluid balance and body temperature. Functions of the brain are responsible for cognition, emotion, memory, motor learning and other sorts of learning. The brain is primarily made up of two types of cells: glia and neurons.
Social psychologists	Social psychologists study the nature and causes of human social behavior, emphasizing on how people think and relate towards each other.
Social role	Social role refers to expected behavior patterns associated with particular social positions.
Zimbardo	Zimbardo is best-known for his Stanford prison experiment. The experiment led to theories about the importance of the social situation in individual psychology that are still controversial today.
Psychological test	Psychological test refers to a standardized measure of a sample of a person's behavior.
Psychosomatic	A psychosomatic illness is one with physical manifestations and perhaps a supposed psychological cause. It is often diagnosed when any known or identifiable physical cause was excluded by medical examination.
Random assignment	Assignment of participants to experimental and control groups by chance is called random assignment. Random assigment reduces the likelihood that the results are due to preexisiting systematic differences between the groups.
Norms	In testing, standards of test performance that permit the comparison of one person's score on the test to the scores of others who have taken the same test are referred to as norms.
Punishment	Punishment is the addtion of a stimulus that reduces the frequency of a response, or the removal of a stimulus that results in a reduction of the response.
Autonomy	Autonomy is the condition of something that does not depend on anything else.
Attitude	An enduring mental representation of a person, place, or thing that evokes an emotional response and related behavior is called attitude.
Informational	Informational influence is the use of others' behaviors or opinions as information in forming

influence	one's own judgment about the objective nature of an event or situation.
Normative influence	The normative influence is the effect on an individual that results from a concern about what others will think of them if they behave in a certain way or express a certain belief.
Muzafer Sherif	Muzafer Sherif studied the origin of prejudice in social groups and conducted the famous Robbers Cave experiment on group hostility.
Self-worth	In psychology, self-esteem or self-worth refers to a person's subjective appraisal of himself or herself as intrinsically positive or negative to some degree.
Asch	Asch conducted groundbreaking studies on independence and conformity under group pressure. His most famous experiments involved having subjects judge the relative length of lines after hearing other subjects give incorrect judgments on purpose.
Visual perception	Visual perception is one of the senses, consisting of the ability to detect light and interpret it. Vision has a specific sensory system.
Confederate	Someone who is posing as a participant in an experiment but is actually assisting the experimenter is a confederate.
Script	A schema, or behavioral sequence, for an event is called a script. It is a form of schematic organization, with real-world events organized in terms of temporal and causal relations between component acts.
Stimulus	A change in an environmental condition that elicits a response is a stimulus.
Human nature	Human nature is the fundamental nature and substance of humans, as well as the range of human behavior that is believed to be invariant over long periods of time and across very different cultural contexts.
Nonconformity	Nonconformity occurs when individuals know what people around them expect but do not use those expectations to guide their behavior.
Group polarization	The solidification and further strengthening of a position as a consequence of a group discussion is called a group polarization effect.
Social psychology	Social psychology is the study of the nature and causes of human social behavior, with an emphasis on how people think towards each other and how they relate to each other.
Groupthink	In a groupthink situation, each member of the group attempts to conform his or her opinions to what they believe to be the consensus of the group.
Polarization	Polarization is the process of preparing a neuron for firing by creating an internal negative charge in relation to the body fluid outside the cell membrane.
Social comparison	Social comparison theory is the idea that individuals learn about and assess themselves by comparison with other people. Research shows that individuals tend to lean more toward social comparisons in situations that are ambiguous.
Irving Janis	Irving Janis is most famous for his theory of "groupthink" which described the systematic errors made by groups when taking collective decisions.
Janis	Janis is famous for his theory of "groupthink" which described the systematic errors made by groups when taking collective decisions. He also collaborated with Carl Hovland on his studies of attitude change, including the sleeper effect.
Society	The social sciences use the term society to mean a group of people that form a semi-closed (or semi-open) social system, in which most interactions are with other individuals belonging to the group.
Seizure	A seizure is a temporary alteration in brain function expressed as a changed mental state,

	tonic or clonic movements and various other symptoms. They are due to temporary abnormal electrical activity of a group of brain cells.
Gene	A gene is an ultramicroscopic area of the chromosome. It is the smallest physical unit of the DNA molecule that carries a piece of hereditary information.
Reasoning	Reasoning is the act of using reason to derive a conclusion from certain premises. There are two main methods to reach a conclusion,deductive reasoning and inductive reasoning.
Reciprocity	Reciprocity, in interpersonal attraction, is the tendency to return feelings and attitudes that are expressed about us.
Evolution	Commonly used to refer to gradual change, evolution is the change in the frequency of alleles within a population from one generation to the next. This change may be caused by different mechanisms, including natural selection, genetic drift, or changes in population (gene flow).
Nurture	Nurture refers to the environmental influences on behavior due to nutrition, culture, socioeconomic status, and learning.
Innate	Innate behavior is not learned or influenced by the environment, rather, it is present or predisposed at birth.
Collectivism	Collectivism is an emphasis on the group, as opposed to the individual. It is syndrome of attitudes and behaviors based on the belief that the basic unit of survival lies within a group, not the individual.
Empathy	Empathy is the recognition and understanding of the states of mind, including beliefs, desires and particularly emotions of others without injecting your own.
Empathy-altruism hypothesis	The empathy-altruism hypothesis suggests that prosocial behavior is motivated solely by the desire to help someone in need.
Dependent variable	A measure of an assumed effect of an independent variable is called the dependent variable.
Bystander intervention	A bystander will often intervene if another person is in need of help: this is known as bystander intervention. They will often do this for complete strangers, sometimes even at great personal risk.
Diffusion of responsibility	Diffusion of responsibility is a social phenomenon which tends to occur in groups of people above a certain critical size when responsibility is not explicitly assigned.
Attention	Attention is the cognitive process of selectively concentrating on one thing while ignoring other things. Psychologists have labeled three types of attention: sustained attention, selective attention, and divided attention.
Lorenz	Lorenz demonstrated how incubator-hatched geese would imprint on the first suitable moving stimulus they saw within what he called a "critical period" of about 36 hours shortly after hatching. Most famously, the goslings would imprint on Lorenz himself .
Species	Species refers to a reproductively isolated breeding population.
Predisposition	Predisposition refers to an inclination or diathesis to respond in a certain way, either inborn or acquired. In abnormal psychology, it is a factor that lowers the ability to withstand stress and inclines the individual toward pathology.
Hypothesis	A specific statement about behavior or mental processes that is testable through research is a hypothesis.
Emotion	An emotion is a mental states that arise spontaneously, rather than through conscious effort. They are often accompanied by physiological changes.

Neurotransmitter	A neurotransmitter is a chemical that is used to relay, amplify and modulate electrical signals between a neurons and another cell.
Serotonin	Serotonin, a neurotransmitter, is believed to play an important part of the biochemistry of depression, bipolar disorder and anxiety. It is also believed to be influential on sexuality and appetite.
Amygdala	Located in the brain's medial temporal lobe, the almond-shaped amygdala is believed to play a key role in the emotions. It forms part of the limbic system and is linked to both fear responses and pleasure. Its size is positively correlated with aggressive behavior across species.
Personality	Personality refers to the pattern of enduring characteristics that differentiates a person, the patterns of behaviors that make each individual unique.
Personality trait	According to the Diagnostic and Statistical Manual of the American Psychiatric Association, a personality trait is a "prominent aspect of personality that is exhibited in a wide range of important social and personal contexts. ...".
Empirical	Empirical means the use of working hypotheses which are capable of being disproved using observation or experiment.
Intentionality	Brentano defined intentionality as the main characteristic of "psychical phenomena," by which they could be distinguished from "physical phenomena.". Every mental phenomenon, every psychological act has a content, is directed at an object (the intentional object).
Chronic	Chronic refers to a relatively long duration, usually more than a few months.
Acute	Acute means sudden, sharp, and abrupt. Usually short in duration.
Interdependence	Interdependence is a dynamic of being mutually responsible to and dependent on others.
Prejudice	Prejudice in general, implies coming to a judgment on the subject before learning where the preponderance of the evidence actually lies, or formation of a judgement without direct experience.
Theories	Theories are logically self-consistent models or frameworks describing the behavior of a certain natural or social phenomenon. They are broad explanations and predictions concerning phenomena of interest.
Insight	Insight refers to a sudden awareness of the relationships among various elements that had previously appeared to be independent of one another.
Stanley Milgram	In 1963, Stanley Milgram published the results of his obedience experiment that measured the willingness of a participant to obey an authority who instructs the participant to do something that may conflict with the participant's personal conscience. Ethical considerations ensued.
Milgram	Milgram conducted the Small world experiment (the source of the six degrees of separation concept) and the experiment on obedience to authority.
Paradigm	Paradigm refers to the set of practices that defines a scientific discipline during a particular period of time. It provides a framework from which to conduct research, it ensures that a certain range of phenomena, those on which the paradigm focuses, are explored thoroughly. Itmay also blind scientists to other, perhaps more fruitful, ways of dealing with their subject matter.
Variable	A variable refers to a measurable factor, characteristic, or attribute of an individual or a system.
Learning	Learning is a relatively permanent change in behavior that results from experience. Thus, to

	attribute a behavioral change to learning, the change must be relatively permanent and must result from experience.
Psychiatrist	A psychiatrist is a physician who specializes in the diagnosis and treatment of psychological disorders.
Abnormal behavior	An action, thought, or feeling that is harmful to the person or to others is called abnormal behavior.
Perception	Perception is the process of acquiring, interpreting, selecting, and organizing sensory information.
Heuristic	A heuristic is a simple, efficient rule of thumb proposed to explain how people make decisions, come to judgments and solve problems, typically when facing complex problems or incomplete information. These rules work well under most circumstances, but in certain cases lead to systematic cognitive biases.
Habit	A habit is a response that has become completely separated from its eliciting stimulus. Early learning theorists used the term to describe S-R associations, however not all S-R associations become a habit, rather many are extinguished after reinforcement is withdrawn.
Feedback	Feedback refers to information returned to a person about the effects a response has had.
Population	Population refers to all members of a well-defined group of organisms, events, or things.
Scapegoating	Scapegoating is assigning blame to an individual or group that isn't really responsible, thus alleviating feelings of guilt from responsible parties and/or distracting attention from the need to fix the problem for which blame is being assigned.
Ideology	An ideology can be thought of as a comprehensive vision, as a way of looking at things, as in common sense and several philosophical tendencies, or a set of ideas proposed by the dominant class of a society to all members of this society.
Control group	A group that does not receive the treatment effect in an experiment is referred to as the control group or sometimes as the comparison group.
Mania	Mania is a medical condition characterized by severely elevated mood. Mania is most usually associated with bipolar disorder, where episodes of mania may cyclically alternate with episodes of depression.
Ethnic cleansing	The term ethnic cleansing refers to various policies of forcibly removing people of one ethnic group. At one end of the spectrum, it is virtually indistinguishable from forced emigration and population transfer, while at the other it merges with deportation and genocide.
American Psychological Association	The American Psychological Association is a professional organization representing psychology in the US. The mission statement is to "advance psychology as a science and profession and as a means of promoting health, education , and human welfare".
Authoritarian personality	A personality pattern characterized by rigidity, inhibition, prejudice, and an excessive concern with power, authority, and obedience is called an authoritarian personality.
Propaganda	Propaganda is a specific type of message presentation directly aimed at influencing the opinions of people, rather than to impartially provide information.
Lewin	Lewin ranks as one of the pioneers of social psychology, as one of the founders of group dynamics and as one of the most eminent representatives of Gestalt psychology.
Group dynamics	The term group dynamics implies that individual behaviors may differ depending on individuals' current or prospective connections to a sociological group.
Experimental	Experimental group refers to any group receiving a treatment effect in an experiment.

group	
Generalization	In conditioning, the tendency for a conditioned response to be evoked by stimuli that are similar to the stimulus to which the response was conditioned is a generalization. The greater the similarity among the stimuli, the greater the probability of generalization.
Motivation	In psychology, motivation is the driving force (desire) behind all actions of an organism.
Problem solving	An attempt to find an appropriate way of attaining a goal when the goal is not readily available is called problem solving.
Kelman	Kelman identified three subtypes of conformity: compliance, identification, and internalization.
Normative	The term normative is used to describe the effects of those structures of culture which regulate the function of social activity.
Hormone	A hormone is a chemical messenger from one cell (or group of cells) to another. The best known are those produced by endocrine glands, but they are produced by nearly every organ system. The function of hormones is to serve as a signal to the target cells; the action of the hormone is determined by the pattern of secretion and the signal transduction of the receiving tissue.
Abnormal psychology	The scientific study whose objectives are to describe, explain, predict, and control behaviors that are considered strange or unusual is referred to as abnormal psychology.
Absolute threshold	An absolute threshold is the minimum amount of stimulation required for a person to detect a stimulus fifty percent of the time.
Ciliary muscle	The ciliary muscle is a smooth muscle that affects zonules in the eye (fibers that suspend the lens in position during accommodation), enabling changes in lens shape for light focusing.
Accommodation	Piaget's developmental process of accommodation is the modification of currently held schemes or new schemes so that new information inconsistent with the existing schemes can be integrated and understood.
Cognitive structure	According to Piaget, the number of schemata available to an organism at any given time constitutes that organism's cognitive structure. How the organism interacts with its environment depends on the current cognitive structure available. As the cognitive structure develops, new assimilations can occur.
Assimilation	According to Piaget, assimilation is the process of the organism interacting with the environment given the organism's cognitive structure. Assimilation is reuse of schemas to fit new information.
Piaget	Piaget argued that young children's answers were qualitatively different than older children rather than quantitative. There are two major aspects to his theory: the process of coming to know and the stages we move through as we gradually acquire this ability.
Classical conditioning	Classical conditioning is a simple form of learning in which an organism comes to associate or anticipate events. A neutral stimulus comes to evoke the response usually evoked by a natural or unconditioned stimulus by being paired repeatedly with the unconditioned stimulus.
Conditioned response	A conditioned response is the response to a stimulus that occurs when an animal has learned to associate the stimulus with a certain positive or negative effect.
Conditioned stimulus	A previously neutral stimulus that elicits the conditioned response because of being repeatedly paired with a stimulus that naturally elicited that response, is called a conditioned stimulus.

Acquisition	Acquisition is the process of adapting to the environment, learning or becoming conditioned. In classical conditoning terms, it is the initial learning of the stimulus response link, which involves a neutral stimulus being associated with a unconditioned stimulus and becoming a conditioned stimulus.
Action potential	The electrical impulse that provides the basis for the conduction of a neural impulse along an axon of a neuron is the action potential. When a biological cell or patch of membrane undergoes an action potential, or electrical excitation, the polarity of the transmembrane voltage swings rapidly from negative to positive and back.
Nerve impulse	A nerve impulse is a change in the electric potential of a neuron; a wave of depolarization spreads along the neuron and causes the release of a neurotransmitter.
Synapse	A synapse is specialized junction through which cells of the nervous system signal to one another and to non-neuronal cells such as muscles or glands.
Neuron	The neuron is the primary cell of the nervous system. They are found in the brain, the spinal cord, in the nerves and ganglia of the peripheral nervous system. It is a specialized cell that conducts impulses through the nervous system and contains three major parts: cell body, dendrites, and an axon. It can have many dendrites but only one axon.
Axon	An axon, or "nerve fiber," is a long slender projection of a nerve cell, or "neuron," which conducts electrical impulses away from the neuron's cell body or soma.
Addiction	Addiction is an uncontrollable compulsion to repeat a behavior regardless of its consequences. Many drugs or behaviors can precipitate a pattern of conditions recognized as addiction, which include a craving for more of the drug or behavior, increased physiological tolerance to exposure, and withdrawal symptoms in the absence of the stimulus.
Stereotype	A stereotype is considered to be a group concept, held by one social group about another.They are often used in a negative or prejudicial sense and are frequently used to justify certain discriminatory behaviors. This allows powerful social groups to legitimize and protect their dominant position
Sexism	Sexism is commonly considered to be discrimination against people based on their sex rather than their individual merits, but can also refer to any and all differentiations based on
Ageism	Ageism is bias against a person or group on the grounds of age. When that bias is the primary motivation behind acts of discrimination against that person or group, then those acts constitute age discrimination..
Agoraphobia	An irrational fear of open, crowded places is called agoraphobia. Many people suffering from agoraphobia, however, are not afraid of the open spaces themselves, but of situations often associated with these spaces, such as social gatherings.
Acquired immune deficiency syndrome	Acquired Immune Deficiency Syndrome is defined as a collection of symptoms and infections resulting from the depletion of the immune system caused by infection with the human immunodeficiency virus, commonly called HIV.
Immune system	The most important function of the human immune system occurs at the cellular level of the blood and tissues. The lymphatic and blood circulation systems are highways for specialized white blood cells. These cells include B cells, T cells, natural killer cells, and macrophages. All function with the primary objective of recognizing, attacking and destroying bacteria, viruses, cancer cells, and all substances seen as foreign.
Syndrome	The term syndrome is the association of several clinically recognizable features, signs, symptoms, phenomena or characteristics which often occur together, so that the presence of one feature indicates the presence of the others.
Algorithm	A systematic procedure for solving a problem that works invariably when it is correctly

applied is called an algorithm.

All-or-none
All-or-none indicates a situation in which there are two possibilities (a binary choice set), one of which is 100% and one of which is 0%. It is a phrase commonly used to describe action potentials of neurons, which, if they fire at all, propagate from the beginning to the end of the axonal process.

Threshold
In general, a threshold is a fixed location or value where an abrupt change is observed. In the sensory modalities, it is the minimum amount of stimulus energy necessary to elicit a sensory response.

Amacrine cells
Amacrine cells are interneurons in the retina which operate at the Inner Plexiform Layer (IPL), the second synaptic retinal layer where bipolar cells and ganglion cells synapse. Functionally, they are responsible for complex processing of the retinal image, specifically adjusting image brightness and, by integrating sequential activation of neurons, detecting motion.

Ganglion cell
A ganglion cell is a type of neuron located in the retina of the eye that receives visual information from photoreceptors via various intermediate cells such as bipolar cells, amacrine cells, and horizontal cells. Retinal ganglion cells' axons are myelinated.

Bipolar cell
As a part of the retina, the bipolar cell exists between photoreceptors and ganglion cells. Bipolar cells are so-named as they have a central body from which two sets of processes arise. At one end, they form synapses with either a single cone cell, or a number of rod cells. At the other end, they form synapses with ganglion cells, which fire action potentials along the optic nerve (cranial nerve II). They effectively transfer information from rods and cones to ganglion cells.

Retina
The retina is a thin layer of cells at the back of the eyeball. It is the part of the eye which converts light into nervous signals. The retina contains photoreceptor cells which receive the light; the resulting neural signals then undergo complex processing by other neurons of the retina, and are transformed into action potentials in retinal ganglion cells whose axons form the optic nerve.

Psychological trauma
Psychological trauma involves a singular experience or enduring event or events that completely overwhelm the individual's ability to cope or integrate the emotion involved with that experience. It usually involves a complete feeling of helplessness in the face of a real or subjective threat to life, bodily integrity, or sanity.

Amnesia
Amnesia is a condition in which memory is disturbed. The causes of amnesia are organic or functional. Organic causes include damage to the brain, through trauma or disease, or use of certain (generally sedative) drugs.

Limbic system
The limbic system is a group of brain structures that are involved in various emotions such as aggression, fear, pleasure and also in the formation of memory. The limbic system affects the endocrine system and the autonomic nervous system. It consists of several subcortical structures located around the thalamus.

Anchoring
Anchoring or focalism is a term used in psychology to describe the common human tendency to rely too heavily, or "anchor," on one trait or piece of information when making decisions.

Cognition
The intellectual processes through which information is obtained, transformed, stored, retrieved, and otherwise used is cognition.

Anorexia
Anorexia nervosa is an eating disorder characterized by voluntary starvation and exercise stress.

Consciousness
The awareness of the sensations, thoughts, and feelings being experienced at a given moment is called consciousness.

Preconscious	In psychodynamic theory, material that is not in awareness but that can be brought into awareness by focusing one's attention is referred to as preconscious.
Anxiety	Anxiety is a complex combination of the feeling of fear, apprehension and worry often accompanied by physical sensations such as palpitations, chest pain and/or shortness of breath.
Anxiety disorder	Anxiety disorder is a blanket term covering several different forms of abnormal anxiety, fear, phobia and nervous condition, that come on suddenly and prevent pursuing normal daily routines.
Mental disorder	Mental disorder refers to a disturbance in a person's emotions, drives, thought processes, or behavior that involves serious and relatively prolonged distress and/or impairment in ability to function, is not simply a normal response to some event or set of events in the person's environment.
Archetype	The archetype is a concept of psychologist Carl Jung. They are innate prototypes for ideas, which may subsequently become involved in the interpretation of observed phenomena. A group of memories and interpretations closely associated with an archetype is called a complex.
Association cortex	Region of the cerebral cortex in which the highest intellectual functions, including thinking and problem solving, occur is the association cortex.
Cerebral cortex	The cerebral cortex is the outermost layer of the cerebrum and has a grey color. It is made up of four lobes and it is involved in many complex brain functions including memory, perceptual awareness, "thinking", language and consciousness. The cerebral cortex receives sensory information from many different sensory organs eg: eyes, ears, etc. and processes the information.
Attachment	Attachment is the tendency to seek closeness to another person and feel secure when that person is present.
Attribution theory	Attribution theory is concerned with the ways in which people explain the behavior of others. It explores how individuals "attribute" causes to events and how this cognitive perception affects their motivation.
Shaping	The concept of reinforcing successive, increasingly accurate approximations to a target behavior is called shaping. The target behavior is broken down into a hierarchy of elemental steps, each step more sophisticated then the last. By successively reinforcing each of the the elemental steps, a form of differential reinforcement, until that step is learned while extinguishing the step below, the target behavior is gradually achieved.
Temporal lobe	The temporal lobe is part of the cerebrum. It lies at the side of the brain, beneath the lateral or Sylvian fissure. Adjacent areas in the superior, posterior and lateral parts of the temporal lobe are involved in high-level auditory processing.
Auditory nerve	The vestibulocochlear nerve is the eighth of twelve cranial nerves, and also known as the auditory nerve. It is the nerve along which the sensory cells (the hair cells) of the inner ear transmit information to the brain. It consists of the cochlear nerve, carrying information about hearing, and the vestibular nerve, carrying information about balance.
Cochlea	The Cochlea is the bony tube that contains the basilar membrane and the organ of Corti. The cochlea consists of three fluid-filled chambers - scala tympani and scala vestibuli and scala media.
Nucleus	In neuroanatomy, a cluster of cell bodies of neurons within the central nervous system is a nucleus.
Nerve	A nerve is an enclosed, cable-like bundle of nerve fibers or axons, which includes the glia that ensheath the axons in myelin. Neurons are sometimes called nerve cells, though this term

	is technically imprecise since many neurons do not form nerves.
Peripheral nervous system	The peripheral nervous system consists of the nerves and neurons that serve the limbs and organs. It is not protected by bone or the blood-brain barrier, leaving it exposed to toxins and mechanical injuries. The peripheral nervous system is divided into the somatic nervous system and the autonomic nervous system.
Autonomic nervous system	A division of the peripheral nervous system, the autonomic nervous system, regulates glands and activities such as heartbeat, respiration, digestion, and dilation of the pupils. It is responsible for homeostasis, maintaining a relatively constant internal environment .
Central nervous system	The vertebrate central nervous system consists of the brain and spinal cord.
Sensory receptor	A sensory receptor is a structure that recognizes a stimulus in the environment of an organism. In response to stimuli the sensory receptor initiates sensory transduction by creating graded potentials or action potentials in the same cell or in an adjacent one.
Smooth muscle	Smooth muscle is a type of non-striated muscle, found within the "walls" of hollow organs; such as blood vessels, the bladder, the uterus, and the gastrointestinal tract. Smooth muscle is used to move matter within the body, via contraction; it generally operates "involuntarily", without nerve stimulation.
Gland	A gland is an organ in an animal's body that synthesizes a substance for release such as hormones, often into the bloodstream or into cavities inside the body or its outer surface.
Behavioral therapy	The treatment of a mental disorder through the application of basic principles of conditioning and learning is called behavioral therapy.
Aversion therapy	Aversion therapy is a now largely discredited form of treatment in which the patient is exposed to a stimulus while simultaneously being hurt or made ill. The theory is that the patient will come to associate the stimulus with unpleasant sensations and will no longer seek it out.
Terminal buttons	Terminal buttons are small bulges at the end of axons that send messages to other neurons.
Soma	The soma, or cell body, is the bulbous end of a neuron, containing the nucleus. The cell nucleus is a key feature of the soma. The nucleus is the source of most of the RNA that is produced in neurons and most proteins are produced from mRNAs that do not travel far from the nucleus.
Basilar membrane	The basilar membrane within the cochlea of the inner ear is the part of the auditory system that decomposes incoming auditory signals into their frequency components. This allows higher neural processing of sound information to focus on the frequency spectrum of input, rather than just the time domain waveform.
Hair cells	Hair cells are the sensory cells of both the auditory system and the vestibular system. The auditory hair cells are located within the organ of Corti on a thin basilar membrane in the cochlea of the inner ear.

Printed in the United Kingdom
by Lightning Source UK Ltd.
114859UKS00001B/16